Europan 16
Living Cities
Lebendige
Städte
Ergebnisse
Results

jovis   Europan Deutschland

E 16

Europan 16
Lebendige Städte
Ergebnisse

Europan 16
Living Cities
Results

Inhaltsverzeichnis Content

Europan 16 – mehr als ein europäisches Testlabor

Das Thema von Europan 16 – Lebendige Städte – ließ den Teilnehmerinnen und Teilnehmern zweifelsohne viel Spielraum, eigene inhaltliche Schwerpunkte zu setzen. Doch die Themenstellung barg dieses Mal einen harten Kern, der weder zu übersehen noch zu umgehen war. Die Coronakrise hatte in einem zuvor nicht vorstellbaren weltweiten Testlabor die Bedeutung des öffentlichen Raums für jede Form von Urbanisierung deutlich werden lassen.

Die roten Absperrbänder, mit denen jedes noch so kleine öffentliche Kinderspielgerät während der Lockdown-Phasen unbenutzbar gemacht wurde, bleiben als besonders krasses Beispiel in Erinnerung. Ein lebendig gestalteter, vielseitig nutzbarer und grüner Public Space nahe der eigenen Haustür prägt – vielleicht mehr als wir uns dies vorstellen mochten – die eigene Lebensweise. Er sorgt Tag für Tag für Identifikation mit dem eigenen Wohnumfeld. Fehlt er, fehlt nicht nur der Architektur jede Qualität; die Bebauung selbst wird dann zu einer von der Gesellschaft isolierten Insel.

Dies wäre eine selbstverständliche Feststellung, wenn nicht das Gros heutiger städtischer Entwicklungen den räumlichen Verbindungen zwischen Architektur und Umfeld – aller Rhetorik zum Trotz – zu wenig Aufmerksamkeit schenken würde. Der öffentliche Raum steht generell unter Druck. Das gilt ganz offensichtlich für alle Länder, die sich an E16 beteiligt haben. Gerade auch für die Bewirtschaftung peripherer öffentlicher Räume fehlen längst die Mittel. Dabei steht auf diesen randständigen, auf den ersten Blick unauffälligen Flächen die Qualität der künftigen Biodiversität auf dem Spiel, wie die vielfältigen Debatten um das Anthropozän deutlich machen.

Für diese Vernachlässigung gibt es nachvollziehbare Gründe: Die Probleme türmen sich, angefangen beim Strukturwandel, der Transformation der Mobilität, der Forderung nach CO_2-Freiheit, der im Zeichen des Kriegs in der Ukraine noch schneller notwendigen energetischen Autarkie bis hin zum Mangel an bezahlbarem Wohnraum. Viele Städte sind bis an ihre Belastungsgrenzen gefordert und haben zu wenig freie Kapazitäten.

Auch ein europaweiter Wettbewerb wie Europan hat keine Wundermittel anzubieten. Aber E16 hat in seiner zweijährigen Laufzeit und mit den jetzt vorliegenden Ergebnissen deutlich gemacht, wie eine beispielhafte Quartiersentwicklung durch die Bündelung und das Zusammendenken herkömmlicher, auf den Einzelfall fokussierter Lösungen neue Synergien freisetzen kann. Nicht selten sind das frühzeitige Einbinden der Bevölkerung und die Konzentration auf wenige, aber dann auch gemeisam vereinbarte Eigenschaften Katalysatoren für eine erfolgreiche Entwicklung. Dabei bezieht sich die Zielsetzung „Living Cities" keineswegs nur auf städtische Ausgangslagen; sie zielt genauso auf den Stadtrand, auf die Kleinstadt und die ländliche Umgebung. Und dort, wo die Planungskapazitäten vielleicht nicht ausreichend zur Verfügung stehen, kann das zeitweilige Einbinden von Knowledge Agents eine große Hilfe sein, wenn es zum Beispiel um die programmatische Aktivierung nicht mehr funktionierender Orts- und Quartierskerne oder Straßen geht.

Insgesamt 40 europäische Städte aus neun Ländern haben sich an E16 beteiligt. Die fünf deutschen Standorte bieten in dieser Runde eine fast beispiellose Breite an gesellschaftlichen und ökologischen, sozialen und wirtschaftlichen Fragestellungen bei ganz unterschiedlichen städtischen Maßstäben. Es geht um die Qualitäten eines neuen, innovativen und gemeinschaftlichen Wohnungsbaus, wie in Wernigerode; um die Reaktivierung von Innenstadtstraßen und der sie begleitenden Bebauung unter Zuhilfenahme von privater Initiative, wie in Selb; um Konzepte für einen Stadteingang mit neuer gemischter Nutzung an einem Ort, der bisher nur als Ort des schnellen Durchgangs und des Gewerbes aufgefallen ist, in Schwäbisch Gmünd; um eine neue Möglichkeit, den Stadteingang zu akzentuieren, in einem viel kleineren, architektonischen Maßstab in Landshut; und um ein neues Quartier, das große Chancen bietet, sich zu einem neuen städtebaulichen Schwerpunkt mit verbindenden Qualitäten zu entwickeln, in Ettlingen.

Das sind fünf beispielhafte Themenstellungen, wie sie heute in ganz Deutschland relevant sind. Der Katalog will dazu beitragen, die oben skizzierte Debatte weiterzuführen. Die thematischen Essays, die den Wettbewerbsergebnissen vorangestellt sind, sollen diese vertiefen.

Kaye Geipel
Stellvertretender Chefredakteur *Bauwelt*, stellvertretender Vorstandsvorsitzender Europan Deutschland e. V.

Saskia Hebert
Dr.-Ing. Architektin BDA, Stadt- und Transformationsforscherin, Mitinhaberin von subsolar* architektur & stadtforschung | Hebert und Lohmann PartG mbB, entwirft konkrete Räume und mögliche Zukünfte, stellvertretende Vorstandsvorsitzender Europan Deutschland e. V.

Michael Rudolph
Station C23, Leipzig, Vorstandsvorsitzender Europan Deutschland e. V.

Europan 16 – More than a European Test Laboratory

The topic of Europan 16, 'Living Cities', undoubtedly gave the participants considerable scope for setting their own focuses with respect to content. But this time the choice of topic contained a 'fixed core' that could not be ignored or sidestepped: the Corona crisis has called attention to the importance of public space for every form of urbanization in a hitherto inconceivable world-wide test laboratory.

The red barrier tape with which islands, no matter how small, of public play equipment for children were made unusable during lockdown phases stick in our minds as a particularly stark example. Green public spaces near one's own door that are designed in a lively manner and can be used in diverse ways shape our individual way of life perhaps more than we imagine. Day after day they give rise to identification with one's personal surroundings. If such spaces are lacking, not only does the architecture lack any quality, but buildings themselves then become islands isolated from society.

This would be a self-evident observation if the majority of urban development today did not give too little attention to these spatial links between architecture and its surroundings – despite all the rhetoric. Public space in general is under pressure, and this quite clearly applies to all the countries that participated in Europan 16. There has long been a lack of funding for the management of peripheral public space in particular. But it is on such marginalized, initially unremarkable areas that the quality of future biodiversity is at stake, as the multifaceted debates about the Anthropocene make clear.

There are clear reasons for this neglect: a mountain of issues, beginning with structural changes, the transformation of mobility, and the call for freedom from CO_2 emissions and energy self-sufficiency – which is needed even more quickly due to the war in Ukraine – to the lack of affordable living space. Many cities are thus being pushed to their stress limits and have too few free capacities.

A Europe-wide competition like Europan is also not in the position to offer any miracle cures. But over its two-year course and with the results now being presented, such as an exemplary development of a district by means of bundling and the incorporation of conventional solutions focussing on individual cases, E16 is able to give rise to new synergies. Quite frequently, involving the population at an early point in time and concentrating on a few but then also jointly agreed upon characteristics serves as a catalyst for successful development. The topic 'Living Cities' thus aims in no way only at urban starting situations, but also targets the urban fringe, small towns, and rural surroundings. And in places where there are insufficient planning capacities, the temporary involvement of 'knowledge agents' can be of great assistance when what is concerned, for instance, is the programmatic activation of town and district cores or streets that no longer function.

A total of forty European cities from nine countries participated in E16. The five German sites in this round offer an almost unparalleled breadth of societal and ecological, social and economic issues with very diverse urban scales. It is about the qualities of new, innovative, and cooperative housing construction, as in Wernigerode; about reactivating city centres and the structures that accompany them with the help of private initiatives, as in Selb; about concepts for an entrance to the city with mixed uses at a location that had hitherto only caught the eye as a place for speedy passage and commerce, as in Schwäbisch Gmünd; about a new possibility to accentuate the entrance to the city on a much smaller architectural scale in Landshut; and about a new district that offers great opportunities to develop into a new urban development focus with connective qualities, as in Ettlingen.

These are five exemplary topics that can be seen throughout Germany today. This catalogue would thus like to contribute to continuing and expanding on the abovementioned debates with the results of the competition as well as the thematic essays prepended to them.

Kaye Geipel
Deputy editor-in-chief of *Bauwelt*, vice chairman of the board of Europan Deutschland e. V.

Saskia Hebert
Dr.-Ing. architect BDA, urbanologist and transformation researcher, co-owner of subsolar* architektur & stadtforschung | Hebert und Lohmann PartG mbB, designs concrete spaces and possible futures, vice chairman of the board of Europan Deutschland e. V.

Michael Rudolph
Station C23, Leipzig, chairman of the board of Europan Deutschland e. V.

Lebendige Städte

Innovative Prozesse und Projekte für die Reaktivierung urbanisierter Räume

Der Wettbewerb Europan 16 „Living Cities – Lebendige Städte" fragt danach, wie wir in den urbanisierten Räumen unserer Städte und Kommunen dem Klimawandel und den vom Menschen verursachten sozialen, wirtschaftlichen und kulturellen Ungleichheiten mit innovativen und integrativen Projekten sowie neuen Planungsprozessen begegnen können.

Ziel des Wettbewerbs ist die Entwicklung von Ideen für vernachlässigte, brachliegende, leere, stigmatisierte oder monofunktional genutzte Flächen, um diese wieder zu lebendigen, integrativen und durchmischten Stadträumen zu transformieren.

Dynamiken der Kreislaufwirtschaft

Die Dynamiken der Kreislaufwirtschaft ermöglichen es, in den Europan-Projekten Elemente der Architektur, der Stadt- und der Landschaftsplanung, Wasser-, Material- und Energiekreisläufe zu berücksichtigen, miteinander zu verbinden und durch ihre Inbezugsetzung neue lebendige Stadträume zu denken und zu planen.

Stadträume werden als komplexe Ökosysteme betrachtet, die Ströme nach innen und außen erzeugen und sich beständig weiterentwickeln. Die Berücksichtigung von Dynamiken der Kreislaufwirtschaft kann auf verschiedenen Ebenen einen Einfluss auf den Entwurfsprozess haben. Fragen der Recyclingfähigkeit, der Wiederverwendung organischer Materialien, der Nutzung erneuerbarer Energien, der Anpassung an den Klimawandel und der Integration von Natur und Biodiversität können dazu beitragen, an den Standorten des Wettbewerbs E16 innovative Projekte und Prozesse anzustoßen.

Die Transformation urbanisierter Stadträume zu Ökosystemen zwischen Natur und Kultur kann langfristig zur Verringerung des ökologischen Fußabdrucks und des Verbrauchs nicht erneuerbarer Ressourcen in den urbanisierten Räumen beitragen.

Dynamiken der Integration

Städte sind heute zunehmend mit Konflikten und Exklusionsprozessen konfrontiert, die aus Ausgrenzung, Marginalisierung und dem Mangel an bezahlbarem Wohnraum, Arbeit, Bildung sowie öffentlichen Dienstleistungen entstehen. Um diesen sozialen Brüchen etwas entgegenzusetzen, sollten derzeit brachliegende, stigmatisierte oder leere Stadträume wieder zu inklusiven Orten transformiert werden. Dabei stehen baulich-räumliche Dynamiken der Integration im Vordergrund, die durch die Artikulation sozialer und ökologischer Anliegen die territoriale Gerechtigkeit unterstützen. Fragen der Zugänglichkeit zu öffentlichen Infrastrukturen und zu bezahlbarem Wohnraum sollten eine vorrangige Rolle spielen und die lebendige Stadtgesellschaft fördern.

Die gemeinsame Sorge um unsere Städte als unmittelbare Lebensumwelt kann die Inklusion fördern, indem derzeit marginalisierte Räume wieder zu Orten des Austauschs, des gemeinsamen Lernens und der biologischen Vielfalt verwandelt werden.

Vesta Nele Zareh
Prof. Dipl.-Ing., Geschäftsführerin Europan Deutschland, Professorin für Stadtplanung an der Hochschule Anhalt

Living Cities

Innovative Processes and Projects for the Reactivation of the Existing Urban Landscape

The competition Europan 16 'Living Cities – Lebendige Städte' asks how we can counter climate change and manmade social, economic, and cultural inequalities in the urbanized spaces of our cities and communities with innovative and inclusive projects and new planning processes?

The goal of the competition is to develop ideas for neglected, derelict, empty, stigmatized, or monofunctionally utilized spaces in order to transform them into vibrant, inclusive, and mixed urban spaces.

Dynamics of the Circular Economy

The dynamics of the circular economy make it possible to consider elements of architecture, urban and landscape planning, water, and material and energy cycles in the Europan projects, to connect them with each other and to think and plan new living urban spaces based on their interrelation.

Urban spaces are viewed as complex ecosystems that generate flows internally and externally and are constantly evolving. Considering the dynamics of the circular economy can have an impact on the design process on a number of levels. Issues connected with recyclability, the reuse of organic materials, the use of renewable energy, adaptation to climate change, and the integration of nature and biodiversity can help trigger innovative projects and processes at the E16 competition sites.

The transformation of urbanized urban spaces into ecosystems between nature and culture can contribute to reducing the ecological footprint as well as the consumption of non-renewable resources in urbanized spaces in the long term.

Dynamics of Integration

Cities today are increasingly confronted with conflicts and processes of exclusion arising from exclusion, marginalization, and a lack of affordable housing, employment, education, and public services. In order to counteract these social disruptions, currently abandoned, stigmatized, or empty urban spaces should be transformed back into inclusive places. The focus here is on structural-spatial dynamics of inclusion that support territorial justice by articulating social and environmental concerns. Issues of accessibility to public infrastructures and affordable housing should play a primary role in fostering vibrant urban societies.

Shared care for our cities as direct living environments can promote inclusion by transforming currently marginalized spaces back into places of exchange, shared learning, and biodiversity.

Vesta Nele Zareh
Prof. Dipl.-Ing., Managing director Europan Germany, Professor of Urban Planning at Anhalt University

E16 Standorte Locations

Revitalisation
1 Alzira (ES)
2 Bassens / Bordeaux Métropole (FR)
3 Bitonto (IT)
4 Douaisis Agglo (FR)
5 Fagerstrand (NO)
6 Klagenfurt (AT)
7 La Porte du Hainaut (FR)
8 Madrid (ES)
9 Namur (BE)
10 Risøy (NO)
11 Varberg (SE)
12 Västerås (SE)
13 **Wernigerode (DE)**

Recovery
14 Almendralejo (ES)
15 Aulnat (FR)
16 Barcelona (ES)
17 Biel / Bienne (CH)
18 Graz (AT)
19 Grenoble (FR)
20 Levanger (NO)
21 Linz (AT)
22 Pont-Aven (FR)
23 Quimper (FR)
24 Roquetas de Mar (ES)
25 **Schwäbisch Gmünd (DE)**
26 Selb (DE)

Care
27 Aalst (BE)
28 Auneuil (FR)
29 Beizama (ES)
30 Région de Bruxelles-Capitale (BE)
31 Carouge (CH)
32 Esparreguera – Colonia Sedó (ES)
33 Ettlingen (DE)
34 Hjertelia (NO)
35 Istres (FR)
36 Karlskoga (SE)
37 Landshut (DE)
38 Limoges (FR)
39 Niort (FR)
40 San Donà Venezia (IT)

Entspannte Urbanität in Stadtlandschaften

Ein Plädoyer für grün-blaue Infrastrukturen und alltagstaugliche Quartiere

Es mag paradox klingen, in Zeiten des Klimawandels, der Digitalisierung und der demografischen Veränderungen sowie mit Blick auf die aktuellen globalen Krisen über „entspannte" Urbanität zu sprechen, wo es doch um die Resilienz von Städten, ihr Rückgrat und ihre Lebenswirklichkeit geht, die mehr denn je bedroht ist, infrage gestellt wird und sich ganz augenscheinlich verändert. Mein Plädoyer zielt gerade deshalb auf ein solches Zukunftsbild der räumlichen Planung.

Städte spielen als Artefakte von Planung, Städtebau und Architektur, als verfasste Gebietskörperschaften, mit Politik und Verwaltung und als Gemeinwesen eine entscheidende Rolle in den sozialen, ökonomischen und ökologischen Transformationen und insbesondere in den aktuellen Krisen. Städte und ihre öffentlichen Infrastrukturen müssen robust und resilient sein. Dabei sind sie auch Labore und Orte, wo Bürgerinnen und Bürger, und damit die Stadtgesellschaft, das Vertrauen in öffentliche Institutionen und gemeinsame Werte behalten, verlieren oder wiedergewinnen können; in einer Zeit, in der Gemeinsinn, kollektiver Ausgleich und das Teilen von Ressourcen zunehmend mehr gelten als Individualisierung – „mehr wir, weniger ich" –, auch wenn es in der Pandemie lange um Distanz und Vermeidung persönlicher Kontakte ging; in einer Zeit, in der die Frage steht, welchen Planeten wir hinterlassen, weil ein wegweisendes Urteil des Bundesverfassungsgerichts vom 24. März 2021 eine Verpflichtung zur Klimaneutralität auch in Bezug auf zukünftige Generationen begründet hat; in einer Zeit, in der sich Extremwetterereignisse in einem bisher unbekannten Ausmaß ereignen und sogar häufen; in einer Zeit, in der seit dem 24. Februar 2022 in der Ukraine in einem Angriffskrieg vor unser aller Augen zahlreiche Städte, und dort vor allem sensible öffentliche Infrastrukturen und Wohnquartiere, zerstört werden und Millionen Menschen auf der Suche nach Schutz oder auf der Flucht ganz elementar auf öffentliche Infrastrukturen wie Verkehrswege, Versorgungssysteme, Krankenhäuser oder Informationskanäle und Betreuungsangebote angewiesen sind.

All diese Auswirkungen der globalen Krisen zeigen, dass weniger die klassischen Schwarzpläne des Städtebaus, sondern vielmehr die blau-grünen Raumsysteme und öffentlichen Infrastrukturen der Städte herausgefordert sind. Das betrifft Gewässer, Grünbereiche, Mobilitäts- und Versorgungsinfrastrukturen sowie Bildungs- und Kulturlandschaften gleichermaßen.

In den Quartieren – sowohl bei der Planung als auch bei ihrem Bau, aber vor allem in ihren Perspektiven im Bestand – sind Alltagstauglichkeit und solidarisch-produktive Nachbarschaften für den sozialen Zusammenhalt sowie als ökonomische Existenz und Basis von Wertschöpfung gefragt. Deshalb will ich zwei Thesen formulieren und mit einer Lesart der Stadt als Landschaft beginnen.

Es liegen drei Landschaften übereinander

Zunächst prägt die Topografie der Stadt mit ihrer Lage sowie ihrer unveränderlichen Dimension im Raum, den Höhenlinien, Gewässern und Landschaftselementen den Stadtkörper und das historische Grundmuster der Erschließung. Dies kann als erste Landschaft der Stadt gelesen werden, wie wir sie zum Beispiel auf den Luftbildern und in Geodaten erkennen.

Darüber liegt das Netz der Infrastrukturen in Form von Linien, Punkten sowie kleineren und größeren Flächen. Diese machen das öffentliche Raumsystem der Stadt, die Mobilitäts- und Versorgungssysteme sowie die Standorte und Adressen des Gemeinwesens (Gesundheit, Sicherheit, Abfallentsorgung, Bildung, Kultur usw.) aus. Um dieses Netz geht es, wenn wir von robusten öffentlichen Infrastrukturen sprechen. Diese Grundzüge der Stadt können als ihre zweite Landschaft gelesen werden.

Die hier angesiedelten und eingefügten Bauten oder Liegenschaften mit den zugehörigen Außen- und Innenräumen formen schließlich die dritte Landschaft der Stadt – mit ihren Nutzungsspielräumen und -konflikten, aber auch mit der Verfügbarkeit von Raum und schließlich den auf diese Orte und Räume bezogenen Daten ihrer Bürgerinnen und Bürger. Citi Data, wie sie von Francesca Bria (in der Frankfurter Allgemeinen Zeitung vom 19. Oktober 2020) bezeichnet werden. Sie stellen im Digitalzeitalter ein öffentliches Gut dar, um das hart gerungen wird und das häufig von privaten Tech-Firmen betrieben und kontrolliert wird.

Mit Blick auf dieses komplexe Bild von den drei Landschaften der Stadt wird klar, dass wir im Zusammenhang mit robusten Infrastrukturen auch über Bodenpolitik, die Verfügbarkeit von Raum, Verteilungsgerechtigkeit sowie über sozial-ökologische Standards und die demokratische Nutzung von Daten sprechen müssen.

Grün-blaue Infrastrukturen als Stadtqualitäten

Die öffentlichen Räume bilden als Bewegungsräume, Verbindungswege, Treffpunkte sowie Aufenthalts- und Veranstaltungsorte das tragende Gerüst der Stadt. Anziehungskraft und Verweildauer, aber vor allem sozial gerechte Alltagstauglichkeit werden durch funktionale und gestalterische Qualitäten sowie Sauberkeit und Sicherheit bestimmt. Eine differenzierte Zuständigkeit für die jeweiligen Belange sowie die essenzielle Bedeutung als Bindeglied zwischen den verschiedenen Nutzungen und Adressen erfordern deshalb besondere Anstrengungen, gegebenenfalls auch Formate und Bündelungen, für ressortübergreifendes Handeln.

Zugleich unterliegt der Strukturwandel der Städte den globalen Anforderungen von Klimaschutz und Klimaanpassung. Deshalb kommt der Pflege, Anreicherung und Weiterentwicklung einer nachhaltigen Freiraum- und Grünausstattung eine zentrale Rolle zu. Neben vorhandenen Anlagen sind insbesondere neue Potenziale in stark versiegelten Stadt- und Verkehrsräumen, z.B. auch auf großen Dächern oder an geeigneten Fassaden, zu erschließen. Überhitzte Stadträume erfordern Kühlung durch Grün, aber auch frei zugängliche Trinkwasserangebote.

Schließlich sei auf die Bedeutung von Maßnahmen zum Hochwasser- oder Küstenschutz entlang von Flussufern und Deichen hingewiesen, die als kritische Infrastrukturen eine wesentlich größere Aufmerksamkeit erfordern. Das hat zukünftig erhebliche Auswirkungen auf ihre Gestaltung. Dies zeigt das Projekt Waller Sand in Bremen, das eine ausgedehnte Maßnahme zum Küstenschutz in der Überseestadt mit der Gestaltung eines neuen öffentlichen Freiraums verknüpft. In einem neuen Stadtquartier mit einem räumlichen Bezug zum Hafenbetrieb ist ein multicodierter Stadtraum für Freizeitnutzungen entstanden.

An diesen Beispielen zeigt sich, dass wesentliche Parameter eines zukunftsfähigen Städtebaus nicht allein in baulichen Dichten und Gebäudetypologien, sondern vor allem in der Qualität der grün-blauen Räume und Infrastrukturen begründet liegt. So möchte ich jedenfalls entspannte Urbanität verstanden wissen.

Robuste Alltagsquartiere
Sowohl in der inneren Stadt als auch in den Bestandsquartieren und bei der Entwicklung von neuen Quartieren geht es um die Fünf- oder auch 15-Minuten-Stadt, mit einer Nutzungsmischung und autofreier, zumindest autoarmer Erreichbarkeit aller wesentlichen öffentlichen Infrastrukturen.

Ein solcher Ansatz steckt im Konzept von Bildungslandschaften sowie der Unterstützung von Adressen und Aktivitäten des Gemeinwesens, wie er zum Beispiel im Rahmen der Städtebauförderung praktiziert wird. Diese Erfahrungen stehen derzeit Pate bei Strategien für die produktive Stadt in gewachsenen Quartieren oder bei der Konfiguration von neuen Quartieren. Netzwerke aus lokal verankerten, kleinen oder mittleren Unternehmen, Stadtteilinitiativen von Künstlern und Institutionen vor Ort sowie die Stadtteilpolitik und das Quartiersmanagement suchen mit dem Ziel der Stabilisierung solidarischer Nachbarschaften und der Unterstützung lokaler Unternehmen nach neuen Allianzen. Dabei wird das Verhältnis zwischen Erwerbsarbeit und Care-Arbeit neu ausgelotet.

Im Rahmen eines von der GEWOBA 2019 in Bremen ausgelobten studentischen Wettbewerbs mit dem schönen Titel „Alvar-Aalto-Preis" für die Nachverdichtung eines Standorts in der Großsiedlung Neue Vahr wurden genau solche Ideen prämiert: multifunktional nutzbare Freiräume, Erschließungsbereiche und Räume für Co-Working und Nachbarschaftshilfe sowie in dieses System integrierte Wohnformen. Sharing von Raum und Arbeit also. Dieser von der jüngsten Generation von Architektinnen und Architekten ziemlich radikal vorgetragene Anspruch zeigt, dass sich Wertesysteme verändern. Den Bau- und Raumstrukturen der Großsiedlungen, als gebaute Stadtlandschaften im Eigentum gemeinnütziger Wohnungsunternehmen, in denen in den kommenden Jahren auch ein Generationswechsel ansteht, werden Potenziale für robuste Alltagsquartiere zugesprochen.

Insgesamt wollte ich verdeutlichen, dass neben den städtebaulichen Parametern für Quartiere insbesondere die Nutzungsmischung, die sozialen Belange und, im Zeichen des Klimawandels, schließlich die Beiträge zum Klimaschutz auf der Agenda stehen. Die bisher eher auf Gebäude bezogenen Standards müssen deshalb auf die Ebene des Städtebaus erweitert werden. Dann kommen neben dem flächensparenden Bauen, ausreichend dimensionierten Freiräumen und Parametern einer zukunftsfähigen Mobilität noch die Aspekte Energieerzeugung und -verbrauch hinzu.

Iris Reuther
Prof. Dr.-Ing., Architektin und freie Stadtplanerin 1992–2013 mit dem Büro für urbane Projekte in Leipzig, 2004–13 Professur für Stadt und Regionalplanung an der Universität Kassel, seit 2013 Senatsbaudirektorin der Freien Hansestadt Bremen

Relaxed Urbanity in Urban Landscapes

A Plea for Green-Blue Infrastructures and Districts Suitable for Everyday Life
Speaking about a 'relaxed' urbanity in an era of climate change, digitization and demographic changes, as well as with a view to the current global crises might sound paradoxical. When what is really concerned is the resilience of cities, their backbone, and their life reality, which is more endangered than ever, is being called into question, and is undergoing clear changes. My plea thus aims at such a picture of the future of spatial planning.

As artefacts of planning, urban development, and architecture, as public authorities with a policy and administration, and as polities, cities play a decisive role in social, economic, and ecological transformations and in the current crises in particular.

Cities and their public infrastructures need to be robust and resilient. They are hence also laboratories and places where citizens and thus urban society can retain, lose, or regain trust in public institutions and shared values.

At a time when community spirit, collective exchange, and the allocation of resources are increasingly being regarded as greater than individualization: 'More we, less I' – even though distancing and avoiding personal contact were of importance for a long time during the pandemic. At a time when there is a question of what sort of planet we will leave behind, because a trailblazing ruling by the German Federal Constitutional Court from 24 March 2021 created an obligation to climate neutrality, also with reference to future generations. At a time when extreme weather events are taking place on a hitherto unknown scale and are even increasing. And at a time when, since 24 February 2022, numerous cities and in particular sensitive public infrastructures and residential districts are being destroyed in the war of aggression in Ukraine and additional millions of individuals are searching for protection or rely in a very fundamental way on public infrastructures like traffic routes, supply systems, hospitals, or channels of information and care services.

All these effects of global crises show that what are needed are not so much the classic figure-ground plans of urban planning, but instead many more blue-green spatial systems and public infrastructures of cities. This applies equally to bodies of water, green areas mobility and supply infrastructures, and educational and cultural landscapes.

In city districts – as well as in their planning and construction, but especially with respect to their perspectives on their existing inventory – what are needed are everyday usability and solidarity and productive neighbourhoods for social cohesion as well as an economic existence and a basis for the creation of value. This is why I want to formulate two theses and begin with an approach to reading the city as a landscape.

Three Landscapes Situated on Top of One Another
The topography of a city with its location and unchanging dimensions in space, its contours, bodies of water, and landscape elements, is the first thing that shapes the urban corpus and its basic historical patterns of development. This can be read as the 'first landscape' of the

city, as we recognize it, for instance, in aerial photos and in geographical data.

Over it lies the network of infrastructures in the form of lines, points, and smaller and larger areas. They constitute the system of the public space of a city, its mobility and supply systems, and locations and addresses for the community (health, safety, waste disposal, education, culture, et cetera). When we speak about robust public infrastructures, we are talking about this network. These basic characteristics of a city can be read as its 'second landscape'.

Finally, the buildings and properties situated and inserted here, along with their interior and exterior spaces, form the 'third landscape' of the city. With their utilization options and conflicts, but also with the availability of space, and last but not least the data on citizens related to these locations and spaces. In the digital age, 'Citi Data', as Francesca Bria has called this (in the Frankfurter Allgemeine Zeitung of 19 October 2020), represents a public good that is fought for and often operated and controlled by private tech companies.

Based on this complex picture of the three landscapes, it becomes clear that we have to plead for robust infrastructures and also talk about land policy, the availability of space, distributive justice, and about social-ecological standards and the democratic use of data.

Green-Blue Infrastructures as Urban Qualities

As spaces for movement, connecting paths, meeting places, and places for events and spending time, public spaces form the supporting framework of the city. Attractiveness and time spent there, but in particular socially equitable suitability for everyday use are determined by functional and design-related qualities as well as by cleanliness and safety. Differentiated responsibility for the respective concerns as well as the essential importance as a connective link between different uses and addresses thus call for particular efforts, and possibly also formats and bundling for coordinated action.

At the same time, the structural transformation of cities must satisfy the global calls for climate protection and climate adaptation. Maintaining, augmenting, and further developing a sustainable equipping of open and green spaces is thus a central task. Besides existing sites, particularly new potentials in heavily sealed urban and traffic spaces, for instance, on large roofs or suitable façades as well, also have to be developed. Overheated urban spaces require cooling by means of greenery, but also freely accessible offers of drinkable water.

Finally, it is necessary to point to the importance of measures to protect against flooding along riverbanks and dykes, which require considerably more attention than critical infrastructures. This has significant impacts on their future design. This is illustrated by the Waller Sand project in Bremen, which combines an extensive coastal protection measure in Überseestadt with the design of a new public open space. A multi-coded urban space for leisure uses has been created in a new urban quarter with a spatial relationship to the port operations.

Another topic of urban landscapes with a potentially high groundwater level is rainwater management in dense city centres, at heavily sealed locations in transformation, and in existing districts. Here, the developed system of greenery and bodies of water is renatured and adapted and frequently expanded within the framework of the creation of new public squares and urban spaces. These requirements also have an impact on the design and usability of such sites.

Based on such examples, it becomes clear that an important parameter of a future-oriented urban development is derived not only from structural density and building typologies, but also particularly from the quality of green-blue spaces and infrastructures. This is how I, in any case, would like to regard 'relaxed urbanity'.

Robust Everyday Districts

What is important both in city centres, but also in existing districts and in the development of new districts in particular is the five- or also fifteen-minute city, with a mix of utilizations and an accessibility of all important public infrastructures without a car or at least in a car traffic-limited manner.

Such an approach is found in the concept of educational landscapes as well as in support for the addresses and activities of the community, as is practiced, for instance, within the framework of urban development funding.

Such experiences are what stand behind strategies for the productive city in developed districts or the configuration of new districts. Networks of locally anchored small or mid-size businesses, district initiatives by local artists and institutions, as well as district policy and neighbourhood management offices are seeking new alliances with the aim of stabilizing solitary neighbourhoods and supporting local businesses. The relationship between gainful employment and care work is thus being sounded out anew.

Within the framework of one of the student submissions for the retroactive densification of a site in the large Neue Vahr settlement, which was awarded a prize by the GEWOBA 2019 in Bremen with the lovely title 'Alvar Aalto Prize', precisely such ideas were highlighted: open spaces that can be used in a multifunctional manner, development areas, and spaces for co-working and neighbourhood assistance as well as forms of housing integrated within this system, hence a sharing of space and work. This quite radically presented aspiration of the youngest generation of architects shows that value systems are changing. The building and spatial structures of large settlements as built urban landscapes owned by non-profit housing associations, where a change of generations is foreseen in the coming years, have to be given the capabilities of robust everyday districts.

On the whole, I want to make it clear that what is on the agenda besides the urban development parameters for districts, is a mix of uses, social concerns, and contribution to climate protection in connection with climate change. The standards, which have hitherto applied to buildings, thus have to be expanded on the level of urban development. In addition to space-saving construction, suitably dimensioned open spaces, and parameters for a future-oriented mobility, there are then also the aspects of the generation and use of energy.

Iris Reuther
Prof. Dr.-Ing., architect and independent urban planner; 1992–2013 with the Büro für urbane Projekte in Leipzig; 2004–13 professor of urban and regional planning at the University of Kassel; since 2013 Senate Building Director of the Free Hanseatic City of Bremen

1

2

3

4

1 Der städtebaulich neu entwickelte Teil der Bremer Überseestadt im Kontext des weiterhin genutzten Holz- und Fabrikenhafens

2 Die neue Hochwasserschutzanlage wurde in ihrer notwendigen Lage und Dimensionierung als neuer Park und Freizeitort ausformuliert

3 Die Hochwasserschutzmauer und Deichlinie ist zugleich eine multifunktional nutzbare Sitzbank, die sich über die gesamte Länge des neuen Parks erstreckt

4 Einen Teil des Parks entlang des Hafenbeckens prägen heimische pflegeextensive Pflanzen auf den überlieferten Konturen

1 The part of the Überseestadt in Bremen that has undergone new urban development within the context of the wood and factory harbour, which is still in operation

2 The new flood protection system, with its necessary position and dimensioning, has been formulated as a new park and recreation area

3 The flood protection wall and dyke line is simultaneously a multifunctional seating bench that can be used from several sides and extends over the entire length of the new park

4 One section of the park along the harbour basin is characterized by low-maintenance indigenous plantings positioned on the given contours

Europan und die europäische Stadt

Europan ist der größte Architektur und Städtebauwettbewerb für junge interdisziplinäre Planerteams in Europa, und die Neue Leipzig-Charta ist das Leitbild der europäischen Stadtentwicklungspolitik. Wie passen beide Initiativen zusammen und welche Auswirkungen hat dies auf die Städte?

Europan 16 „Living Cities – Metabolic Vitalities and Inclusive Vitalities" möchte neue Ideen für mindergenutzte, brachgefallene oder monofunktionale Flächen entwickeln. Die Teilnehmenden sind aufgerufen, Projekte und Prozesse zu entwerfen, die lebendige und inklusive Quartiere befördern. Hierbei sind Aspekte der Kreislaufwirtschaft im Sinne der Metabolismus-Theorie zu berücksichtigen.

Die „Neue Leipzig-Charta – die transformative Kraft der Städte für das Gemeinwohl" ist das Leitdokument für eine nachhaltige Stadtentwicklungspolitik in Europa. Das Leitbild wurde 2007 durch die für Stadtentwicklung zuständigen Ministerinnen und Minister der europäischen Mitgliedsstaaten verabschiedet und 2020 grundlegend aktualisiert. Im Dokument werden die drei Dimensionen – gerecht, grün und produktiv – in Anlehnung an die drei Dimensionen der Nachhaltigkeit – sozial, ökologisch und ökonomisch – als Ziele einer guten Stadtentwicklung beschrieben. Darüber hinaus werden fünf Grundprinzipien der gemeinwohlorientierten Stadtentwicklung formuliert. Beide Initiativen scheinen den Fokus auf unterschiedliche Themen zu legen und dennoch gibt es Gemeinsamkeiten.

Transformation und lebendige Städte

Die Städte befinden sich seit jeher in einem stetigen Prozess der Anpassung und Weiterentwicklung. Hierbei stellen der demografische, klimatische, strukturelle und gesellschaftliche Wandel, die Integration und die Zuwanderung ebenso wie die Digitalisierung Städte fortlaufend auf eine Bewährungsprobe. Transformation ist somit kein neuer Prozess, sondern der Regelfall.

Mit Blick auf die Geschichte der europäischen Stadt sind lebendige und multifunktionale Städte keine Erfindung der Neuzeit. Vielmehr hat sich die Entmischung der Nutzungen, bestärkt durch die Charta von Athen, erst in den vergangenen acht Jahrzehnten vollzogen. Diese Entwicklung gilt es nun wieder umzukehren. Und obwohl die nutzungsgemischte und lebendige Stadt schon seit 15 Jahren als Leitbild in der Fachwelt anerkannt ist, ist die Transformation der gebauten Umwelt alles andere als einfach. Neue Ideen und Prozesse aus den Arbeiten von Europan können diese Transformation unterstützen.

Gemeinwohl und Inklusion

Der Begriff des Gemeinwohls ist in der Leipzig-Charta auf die Aspekte Gleichheit und Gerechtigkeit gerichtet. Insbesondere die Teilhabe von benachteiligten Bevölkerungsgruppen und den Zugang zu Angeboten der Grundversorgung (Gesundheit, Wohnraum, Energie usw.) gilt es sicherzustellen. Inklusion, wie in der Beschreibung von Europan als Ziel formuliert, wäre somit ein Bestandteil der gerechten Stadt im Sinne der Leipzig-Charta.

Die Herausforderung besteht auch bei diesem Thema nicht in der Formulierung des Ziels, sondern in der Umsetzung. Wie lässt sich eine gerechte und inklusive Stadt gewährleisten?

Nachhaltigkeit und Metabolismus

Während sich das Konzept der Nachhaltigkeit auf den Ressourcenverbrauch konzentriert, zielt das des Metabolismus auf flexible und erweiterbare Strukturen. Die Gemeinsamkeiten bestehen darin, dass beide Konzepte Bezug auf Prozesse der Natur nehmen und daraus das Prinzip der Kreislaufwirtschaft abgeleitet werden kann. Insofern ist beides nicht miteinander gleichzusetzen, kann aber zu ähnlichen Lösungsansätzen im Bauwesen führen.

Der Deutsche Städtetag hat sich für eine Entscheidungskaskade aus Bestandserhalt, Bestanderneuerung und als Ultima Ratio für den Neubau ausgesprochen, wenn eine Lösung im Bestand nicht möglich ist.

Dieses Vorgehen würde sowohl dem Konzept des Metabolismus gerecht, da es auf flexible und anpassbare Strukturen im Bestand setzt, als auch den Zielen der Nachhaltigkeit, da es den Ressourcenverbrauch durch die Um- und Nachnutzung des Bestands reduziert.

Herausforderungen für die Städte

Die verfolgten Zielsetzungen der beiden Initiativen sind ähnlich, allerdings sind die Herangehensweisen unterschiedlich. Während sich die Leipzig-Charta mehr an die politischen Entscheider und die bereits etablierten Planerinnen und Planer richtet, versucht Europan, durch einen kreativen Bottom-up-Ansatz neue Ideen und Projekte der jungen Planerinnen und Planer umzusetzen. Beide Ansätze sind wichtig – zum einen die politische und fachliche Rückendeckung und zum anderen die innovativen Ansätze in der Entwicklung vor Ort.

Die Städte als Akteure und Orte der Transformation müssen alle unterschiedlichen Entwicklungen und Trends rechtzeitig erkennen, ressortübergreifende, integrierte Strategien entwickeln und darauf basierend Maßnahmen umsetzen. Dies alles ist im Spannungsfeld einer zunehmend polarisierenden gesellschaftlichen Entwicklung und geringer werdender finanzieller Mittel keine einfache Aufgabe.

Die schwierige Aufgabenstellung macht es erforderlich, erprobte Instrumente und Vorgehensweisen auf den Prüfstand zu stellen. Die Herausforderungen der Zukunft unterscheiden nicht nach Ressortzuständigkeiten und Aufgabengebieten, sondern stellen Querschnittsaufgaben dar, die dazu auffordern, manche Lösungsansätze anders zu betrachten. Offenheit und Mut sind daher ebenso zur Bewältigung der Herausforderungen notwendig wie flexible und rechtssichere Instrumente, eine querschnittsorientierte, leistungsfähige Verwaltung und integrierte Konzepte sowie die entsprechenden Förderansätze.

Europan kann dabei unterstützen, das Bauwesen in den Städten kreativer zu denken, neue Lösungen zu schaffen und dadurch gleichzeitig den Nutzen für die Bürgerinnen und Bürger zu steigern sowie die Belastungen für Umwelt und Klima zu reduzieren. Dafür ist es wichtig, die guten Ansätze aus Europan enger mit der kommunalen Praxis zu verbinden, sodass Auftraggeber und Auftragnehmer von Anfang an enger zusammenarbeiten.

Timo Munzinger
Dr.-Ing., MBA, Referent für Städtebau, Hochbau, Stadtplanung, Stadtentwicklung und Baukultur beim Deutschen Städtetag und Städtetag Nordrhein-Westfalen

Europan and the European City

Europan is the biggest architecture and urban planning competition for young interdisciplinary teams of planners in Europe and the new Leipzig Charter is the mission statement for European urban development policy. How do the two initiatives fit together and what effects does this have on cities?

The Europan 16 competition 'Living Cities – Metabolic Vitalities and Inclusive Vitalities' is aimed at the development of new ideas for underused and mono-functional areas as well as wastelands. The participants are called upon to design projects and processes that give rise to lively and inclusive districts. Aspects relating to the circular economy in line with metabolism theory should also be taken into account.

The 'New Leipzig Charter – The Transformative Power of Cities for the Common Good' is the guidance document for sustainable urban development policies in Europe. The mission statement was first adopted in 2007 by the ministers responsible for urban development in the European member states and was updated substantially in 2020. In the document, the three dimensions of equitable, green, and productive with the three dimensions of sustainability, thus the social, ecological, and economical, are described as the aims of good urban development. Moreover, five basic principles of an urban development that is oriented towards the common good are also described. At first glance, the two initiatives share little in common and focus on different topics. But upon closer examination, there are some commonalities.

Transformation and Living Cities

Cities have always found themselves in an on-going process of adaptation and further development. Demographic, climactic, structural, and social change, integration and immigration, as well as the digitization of cities are thus continually being put to the test. Transformation is thus not a new process but instead the norm.

Within history, lively and multifunctional cities are not a new invention. The separation of uses inspired by the Charter of Athens has instead first taken place in the last eight decades. This development now has to be reversed. But even though the living city of mixed uses has already been recognized as an objective in the specialist world for the past fifteen years, transforming the built environment is anything but simple. New ideas and processes from the works submitted to Europan can, however, assist in advancing this transformation.

The Common Good and Inclusion

The concept of the common good in the Leipzig Charter focuses on the aspects of equality and justice. What has to be ensured is the participation of disadvantaged population groups and access to the offerings of basic supply and care (health, living space, energy, et cetera). Inclusion as it is formulated as an objective in the description of Europan would thus be a component of the equitable city in line with the Leipzig Charter.

In the case of this topic, the challenge also consists not of how the objective is formulated, but instead of the implementation on site. How can an equitable and inclusive city be guaranteed?

Sustainability and Metabolism

While the concept of sustainability focuses on the consumption of resources, the concept of metabolism aims at flexible and expandable structures. The commonalities consist more of the fact that both concepts refer to processes in nature and the ability to derive the principles of a circular economy from them. To this extent, the two concepts cannot be equated with one another, but can nevertheless lead to similar approaches to solutions in construction.

The Deutsche Städtetag (German Association of Cities) has advocated a cascade of decisions consisting of preservation of existing buildings, renovation of existing buildings and, as a last resort, new constructions if a solution in the existing buildings is not possible.

This course of action would fulfil not only the concept of metabolism, since it focuses on flexible and adaptable structures in the existing inventory. It also meets the objective of sustainability, since it reduces the consumption of resources by the repurposing and subsequent use of the existing inventory.

Challenges for Cities

As previously presented, the objectives pursued by the two initiatives are similar, even though the approaches differ. While the Leipzig Charter addresses more political decision-makers and already established planners, Europan strives to realize new ideas and projects by young planners by taking a creative bottom-up approach. Both approaches are important – political and specialist support on the one hand and innovative approaches to development on site on the other.

As protagonists and places of transformation, cities are confronted with a wide range of different challenges. They have to recognize the different developments and trends at the right time, develop integrated, interdisciplinary strategies, and implement measures based on them. This is not an easy task in the field of tension between an increasingly polarized development of society and more and more limited financial resources.

The obviously challenging task makes it necessary to put tried and tested instruments and approaches to the test and to rethink them. The challenges of the future do not differ based on departmental responsibilities and fields of activity, but are instead presented as cross-sectional tasks that sometimes make it necessary to think differently about some approaches. Openness and courage are thus just as necessary to meet the challenges as flexible and legally compliant instruments, efficient management oriented across sectors, and integrated concepts as well as corresponding funding approaches.

Europan can thus support the construction sector in thinking more creatively in cities, produce new solutions, and thus increase the benefits for citizens and reduce stresses on the environment and the climate at the same time. To do so, it is important to bring the good approaches from Europan closer to the practice of municipalities so that contracting authorities and firms work together more closely from the very beginning.

Timo Munzinger
Dr.-Ing., MBA, policy advisor for urban development, architecture, urban planning, and building culture at the Association of German Cities and Association of Cities and Towns in North Rhine-Westphalia

1

2

1   Europan-Workshop mit Finalisten
    E16 in Wernigerode, April 2022
2   Europan-Standortbesichtigung
    E16, Mai 2021

3   Umbau statt Abriss, Sanierung
    alter Schweinestall, Sommerschule
    Universität Kassel, 2020
4   Klimaanpassung in Freiräumen –
    pflegeextensive Pflanzungen,
    Arbeiten mit Bestandsbäumen,
    Beispiel: Mitmachpark Weinstadt

3

4

1 Europan workshop with the
finalists for E16 in Wernigerode,
April 2022
2 Europan site visit E16, May 2021

3 Conversion instead of demolition,
renovation of an old pigsty,
Summer School of the University
of Kassel, 2020
4 Climate adaptation in open
spaces – low-maintenance plantings, work with existing trees,
example: Mitmachpark Weinstadt

DE

Ergebnisse
in Deutschland

Results
in Germany

Ettlingen (DE)

Standort

Für das Entwicklungsareal soll im Sinne der Neuen Leipzig-Charta für gemeinwohlorientierte Stadtentwicklung in Europa eine Transformation eingeleitet werden, die ein lebendiges Quartier mit Wohn- und Arbeitsplätzen und mit eigener Identität herstellt. Hierbei ist der Neubau des Betriebshofs der Albtal-Verkehrsgesellschaft als vordefinierter Baustein unterzubringen, weil dessen heutiger Standort, in der zentralen Innenstadt, verlegt wird. Mit der ergänzenden Quartiersentwicklung des ehemaligen ELBA-Areals und des Bahnhofs Ettlingen-West sollen die „losen Enden" der angrenzenden Quartiere und Nutzungen aufgegriffen und zu einem stimmigen Nutzungs- und Strukturkonzept verwoben werden. Grundlage ist ein bestehender städtebaulicher Rahmenplan.

Der Standort bietet die Möglichkeit, einen Entwicklungsimpuls zu setzen, in Teilen Stadtreparatur zu leisten und einen neuen Stadtbaustein einzufügen. Mit der Quartiersentwicklung können der Stadtgesellschaft – neben dem neuen Betriebshof – bisher nicht zugängliche Flächen zurückgegeben sowie Raum für ca. 2.000 Arbeitsplätze, etwa 200 preisgünstige Mietwohnungen und ergänzende Nutzungen geschaffen werden.

Mit der Erschließung des Geländes können Defizite im Verkehrsnetz behoben, der Bahnhof kann als Ort des Ankommens ausgestaltet werden. Im Sinne einer doppelten Innenentwicklung sollen auch Beiträge zu Klimaanpassung, Klimaschutz und Mobilitätswende geleistet werden. Der Betrachtungsraum ist heute Übergangsbereich zwischen der kompakten Kernstadt und den großflächigen Strukturen des Industriegebiets „West". Die Lage, in direkter Nähe zur Innenstadt und die gute Verkehrsanbindung erhöhen den Wandlungsdruck auf diesen Stadtraum. Die Rheintalbahn wirkt stark trennend und ist als Lärmquelle relevant, bietet aber gleichzeitig ein hohes Erschließungspotenzial.

Es soll ein städtebaulicher Entwurf erarbeitet werden, der die Ziele des Rahmenplans konkretisiert, Aussagen zur städtebaulichen Struktur (Körnung, Höhenentwicklung usw.) enthält, Vorschläge zu Gebäudetypologien macht und die Grün- und Freiräume weiter ausformuliert. Der Stadtbereich soll auch weiterhin stark durch Arbeiten geprägt sein. Es ist erklärtes Ziel, die flächenbezogene Arbeitsplatzdichte zu erhöhen und so auch für ergänzende Nutzungen Raum zu schaffen, damit ein lebendiges Stadtleben gelingen kann. Auch für Büro- und Dienstleistungsnutzungen sind Umfeldqualität, Nahversorgung, soziale Einrichtungen sowie grüne Frei- und Begegnungsräume Standortvorteile und mitunter Kriterien für die Attraktivität eines Arbeitgebers. Insofern sollen Straßen und Plätze mit entsprechenden Aufenthalts- und Freiraumqualitäten geplant werden.

Im städtebaulichen Entwurf sollen die drei Grundprinzipien der Neuen Leipzig-Charta – die gerechte Stadt, die grüne Stadt und die produktive Stadt – als Leitgedanken des E16 konkret angewandt werden. Der angrenzende Bahnhof soll als Intermodalknoten (Mobilitätshub) und als Ort für Ankommende ausgebaut und die Adressbildung insgesamt verbessert werden.

Location

In line with the 'New Leipzig Charter' for European cities, the aim is to initiate a transformation for the urban area in order to give it a new identity. This envisages the new building for the Albtal-Verkehrsgesellschaft depot being accommodated in a predefined building block, because it has to be relocated from its location in the middle of the town centre. An urban development framework plan provides the basis for this.

In conjunction with the district development of the former ELBA site and the railway station, the 'loose ends' of adjacent districts and utilizations are also supposed to be taken up and woven into a coherent use and structure concept.

The site offers the opportunity to generate development momentum, to carry out urban renovation in places, and to introduce new urban components. In addition to providing space for the new depot, this district development will facilitate the incorporation of previously inaccessible areas into the urban community, and will create space for about 2,000 jobs, roughly 200 affordable rental units, and other uses.

The development of the site itself will remedy shortcomings in the transport network and create a new atmosphere for the station as a place of arrival. Such a twofold inner development can also contribute to climate change adaptation, climate protection, and the mobility transition. The project area, in the immediate vicinity of the town centre on the one hand and its good transport connections on the other, increase the pressure for change in this urban area. It is expected that it will develop into the city's strongest 'conversion zone'.

The railway station will be developed as an intermodal hub with improved connections to the surrounding transport network. The main line of the Rhine Valley Railway has a strong dividing effect and is a source of noise, but also offers great development potential. The aim is to develop an urban design draft that substantiates the objectives of the framework plan, specifies the urban structure (gradation, height development, et cetera), makes proposals with respect to building typologies, and formulates the green and open spaces further.

The urban area should continue to be strongly typified by 'work'. The declared aim, however, is to increase the density of workplaces and thus create space for complementary uses, so that lively urban life can emerge. The quality of the surroundings, local amenities, social facilities, and green open spaces are also locational advantages for office and service uses and at times criteria for the attractiveness of an employer.

Streets and squares should thus be planned with corresponding amenities and open space qualities. The three basic principles of the New Leipzig Charter – the 'Just City', the 'Green City', and the 'Productive City' – should be applied to the urban design in particular as the guiding principles of Europan 16. To this end, the image profile of this urban space must be improved in order to make it an urban pivot for the different transport interconnections that is proportionate to its function and significance.

Bevölkerung   Inhabitants
ca. 39.000

Betrachtungsraum   Study Site
64 ha

Projektgebiet   Project Site
16,4 ha

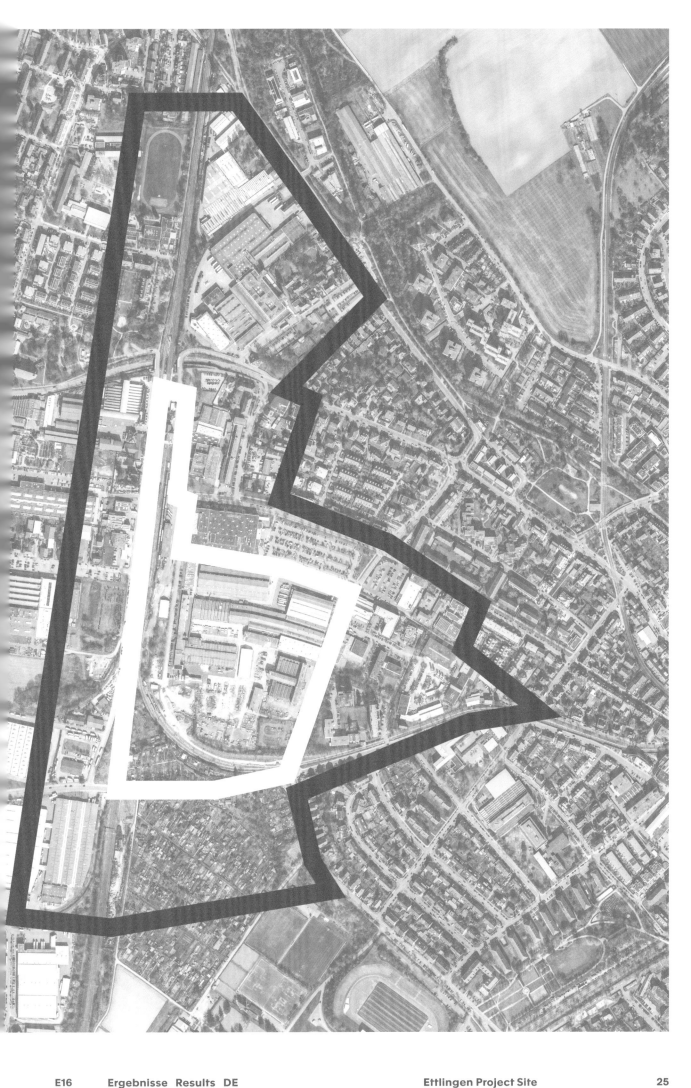

Multilayer City

Projekt

Multilayer Architecture ist eine Methode der Softwareentwicklung, bei der die Software aus verschiedenen, sich überlappenden Ebenen aufgebaut wird, die ineinandergreifen und gemeinsam das fertige Programm bilden. Die Multilayer City besteht ebenfalls aus verschiedenen Konzepten, die in ihrer Verbindung ein neues, vielschichtiges System auf dem ehemaligen ELBA-Gelände bilden und so den fertigen Entwurf darstellen.

Die konzeptuelle Idee ist die Schaffung eines resilienten, nachhaltigen Stadtteils, der vor allem neue Formen des Arbeitens, aber auch des Lebens ermöglicht. Der IT-Sektor hat hier einen besonderen Stellenwert. Auf dem ehemaligen ELBA-Gelände wird unter Einsatz verschiedener Konzept-Layers ein neues urbanes Viertel geschaffen, das mit neu entwickelter Urbanität und Charisma den Westen von Ettlingen mit der ganzen Stadt vereint.

Im Sinne des Themas von Europan 16, Living Cities – Lebendige Städte, ist das Ziel des Projekts die Schaffung einer resilienten urbanen Gemeinschaft, der es gelingt, existenzfähig und lebenswert zu sein, selbst unter sich verändernden Bedingungen, und zudem Ettlingen in seiner Gesamtheit positiv zu beeinflussen.

Der Gesamtentwurf besteht aus den drei zentralen Concept Layers: New Work, Mobilität und Circular Systems sowie grüner und blauer Infrastruktur.

Team

Wir – Sabine Tastel, Björn Simon, Jannik Mause, Milena Zampich, Fabius Kerstein, Tobias Trutzenberger, Tim Pertl, Sabine Wittmann, Nele Lesemann – sind ein Team aus acht Studentinnen und Studenten der Universität Kassel mit einem Dozenten als Vertreter des Teams. Nach unseren BA-Abschlüssen beschlossen wir, ein eigenes Projekt als interdisziplinäres Team zu organisieren, um unsere erlernten Fähigkeiten anzuwenden. Der Wettbewerb Europan 16 bot die perfekte Gelegenheit für uns und unser Ziel. Wir suchten also an unserer Universität nach Studierenden im Bereich Stadtplanung und Architektur, konnten jedoch niemanden aus dem Fachbereich Landschaftsplanung finden, der oder die sicher ebenfalls eine Bereicherung für das Team gewesen wäre. Da wir einander bereits aus vorherigen Kursen kannten, gingen wir davon aus, dass die Zusammenarbeit von sieben Master-Studentinnen und -Studenten, einem Bachelor-Studenten und einem Dozenten gut funktionieren würde, da unterschiedliches Fachwissen zum Einsatz kommen konnte.

Project

Multi-tier architecture is a software architecture in which software components are built up in overlapping tiers or layers that interlock and together produce the finished program. The Multilayer City is also built up from various concepts, the interconnection of which forms a new multi-layered system on the former ELBA site and represents the finished design.

The conceptual idea is the creation of a resilient, sustainable urban district, which facilitates not only new forms of working in particular, but also of living. The IT sector is a specific focus here. With the help of several concept layers, a new urban district is being created on the former ELBA site, which, with its newly developed urbanity and charisma, succeeds in uniting the west of Ettlingen with the city as a whole.

In line with the Europan 16 theme, 'Living Cities', the goal of the project is to create a resilient urban community that manages to remain viable and liveable even under changing conditions and, moreover, to positively influence Ettlingen as a whole.

The overall design is composed of three, thus central concept layers: New Work, Mobility and Circular Systems, and Green and Blue Infrastructure.

Team

We – Sabine Tastel, Björn Simon, Jannik Mause, Milena Zampich, Fabius Kerstein, Tobias Trutzenberger, Tim Pertl, Sabine Wittmann, Nele Lesemann – are a team of eight students from the University of Kassel with a university instructor as team representative. After completing our BA degrees, our goal was to do a self-organized project as an interdisciplinary team in order to apply the skills learned. The Europan 16 competition was perfect for us and our intention. So, we looked for other urban planning and architecture students at our university who were interested in participating in this project. Unfortunately, we were unable to find someone who specializes in landscape architecture, which would have been a great addition to the team. Since we knew each other from previous courses, we assumed that working together in a team of seven master's students plus one bachelor's student and an instructor could work well and enable us to apply our individual expertise.

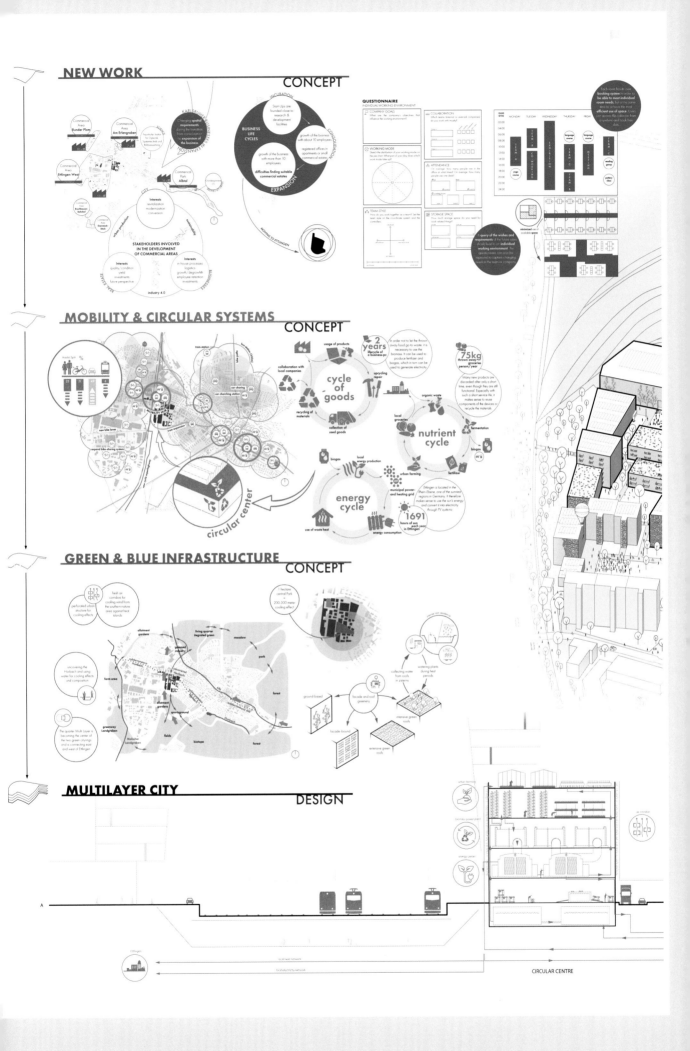

NEW WORK
CONCEPT

MOBILITY & CIRCULAR SYSTEMS
CONCEPT

GREEN & BLUE INFRASTRUCTURE
CONCEPT

MULTILAYER CITY
DESIGN

MULTILAYER CITY

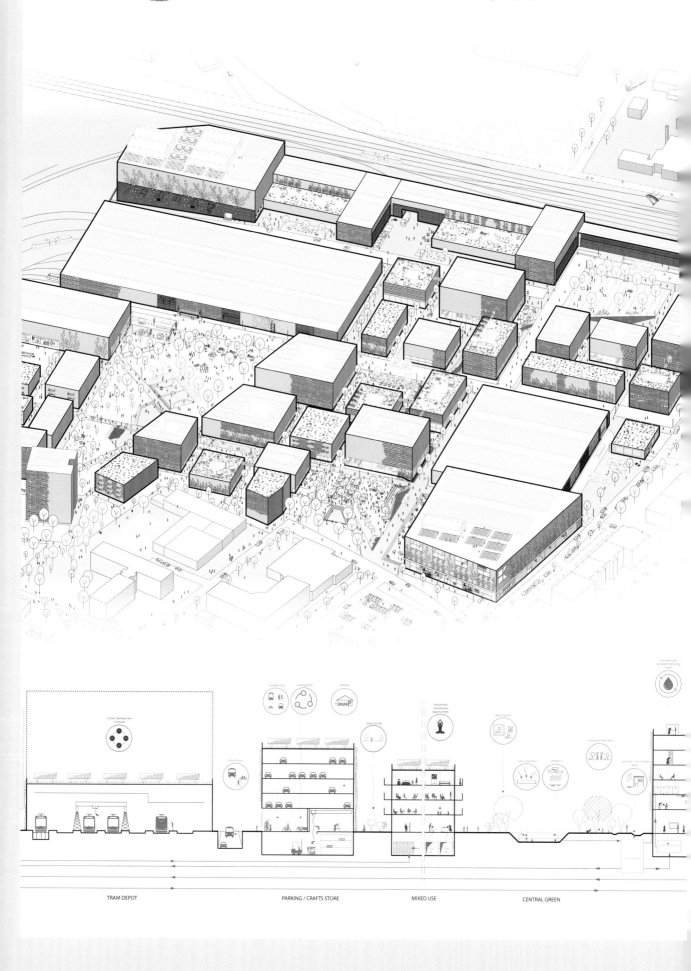

TRAM DEPOT   PARKING / CRAFTS STORE   MIXED USE   CENTRAL GREEN

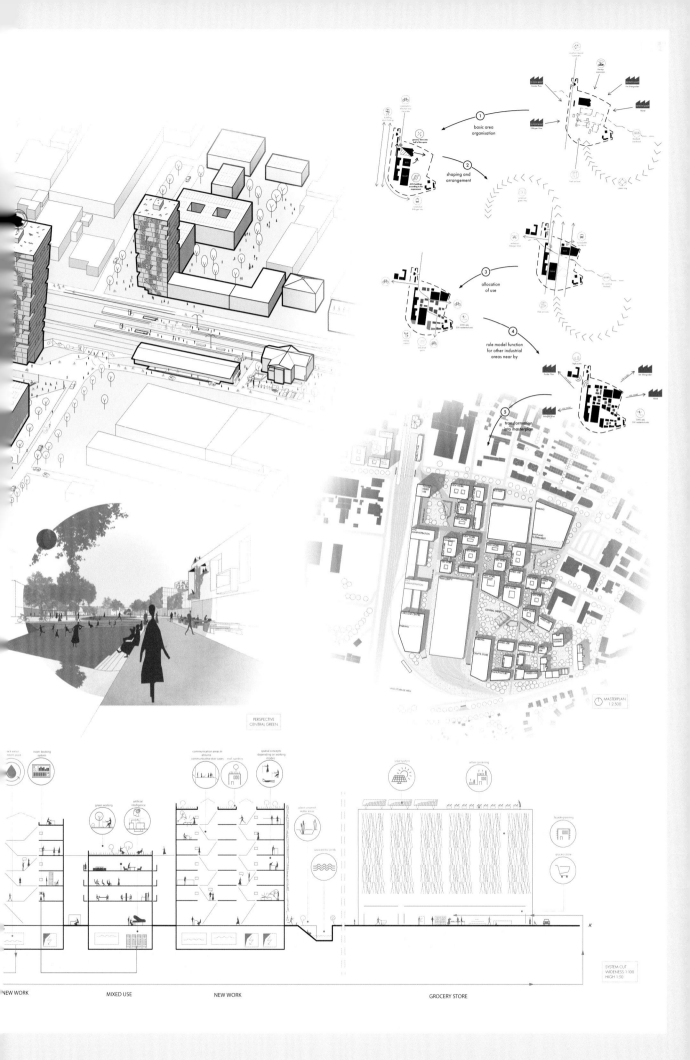

PERSPECTIVE
CENTRAL GREEN

MASTERPLAN
1:2.500

NEW WORK   MIXED USE   NEW WORK   GROCERY STORE

Querbeet

Projekt

Nachhaltigkeit und Klimaschutz sind die Leitthemen unserer Zeit, auf die sich das Konzept für das neue ELBA-Areal stützt.

Es wird ein Quartier entwickelt, welches nach dem Motto „Querbeet" ganz verschiedene Menschen und unterschiedliche Aspekte des großen Themenfelds der Gesundheit von Menschen und Erde zusammenbringt und von den daraus erwachsenden Synergien lebt.

Übergeordnete Themen sind Wohnen und Arbeiten; eine besondere Rolle kommt dem Forschungscampus zu, welcher sich mit der Produktion von Lebensmitteln und Energie, aber auch mit der Produktion und Vermittlung von Wissen beschäftigt. Er beherbergt Universität, Laborräume und Forschungsfelder sowie Gewächshäuser auf dem Dach des Forschungszentrums. Neben der Universität profitieren auch Biotechnologieunternehmen von den diversen Räumen, die der Forschung gewidmet sind.

Das Verhältnis von Baufeldern und Freiflächen ist ausgeglichenen. Einer starken Versiegelung des Gebietes wird durch die Freiraumgestaltung entgegengewirkt. Grünanlagen auf den öffentlichen Plätzen, grüne Erschließungsachsen sowie Fassaden- und Dachbegrünung sorgen – trotz der hohen baulichen Dichte – für ein gutes Mikroklima.

Ein zentrales Motiv des Entwurfs ist eine Abfolge von Plätzen, denen unterschiedliche Themen der gesunden Stadt zugewiesen sind. Sowohl der Bahnhofsplatz im Norden als auch die *Arena* im Süden sind gut funktionierende Quartierseingänge. Wer vom Bahnhof kommt, wird von der alten ELBA-Halle als Eingangstor empfangen und gelangt über die *Passage* zum *Forum*. Das Forum bildet den Schnittpunkt aller im Quartier vorhandenen Nutzungen.

Die Arena im Süden ist dem Thema Aktivität gewidmet, hier können verschiedenste sportliche Aktivitäten stattfinden, um diverse Nutzergruppen zu vereinen.

Team

Wir – Isabel Gierok, Nina Pfeiffer, Marleen Wenkow, Todor Nachev – sind eine Gruppe von drei Architekturstudentinnen und einem Architekten, die zurzeit verstreut in Deutschland, in München, Mainz und Darmstadt, leben. Im letzten Jahr haben wir zusammen am Standort Ettlingen des Europan-Wettbewerbs gearbeitet. Unser Konzept mit dem Titel „Ettlingen Querbeet" spiegelt unseren gemeinsamen Anspruch an die Planung wider, Architektur und Stadtplanung nachhaltig zu gestalten. Eine zukunftsfähige Stadt muss in unserem Verständnis aus dem Bestand heraus entwickelt werden, indem auf bestehende räumliche und soziale Strukturen sensibel eingegangen wird. Dabei ist es notwendig, innovative Lösungsansätze zu verfolgen, denen ein bewusster Umgang mit der Umwelt zugrunde liegt.

Project

Sustainability and climate protection are key topics of our time, and the basis for our concept for the new ELBA site.

What will be developed is a district that, based on the motto 'Querbeet' (at random), brings together very diverse individuals and aspects of the large thematic field of the health of people and the earth and is influenced by the synergies that thus develop.

Housing and work are superordinate topics. A special role is assigned to the research campus, which occupies itself not only with the production of food and energy, but also with the production and mediation of knowledge. It accommodates a university, laboratory spaces, and fields and greenhouses for research on the roof of the research centre. Besides the university, biotech firms also benefit from the diverse spaces dedicated to research.

There is a balanced relationship between construction fields and open spaces. Large-scale sealing of the area is countered by the design of the open space. Green areas on the public squares, green access routes, and greened façades and roofs ensure a good microclimate – despite the high building density.

A sequence of public squares, to which different topics relating to the healthy city are assigned, is a central motif in the design. Both the railway station square in the north as well as the 'Arena' in the south are well-functioning entrances to the district. People coming from the railway station are received by the old ELBA hall as an entrance gate and reach the 'Forum' via the 'Passage'. The 'Forum' forms the point of intersection for all the uses found in the district.

The 'Arena' in the south is dedicated to the topic of activity. Diverse sports activities can take place here, with the aim of bringing a wide range of groups of users together.

Team

We – Isabel Gierok, Nina Pfeiffer, Marleen Wenkow, Todor Nachev – are a group consisting of three architecture students and one architect, who are currently spread out around Germany, and live in Munich, Mainz, and Darmstadt. Over the past year, we worked together on the Ettlingen site of the Europan competition. Our concept, with the title 'Ettlingen Querbeet', reflects our shared planning objective of designing architecture and urban development sustainably. A sustainable city, as we understand it, must develop based on the existing situation by dealing with spatial and social structures that are already present in a sensitive way. In doing so, it is necessary to pursue innovative approaches to solutions, which include a deliberate approach to dealing with the environment.

ETTLINGEN QUERBEET___ Europan 16 - Living Cities

Sustainability and climate protection are the key themes of our time, on which the concept for the new ELBA site is based. A quarter will be developed, which brings together different people and aspects of the great topic of human and earth health and lives on synergies between them according to the motto "Querbeet." Overriding themes are living and working, but the heart of the district is the research campus, which deals with the production and transmission of knowledge. In addition to the university, biotechnology companies also benefit from the various facilities dedicated to research.

Concept

Research centre as a lighthouse

Development of volumes

Zoning of uses

Open spaces + sequence of places

System of passage

Concept of urban planning

site plan1_1000

ETTLINGEN QUERBEET___ Europan 16 - Living Cities

Living in the Querbeet-Quartier is characterized by two different types of living, which allow the intermingling of different groups of residents by creating meeting spaces and communal areas. The arcade house offers in the upper floors 1-4 room apartments with cut-out loggias as a private outdoor space. The communicative cooking and dining area is oriented towards the arcade, while the bedrooms and living rooms are located in the more protected part of the apartments. On the ground floor, in addition to the communal washing, bicycle and multifunctional rooms, there are studio apartments, which extend over two floors and can also be accessed via the arcade on the 1st floor. The more private living and sleeping rooms can be found in the studio on the gallery floor, as the more public workrooms on the ground floor are oriented towards the street. The adjacent terraces offer space for exhibitions. In addition to its development functions, the wide arcade offers spacious living areas where residents can meet and exchange views.

ground floor 1_600

Access to the acarde house

studio apartment

The deep house offers space for experimental living with a focus on community. Two residential units are each spread over two floors and with their cluster floor plans allow for shared flats with up to 10 separate rooms with private bathrooms. The area between the living cubes is shared and serves for example as a kitchen, dining and living room.

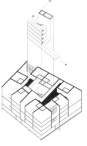

Access to the deep house

6er residential community

section a-a 1_600

ETTLINGEN QUERBEET___ Europan 16 - Living Cities

section b-b 1_600

AWG Rausenbach
Forschungsdach
Forschungshof
open air Kino
Bibliothek der Dinge
Passage
Forum
Co-Working
Gründer HUB
Bioteschgewerbe
Querbeet
Arena
Boderhalle
Tiefes Haus
KiTa
Landwergarghaus

Isometry without scale

Concept of passage

Roof:
intensive greening

Facade:
Photovoltaics

Greenhouse
Grid

Facade:
Ground-based
Greening

Ceiling
Overview

Carrying structure
Wood / Hybrid

Materials & Raw Materials

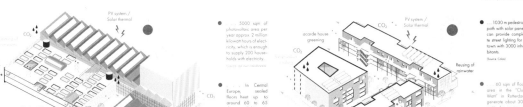

PV system /
Solar thermal

CO_2

5000 sqm of photovoltaic area per year approx. 2 million kilowatt hours of electricity, which is enough to supply 200 households with electricity.

In Central Europe, sealed floors heat up to around 60 to 65 degrees Celsius in summer, and the energy could be used to supply a swimming pool.

Busdepot &
E-Charging

Facade
greening

Neighbourhoods
greening

acarde house
greening

PV system /
Solar thermal

Reusing of
rainwater

Facade
greening

Vehicle
integrated PV

Neighbourhoods
greening

1030 m pedestrian path with solar panels can provide complete street lighting for a town with 3000 inhabitants.

60 sqm of floor area in the "Club Watt" in Rotterdam generate about 300 watts by means of kinetic energy. That's enough to power the DJ desk and the lighting in the station pub.

Basically, the aim is to develop a climate-neutral neighborhood by mainly supplying it with renewable energies. With regard to the heart of the design, the research center, for example, electricity is to be operated by PV systems. The reuse of rainwater can also be useful for the irrigation of the various plants. In addition, it can also be used for toilets in the apartment blocks. Repeated openings of the building structure also ensure adequate ventilation. In order to create a pleasant microclimate, the facades are to be greenery and, in general, a neighborhood planting is to extend over the entire area. After all, despite the new industry, no areas should be created that heat up excessively and do not benefit people.

QUERBEET

elevation Dieselstraße 1_600

Landshut (DE)

Standort

Die Stadt Landshut ist eine kreisfreie Stadt, regionales Oberzentrum und Hauptstadt des Regierungsbezirks Niederbayern. Auf lange Sicht plant Landshut die Umsetzung eines Stadtentwicklungsplans. In Zukunft soll nicht nur auf gegebene Umstände reagiert werden, sondern die Entwicklung durch gezielte Untersuchungen und Arbeitsprozesse bereits im Vorfeld positiv gelenkt werden. Dazu zählt auch eine frühzeitige Beteiligung der Bürgerinnen und Bürger an verschiedenen Themen der Stadt. Ein neues Konzept für die ehemalige JVA könnte somit auch einen Teil des Stadtentwicklungsprozesses darstellen.

Gegenstand des Wettbewerbs ist das Gelände der ehemaligen Justizvollzugsanstalt Landshut am Rande der Landshuter Innenstadt. Das Gefängnis wurde 1905 bis 1907 als modernes, mittelgroßes Gefängnisgebäude für 180 Gefangene errichtet. Der Gebäudekomplex wurde seit dem Auszug der Gefangenen im Jahr 2008 nur noch temporär genutzt, steht seit mehreren Jahren leer und wurde 2012 unter Denkmalschutz gestellt. Ziel des Wettbewerbs ist es, das Gebäude und den Ort zu transformieren, zu erschließen und in die Stadt zu integrieren, einen Prozess für diese Transformation zu entwerfen und neue Programme zu definieren. Gefragt sind innovative Ideen dafür, wie man mit dem alten Gebäude umgehen kann.

Das Betrachtungsgebiet umfasst die Promenade entlang der Isar, die unmittelbar angrenzende Grieserwiese (derzeit ein Pkw-Stellplatz), die Parkanlage und eine große Veranstaltungswiese, den Zugangsbereich zur historischen Innenstadt mit oberem Stadtbereich (Dreifaltigkeitsplatz) und die Burg Trausnitz. Im Wettbewerb sollen innovative Ideen zur zukünftigen Entwicklung des Betrachtungsraums und insbesondere des Projektgebietes aufgezeigt werden. Diese entsprechen in den Statuten von Europan Europa den Maßstabsebenen S/M und L. Dabei gilt es, ein passendes Nutzungsprogramm zu entwickeln und dieses in eine hervorragende architektonische, städtebauliche und freiraumplanerische Lösung zu überführen. Unter dem Europan-16-Titel „Living Cities – Lebendige Städte" sollen nachhaltige, gemischte und sozial-integrale Stadträume entstehen.

Gewünscht werden entsprechende Aussagen zur räumlichen und programmatischen Verknüpfung mit der Gesamtstadt, zur möglichen Beteiligung der Bevölkerung (Teilhabe), zu neuer Mobilität und zu den Themen Dynamiken der Kreislaufwirtschaft und Dynamiken der Integration.

Ziel ist es, den Ort mit historischem Bauwerk wieder lang anhaltend belebter und attraktiver zu gestalten. Die Stadt möchte sich im Vorfeld nicht auf eine bestimmte Nutzung festlegen und ist offen für verschiedenste Ideen. Gesucht werden innovative Ideen für eine programmatische Belegung und insgesamt Ansätze, die eine hohe Aufenthaltsqualität generieren. Das Gelände soll dabei behutsam geöffnet werden, sich fortan in das Stadtgefüge integrieren und eine adäquate Eingangssituation in Richtung Stadtkern ausbilden.

Location

The town of Landshut is an independent town, regional centre, and capital of the Lower Bavaria administrative district. In the long term, the city of Landshut aims to implement an urban development plan. The future objective is not only intended as a reaction to existing circumstances, but is also meant to direct the town's development in a positive way based on targeted research and operating procedures. This also includes the early involvement of citizens in various issues affecting the town. A new concept for the former prison could thus also form part of an urban development process that links new ideas with historical settings and thus redefines the approach to the city.

The subject of the competition is the site of the former Landshut correctional facility on the edge of central Landshut. The prison was built 1905 to 1907 as a modern, medium-sized prison with space for 180 prisoners, and the complex has been a listed building since 2012. It stands on the main development axis leading to Landshut's historic town centre from the south, and work on the project should take this context into account. The project site nevertheless needs to be approached with an open mind. All sorts of uses are conceivable. Since ceasing operations in 2008, the existing building has only been used temporarily, and has been completely empty for several years. The aim of the competition is to transform the building and the site, to open it up and integrate it into the city, to design a process for this transformation, and to define new programs. What are needed are innovative ideas for how to deal with the old building. The study site includes the Isarpromenade, the directly adjoining Grieserwiese, a park and a large event lawn, the access area to the historic town centre and the upper part of the town (Dreifaltigkeitsplatz), and Trausnitz Castle.

The competition sets out to demonstrate innovative ideas for the future development of the study site (red area) and, in particular, the project site (yellow area). This corresponds to the scale levels S/M and L in the Europan Europa statutes. The aim is to develop a suitable utilization program and to translate it into an outstanding architectural, urban planning, and open space planning solution.

Under the Europan 16 title 'Living Cities', sustainable, mixed, and socially integral urban environments are to be created. Corresponding statements are desired on the spatial and programmatic linkage with the city as a whole, on the possible participation of the population (stakeholding), on new mobility, and on the topics of the 'dynamics of the circular economy' and the 'dynamics of integration'.

The aim is to make the location more lively and attractive again in the long term. At the same time, the town does not want to commit to a specific use in advance. This means that all sorts of ideas and implementations are conceivable. Approaches that seek to generate a high amenity value and innovative ideas for programmatic occupancy, to open up the site, and to integrate it into the urban fabric in the longer term are also desired.

Bevölkerung   Inhabitants
72.865

Betrachtungsraum   Study Site
16 ha

Projektgebiet   Project Site
1 ha

Archive of European Culture

Projekt

Archive of European Culture ist ein Entwurfsvorschlag für die Umgestaltung des alten Gefängnisses in Landshut. Als neuartiges Datenzentrum soll seine Funktionalität mit einer Initiative der EU in Verbindung gebracht werden, welche das Ziel hat, unser gemeinschaftliches Kulturerbe digital zu bewahren und zu erhalten.

Dass ein Gefängnis im Sinne seiner typologischen Eigenschaften auch als Aufbewahrungsort genutzt werden kann, war der Ausgangspunkt für die Idee, das Gebäude als Archiv zu konzipieren – ehemals gebaut, um die Umgebung vor seinen Gefangenen zu schützen, könnte es umgekehrt auch wertvolle Dinge vor anthropologischen und ökologischen Bedrohungen abschirmen.

Aus urbaner Hinsicht ist das Projektareal ideal für eine solche Funktion: Durch eine fortlaufende Veränderung der Mitgliedsländer bewegt sich das geografische Zentrum der EU immer weiter Richtung Landshut, was nach einer zentralen Funktion fragt. Die Stadt Landshut hat auch eine ideale Infrastruktur: mit nur 30 Minuten zum Flughafen München, der Flutmulde, welche die Stadt vor ernsthaften Überströmungen bewahrt, und der Hochschule für angewandte Wissenschaften, welche Forschung und Wartungsarbeiten durchführen könnte, um das Archiv in Betrieb zu halten.

Die Entwurfsstrategie besteht aus zwei aufeinanderfolgenden Phasen. Zuerst wird das Gefängnis zum digitalen Archiv umstrukturiert; die oberen Etagen des Gebäudes werden für das Publikum geschlossen, um Platz für die Serverräume zu schaffen. Das Erdgeschoss dahingegen wird als öffentliches Forum – eine Schnittstelle zwischen Besucher und Archiv – umstrukturiert. Danach breitet sich das Projekt in den davorliegenden Park aus. Ein Zusammenspiel von bestehenden und neu erstellten Räumlichkeiten bietet Platz für kulturelle Veranstaltungen, um den immateriellen Wert unserer Kultur instand zu halten. Der existierende Turnierplatz wird durch eine permanente Tribüne erweitert, um für vielfältige Festivitäten Platz zu bieten. Das Zeughaus soll als Werkstatt für europäisches Handwerk umfunktioniert werden. Südlich des Parks werden zwei neue Gebäude hinzugefügt: eine Markthalle mit einem gastronomischen Angebot aus verschiedenen europäischen Ländern und ein Theater für größere Veranstaltungen. Zuletzt bildet das neue Plaza eine Verbindung von der Isar bis zum alten Gefängnis und positioniert sich wie ein roter Teppich in Richtung des Zentrums der Stadt Landshut.

Team

AUD-A ist ein Büro für Architektur, Urbanistik und Raumgestaltung, das in Berlin durch Alexandra Heijink und Jorik Bais nach ihrer Arbeitszeit in Amsterdam, New York und Schanghai gegründet wurde. Ihre Arbeit reicht von Möbeldesign bis hin zu wettbewerbsgekrönten urbanen Strategien und zeichnet sich durch einen transdisziplinären Ansatz aus, bei dem verschiedene Praxisfelder holistisch zusammengeführt werden.

AUD-A ist ein Akronym ohne Dogma: Es spiegelt die Überzeugung wider, dass jedes Projekt in seinen Bedingungen einzigartig ist und einen entsprechenden Ansatz erfordert.

Project

The Archive of European Culture is a project that proposes revitalizing the old prison in Landshut by transforming it into a data centre and connecting its functionality to an initiative by the European Union to preserve our European heritage digitally.

Based on the argument that a prison is the ideal typology for safe-keeping, the building is envisioned as an archive – while it was once erected to protect the outside surrounding from its prisoners, it can inversely also protect precious contents from the environment.

On an urban scale, the project site is ideally suited for such a function. Due to an ongoing change in member states, the geographical centre of the European Union is shifting towards Landshut, which thus requires a central function. The city also has an ideal infrastructure, since it is only thirty minutes away from the Munich airport and also close to the nearby 'Flutmulde', which protects the city from severe flooding, and the local university, which would be able to provide the research and maintenance necessary to keep the archive up and running.

The design strategy consists of two consecutive phases. First, the prison will become a digital archive. The upper storeys of the building will be closed off to provide space for the server towers, while the ground floor will serve as a public forum. In the second phase, the project then expands into the nearby park, where a variety of added structures will provide additional space to work with and showcase intangible aspects of our culture. In this respect, the design for the park builds on what already exists. The current Turnierplatz will be upgraded with permanent stadium seating to accommodate additional festivities, while the Zeughaus will be transformed into a workshop for European crafts. To the south of the park, two new programs will be added: a food market for European cuisines and a theatre for large performances. Finally, the new plaza establishes a formal connection to the side of the river opposite the prison and serves as a conceptual red carpet towards the centre of the city of Landshut.

Team

AUD-A is a Berlin-based office for architecture, urbanism, and interior design cofounded by Alexandra Heijink and Jorik Bais after gaining work experience in Amsterdam, New York, and Shanghai. Their work ranges from furniture design to competition-winning urban strategies, and is defined by a transdisciplinary approach in which various fields of practice are merged into a holistic tool.

AUD-A is an acronym devoid of dogma: it reflects the belief that the conditions of each project are unique.

Archive_of_European_Culture   //   Landshut_DE

→Initiate//: early 2021 the European Union funded an initiative to digitise our European cultural heritage. This project aims to be its physical archive. Situated near the future geographical centre of the EU and in the digital epicentre of Bavaria, Landshut is the perfect location. In an effort to revitalise an old prison without altering its internal structure, cells are rethought as server rooms for data storage. The courtyard of the prison into a public ground floor with various amenities, connecting to the nearby park which will be used to preserve the cultural manifestations that can't be digitised - traditions, craftmanship & cuisine. Landshut is set to become the epicentre of European culture, displaying what define(d/s) the EU.

aa. 1hr. by car to Munich, 30min. by car to Munich Airport
     1hr. to Isar Valley (silicon valley of Bavaria)

bb. University of Applied Sciences Landshut (technology & business)
     and location of LINK startup hub

cc. 'Flutmulde' provides safety measure to prevent extreme flooding.
     Safety necessity due to future increase of extreme weather

dd. Preservation of a prison -- from archiving prisoners to
     safe-keeping of European cultural data.

ee. 2010   geographical center of EU   2020   2030 ?
                  shifting towards
                  Landshut

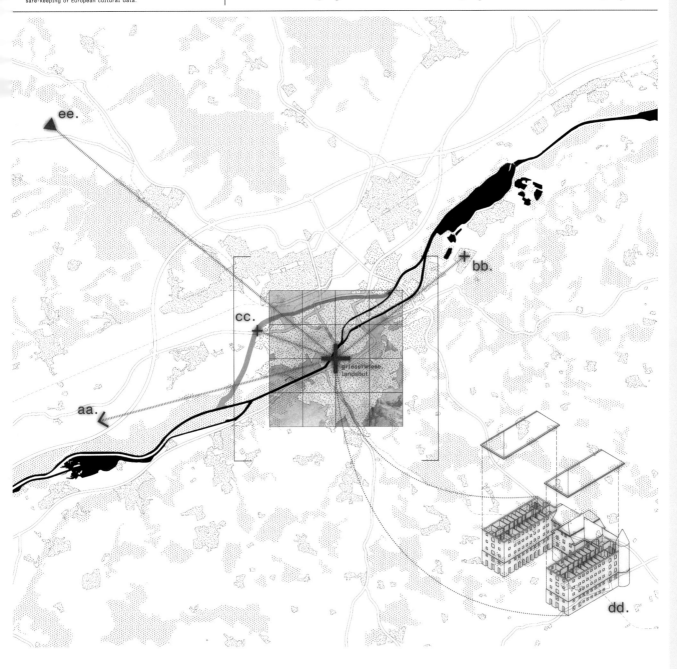

Archive_of_European_Culture   //   Landshut_DE

01. Forum: former prison reinstated as data-centre; keeping our cultural heritage data safe. Uplink to satellite provides global access for research.

02. Workshop: existing 'Zeughaus' used as a space to practice and teach European crafts.

03. Arena: Turnierplatz upgraded with permanent track and stadium seats to accommodate various sports events.

04. Stage: pavilion reused as small concert stage for small romantic gatherings.

05. Food court: to learn about and enjoy various European cuisines. Centre courtyard to be used for markets and for restaurant tables.

06. Theatre: for larger performances and open-air concerts. Used throughout the year both spontaneously and organised.

07. Monument: celebrating the EU. The watchtower provides an overview of the park. Can be used for light shows etc.

08. Uplink: the data stored in the archive can be accessed by all citizens of the EU.

Section of the Forum, the former prison and Wittstraße

1:250 on A1

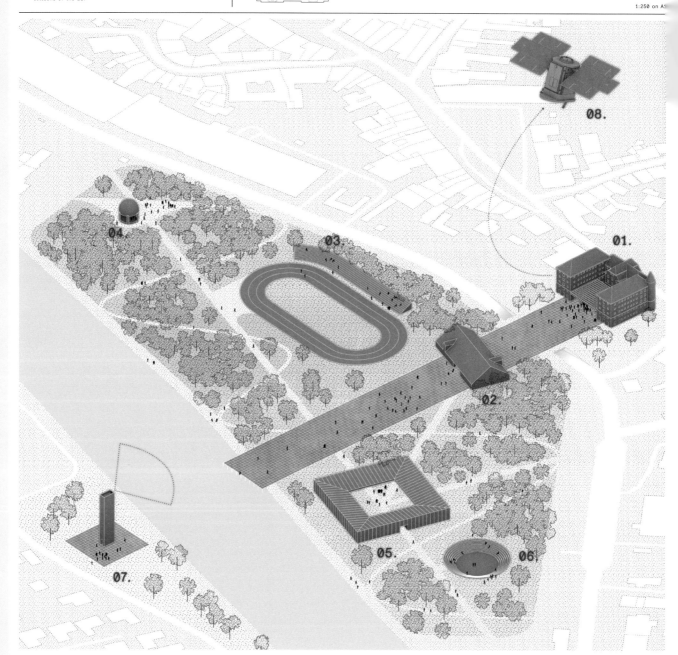

Archive_of_European_Culture   //   Landshut_DE

FP.01 - Public forum

FP.02 - Servers for data storage

1:350 on A1

CELL / A034

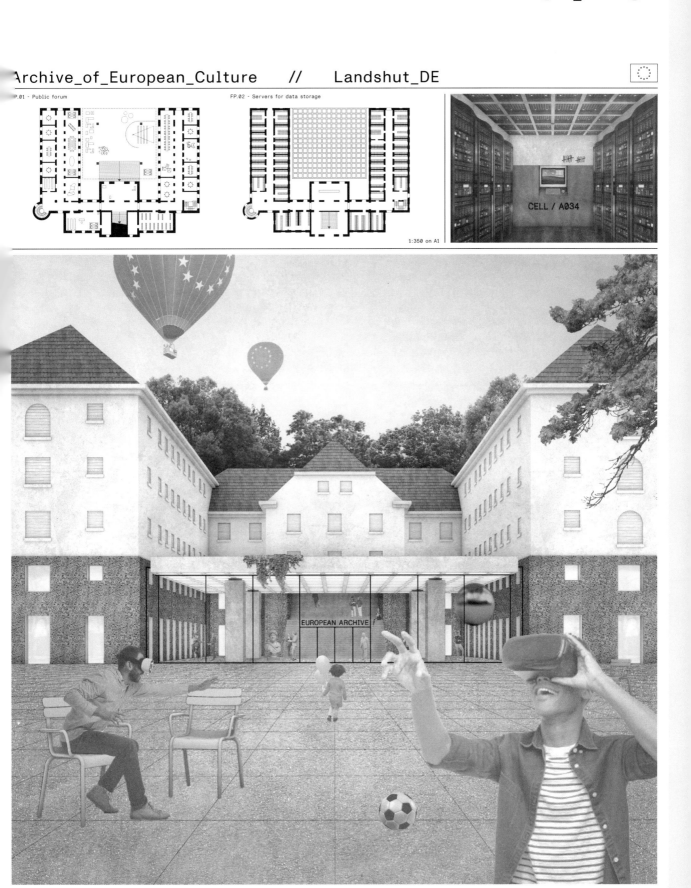

Medieval Experimentarium

Projekt

Medieval Experimentarium füllt das historische Ambiente des alten Gefängnisbaus von Landshut mit neuem Leben. Eine leichte Stahlkonstruktion, ein strukturelles Gegenstück zu den beiden Gefängnisflügeln, wird in den Hof eingefügt und dient dort als Stützsystem – zusammen werden die beiden Strukturen zu einem kulturellen Katalysator für die Stadt und ihre aufstrebende kreative Szene.

Einerseits soll das bestehende Gebäude wiederhergestellt und in ein kreatives Experimentarium umgewandelt werden – Ateliers, temporäre Schlafplätze, Gemeinschaftsräume und Ausstellungssäle. Andererseits bildet die neue Struktur einen vertikalen öffentlichen Raum – eine Promenade entlang der alten Fassaden auf verschiedenen Ebenen, die von außen Zugang zu allen Geschossen bietet und gleichzeitig eine große kollektive Halle im Zentrum überdeckt. Am Rande des historischen Stadtzentrums gelegen, wird Medieval Experimentarium buchstäblich zu einem Tor zur Stadt und bietet über die Promenade einen neuen Zugang zur historischen Stadt, der nicht mehr rund um das geschlossene Gefängnisgelände herum führt, wie in den vergangenen hundert Jahren.

Die neue Struktur der vertikalen Promenade dient nicht nur als archäologisches Gerüst für das alte Gefängnis, es schützt gleichzeitig auch das historische Gebäude und führt Besucherinnen und Besucher näher an dieses heran. Der Bau erinnert an die gotischen Gewölbe aus der mittelalterlichen Geschichte von Landshut – offene Galerien umgeben den großen öffentlichen Raum, die skelettartigen Bögen sind von Hunderten duftender Kletterpflanzen berankt, geschützt wird er von einem transparenten doppelten Walmdach – mit der Zeit wird das gesamte Gebäude zu einer überwachsenen gotischen Kathedrale im Freien werden, bereit, die traditionellen Landshuter Mittelalterfeste zu beherbergen!

Das Projekt befasst sich mit zukünftigen Mehrnutzungsmodellen in denen Menschen in einem zirkulären, selbstversorgenden System miteinander leben, lernen, arbeiten, spielen und wachsen. Gründerinnen und Gründer, temporäre Bewohner und Tagesgäste, alle sind Teil eines dynamischen Zusammenlebens innerhalb neu entstandener hybrider Ökosysteme des Experimentariums, hervorgegangen aus Synergien zwischen Alt und Neu, Natur und Kultur.

Team

AKVS Architecture wurde 2013 von Anđela Karabašević und Vladislav Sudžum, einer Architektin und einem Ingenieur, gegründet, die beide über einen mathematischen Hintergrund verfügen. In Forschung und Planung legt das Büro den Schwerpunkt auf atmosphärische räumliche Systeme, die ihren Benutzerinnen und Benutzern eine Vielzahl an Erfahrungen ermöglichen. Im Laufe der Jahre haben die Planer an mehr als 40 Architekturwettbewerben teilgenommen, darunter Europan 13 und Europan 15, mit Projekten, die vielfach ausgezeichnet wurden und sich zum Teil in der Entwicklungsphase befinden. 2021 begannen sie mit einem Projekt für das kreativ-innovative multifunktionale Zentrum „Ložionica", dem Wiederaufbau und der Neunutzung verlassener historischer Gebäude des Belgrader Bahnhofs – dem Lokschuppen mit Drehscheibe –, nachdem sie zuvor in einem internationalen Wettbewerb den ersten Preis gewonnen hatten.

Project

The Medieval Experimentarium infuses life into the historical milieu of the old prison building in Landshut. A light steel structure, a skeletal double of the two prison wings, is inserted into its courtyard to act as a support system – together the two structures become a cultural catalyst for the town and its emerging creative scene.

The aim on the one hand is to reconstruct and transform the existing building into a creative experimentarium – with studios, temporary dormitories, collective spaces, and exhibition halls. On the other, the new structure forms a vertical public space – a promenade along the old façades on multiple levels, which allows access to all floors from the outside, and covers a large collective Grand Hall in its centre. Located on the edge of the historical city centre, the Medieval Experimentarium literally becomes a gateway to the city, and provides access to the historical town through the Experimentarium via a promenade, and not around the enclosed prison site, as has been the case for the past 100 years.

The new structure of the Vertical Promenade serves as an archaeological scaffolding for the old prison, while protecting the historical building as well as bringing the visitors closer to it at the same time. The structure recalls the Gothic domes of Landshut's medieval history – open galleries surround the large central public space, its skeletal arches are covered with hundreds of aromatic climbing plants, and it is protected with a transparent double-hipped roof – over time, the whole building will thus become an overgrown Gothic cathedral in the open, a perfect place to host Landshut's traditional medieval festivals!

The project speculates about future cohabitation models, where people live, learn, work, play, and grow together in one circular, self-sustained system. Creators, temporary tenants, and daily visitors are all part of a vibrant coexistence within the newly formed hybrid ecosystems of the Experimentarium, generated by symbiotic synergies between the old and the new, nature and culture.

Team

AKVS architecture was founded by Anđela Karabašević and Vladislav Sudžum in 2013, an architect and an engineer, both with a background in mathematics. The studio's research and designs focus on atmospheric spatial systems that offer multiplicities of experiences for their users. Over the years, they have participated in over 40 architectural competitions, including Europan 15 and Europan 13, and many of their contributions have received awards and some are now in the design development stage. In 2021 they began working on a project for the creative-innovative multifunctional centre 'Ložionica' – the reconstruction and re-use of the abandoned historical buildings of the Belgrade Railway Station – the old turntable and railway depot, after receiving first prize in an international competition earlier that year.

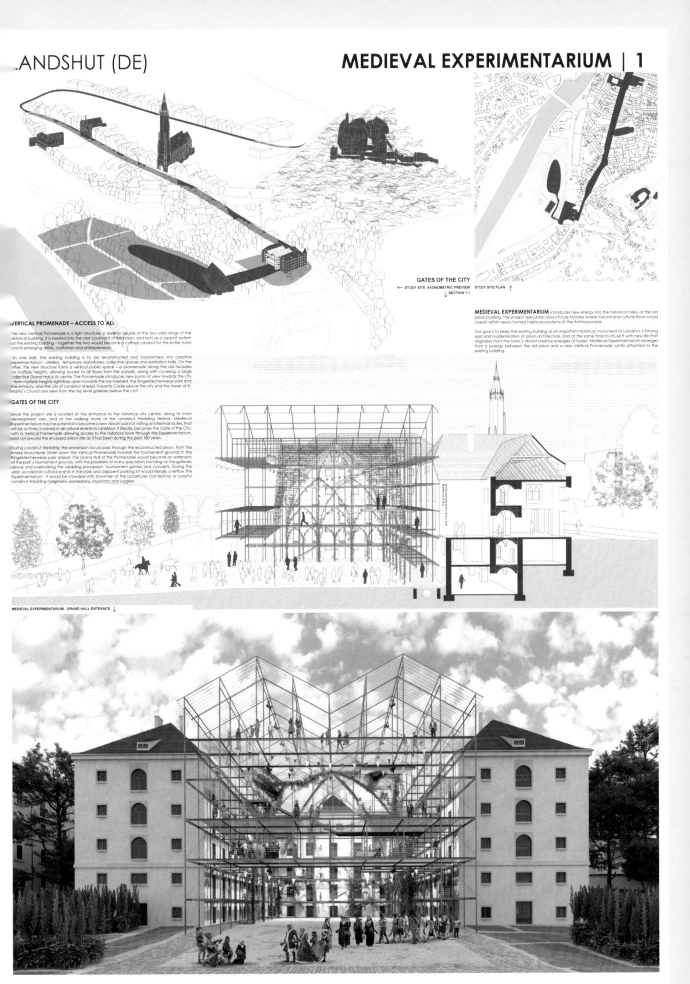

GATES OF THE CITY

← STUDY SITE AXONOMETRIC PREVIEW　STUDY SITE PLAN ↑
↓ SECTION 1-1

MEDIEVAL EXPERIMENTARIUM introduces new energy into the historical milieu of the old prison building. The project speculates about future histories where natural and cultural flows would coexist within newly formed hybrid ecosystems of the Anthropocene.

Our goal is to keep the existing building as an important historical monument of Landshut's thriving past and modernization of prison architecture, and at the same time to infuse it with new life that originates from the town's vibrant creative energies of today. Medieval Experimentarium emerges from a synergy between the old prison and a new Vertical Promenade subtly attached to the existing building.

VERTICAL PROMENADE – ACCESS TO ALL

The new Vertical Promenade is a light structure, a skeletal double of the two solid wings of the historical building. It is inserted into the vast courtyard of the prison, and acts as a support system for the existing building – together the two would become a cultural catalyst for the entire town and its emerging artists, craftsmen and entrepreneurs.

On one side, the existing building is to be reconstructed and transformed into creative experimentarium - ateliers, temporary dormitories, collective spaces and exhibition halls. On the other, the new structure forms a vertical public space – a promenade along the old facades on multiple heights, allowing access to all floors from the outside, along with covering a large collective Grand Hall in its centre. The Promenade introduces new points of view towards the city – from multiple heights sight lines open towards the Isar riverbed, the Ringeltscherweise park and the Armoury, and the city of Landshut ahead. Trausnitz Castle above the city and the tower of St. Martin's Church are seen from the top level galleries bellow the roof.

GATES OF THE CITY

Since the project site is located at the entrance to the historical city centre, along its main development axis, and at the walking route of the Landshut Wedding festival, Medieval Experimentarium has the potential to become a new vibrant point of visiting and festival routes, that will be actively involved in all cultural events in Landshut. It literally becomes the Gate of the City, with its Vertical Promenade allowing access to the historical town through the Experimentarium, and not around the enclosed prison site as it has been during the past 100 years.

During Landshut Wedding, the procession would pass through the reconstructed prison, from the Innere Münchener Street down the Vertical Promenade towards the tournament grounds in the Ringeltscherweise park ahead. The Grand Hall of the Promenade would become an extension of the park's tournament grounds, with the possibility of many spectators standing on the galleries above and overlooking the wedding procession, tournament games and concerts. During the year, occasional cultural events in the park and adjacent parking lot would literally overflow the Experimentarium - it would be crowded with showmen of the Landshuter Dult festival, or colorful Landshut Wedding magicians, comedians, musicians and jugglers.

MEDIEVAL EXPERIMENTARIUM - GRAND HALL ENTRANCE ↓

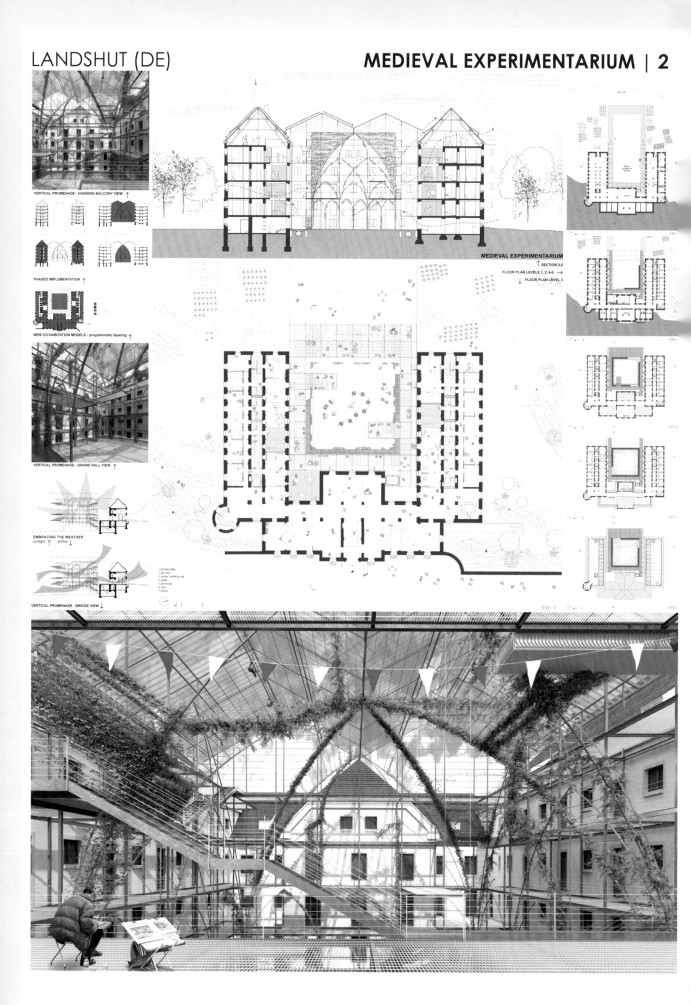

VERTICAL PROMENADE - HANGING BALCONY VIEW ↑

PHASED IMPLEMENTATION ↑

NEW CO-HABITATION MODELS - programmatic layering ↑

VERTICAL PROMENADE - GRAND HALL VIEW ↑

EMBRACING THE WEATHER
sunlight ↑   airflow ↑

VERTICAL PROMENADE - BRIDGE VIEW ↓

MEDIEVAL EXPERIMENTARIUM
↑ SECTION 2-2
FLOOR PLAN LEVELS 1, 2, 4-6 →
↓ FLOOR PLAN LEVEL 3

MEDIEVAL EXPERIMENTARIUM | 3

GRAND HALL - OVERGROWN GOTHIC DOME

We wish to build upon the thriving cultural potential of the town of Landshut on one side, and its rich medieval history and Gothic appearance on the other. The Grand Hall of the Promenade is constructed as a contemporary reinterpretation of a Gothic dome – the large central space is surrounded with galleries, and its higher volume is bounded with skeletal arches overgrown with hundreds of blooming aromatic climbers, with double hipped roof above in polycarbonate.

In summer, when the climbers are at its full growth the Gothic dome takes form in lush greenery, while in winter some of the climbers lose their leaves so that the sunlight can enter deep into the Grand Hall and warm up the space under the glazed roof. The large central open space of the Grand Hall with the bordering galleries on multiple levels from above, and Vertical Promenade's pathways make for a perfect venue for housing some of the city's cultural events and festivals.

EMBRACING THE WEATHER

Vertical Promenade structure is composed of steel frames, wire ropes and steel grate slabs, and covered with large polycarbonate roof, so that it is open to natural airflows and direct sunlight while allowing views in all directions - towards the old prison facades, the fair riverscape with the city ahead and to the sky. Fresh air from the vast agricultural lands and forests, the fair riverbed cold air pathway, as well as from prevailing westerly winds all enter freely into the structure and naturally flow through the hollow prison building.

Being nestled within the old courtyard, it is protected from harsh weather by the prison building itself, and due to its polycarbonate roof it stays accessible in cold weather, acting as a collective vertical garden for both the artists and residents of the Experimentarium as well as for the inhabitants of Landshut.

MONUMENT PROTECTION: OLD AND NEW

With a very peculiar, but careful transformation of the existing building we wish to raise issues about new models for co-habitation in the future - with constant and unpredictable changes of the way we live, how can abandoned historical heritage be preserved and reused at its full potential for future generations?

In the Medieval Experimentarium, the old prison building is kept in its original state from the outside, with the new structure of the Promenade carefully positioned at its close proximity, but not physically attached to it – it is standing independently aside. The Promenade allows new points of perspective towards the old building – it acts as an archeological scaffolding, at the same time protecting the historical building, as well as bringing the visitors closer to it, in order to stay true to the historical prison architecture, we keep the existing spatial configuration, but change the access and walking routes, and open up spaces for more air and light to accommodate new creative programs.

NEW MODELS FOR CO-HABITATION

Natural ecosystems are crucially changed with human activity, and have now become hybrids of both natural processes and human flows (flows of culture and everyday life, of goods, mechanical flows, digital flows...). In turn, architecture itself becomes a complex ecosystem of interweaved flows of multiple types of energies.

Medieval Experimentarium speculates about new models for co-habitation in such future, one where people work, live, play and produce together in one circular self sustained system. Creators, temporary tenants, students, tourists, daily visitors, festival specators, are all part of a productive and vibrant co-existence within newly formed hybrid ecosystems, born from future symbiotic synergies between old and new, nature and culture.

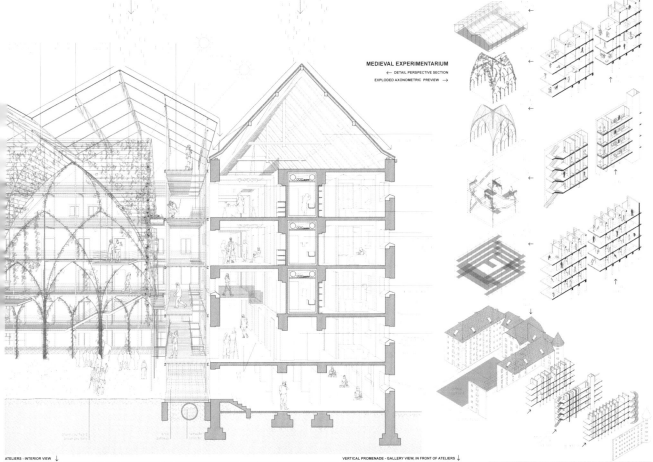

MEDIEVAL EXPERIMENTARIUM
← DETAIL PERSPECTIVE SECTION
EXPLODED AXONOMETRIC PREVIEW →

ATELIERS - INTERIOR VIEW ↓

VERTICAL PROMENADE - GALLERY VIEW, IN FRONT OF ATELIERS ↓

Schwäbisch Gmünd (DE)

Standort

Die Stadt Schwäbisch Gmünd ist ein wichtiger Akteur in der Metropolregion Stuttgart. Die Stadt setzt sich ehrgeizig mit der Zukunft des Bauens, Wohnens und Arbeitens auseinander. In das IBA'27-Netz der Stadtregion Stuttgart sind zwei Projekte aufgenommen worden, u.a. das Projekt „Unbreak my Hardt", das auf einem Beitrag des 2015 durchgeführten Wettbewerbs Europan 13 beruht. An das Areal grenzen die im Rahmen der Landesgartenschau 2014 entwickelten Spiel- und Sportflächen, östlich grenzt das Areal unmittelbar an den historischen Bahnhof, den zentralen Omnibusbahnhof und an die Altstadt. Für den Stadteingangsbereich aus Richtung Stuttgart, der durch die Verlegung der Bundesstraße B29 in einen Tunnel und die Erweiterung des Stadtgartens mit neuen Raumkanten stark veränderte Rahmenbedingungen erhalten hat, werden im Europan 16 neue Ideen und Ansätze zur nachhaltigen Entwicklung gesucht.

Der städtebauliche Entwicklungsbereich „Westliches Stadttor" erstreckt sich in Nord-Süd-Ausdehnung entlang der Bahnlinie am Grünraum Nepperberg bis zur Rems. Das Areal grenzt an die im Rahmen der Landesgartenschau 2014 entwickelten Spiel- und Sportflächen, östlich grenzt es unmittelbar an den historischen Bahnhof, den zentralen Omnibusbahnhof und an die Altstadt an. Es handelt sich bei den teilweise brachliegenden Flächen um große städtebauliche Potenziale, die für alle Mobilitätsformen günstig gelegen und für verschiedenste Nutzungen geeignet sind. Es gilt, diese Potenzialflächen einer neuen Entwicklungsperspektive zuzuführen, welche die dynamische Stadtentwicklung der letzten zehn Jahre räumlich fortsetzt.

Eine abgestimmte Entwicklung der Flächen scheint sowohl inhaltlich-konzeptionell als auch funktional sinnvoll. Die durch den Stadtumbau und die Landesgartenschau geschaffenen Stadtstrukturen mit Grünräumen könnten sich hier weiter nach Westen entwickeln.

Ein städtebauliches Ziel ist ein ansprechend gestalteter Stadtauftritt, der Schwäbisch Gmünd als Mittelzentrum mit oberzentralen Teilfunktionen in der Region Ostwürttemberg, von Stuttgart kommend, repräsentiert.

Das Projektgebiet soll zu einem lebendigen, vielfältigen, nachhaltigen und zukunftsweisenden Quartier transformiert werden, das gleichzeitig einen einladenden Stadteingang ausbildet. Ein Ringschluss des Grünen Bandes vom Wallfahrtsort St. Salvator zum Nepperberg über das Quartier Gleispark, mit einem „Grünen Sprung" über die Bahnstrecke auf das Tunnelgrundstück, und Anschluss nach Süden zum Südufer der Rems sollte mitgeplant werden. Das Areal braucht ein langfristiges städtebauliches Entwicklungsszenario, das Schritt für Schritt umgesetzt werden kann. Entsprechend der Aufgabenstellung „Living Cities – Lebendige Städte" werden Entwurfsbeiträge gesucht, die innovative Ideen und Prozesse aufzeigen und sich mit den Themenschwerpunkten Dynamiken der Kreislaufwirtschaft und Dynamiken der Integration befassen. Ziel ist es, ein gemischtes Quartier zu entwickeln, in dem Baugruppen, Wohnungsbaugenossenschaften, Dienstleistung und neue Produktionsstätten einen Platz finden.

Location

The town of Schwäbisch Gmünd plays an important role in the Stuttgart metropolitan region. It is thus ambitiously addressing the future of building, living, and working. Two projects from Schwäbisch Gmünd have been included in the IBA'27 network of the Stuttgart metropolitan region, including the 'Unbreak my Hardt' project, which is based on an entry from the Europan 13 competition in 2015. New ideas and approaches are being sought here for the area on the Stuttgart-facing side of the town, which has undergone significant changes with the relocation of the B29 federal road into a tunnel and the expansion of the Stadtgarten.

The 'Western Gateway' urban development area extends from the railway line and the green Nepperberg in the north to the Rems River in the south. East of the areas is the historic railway station and central bus station, as well as the historic town centre, which can be reached on foot in ten minutes.

The areas have great urban development potential, are conveniently located for all forms of mobility, and would be suitable for a wide variety of uses. It is important to give these potential areas a new development outlook that carries the dynamic urban development of the last ten years forward in spatial terms.

One urban development goal is a suitably designed town image that presents Schwäbisch Gmünd as a medium-sized centre with regional sub-functions in the East Württemberg region. The currently underused and partially derelict part of the project site needs to be transformed into a lively, diverse, and sustainable neighbourhood. The goal is a lively and future-oriented district that becomes part of the town centre and at the same time provides an inviting entrance to the town.

A plan should also be developed simultaneously for completing the Green Belt ring from the Salvator to the Nepperberg via the Gleispark district, with a 'green leap' over the railway to the tunnel site and a southward connection to the opposite bank of the Rems.

The area requires a long-term urban development process that can be implemented step by step. Its aim should be to develop a mixed district in which groups of buildings, housing cooperatives, service providers, and new production facilities all find a place.

In keeping with the Europan 16 task, 'Living Cities', what are sought are design contributions that demonstrate innovative ideas and processes and address the main topics of the 'dynamics of the circular economy' and the 'dynamics of integration'.

Coordinated development of the project site seems sensible in terms of content and concept and also of function. The urban structures with green spaces that have evolved as a result of urban redevelopment and the State Garden Show could expand westwards here.

Bevölkerung Inhabitants
ca. 61.000

Betrachtungsraum Study Site
138 ha

Projektgebiet Project Site
27 ha

Viriditas ante portas

Projekt

viriditas (lat.) = das Grün; Lebhaftigkeit
ante portas (lat.) = vor den Toren; auch Ausdruck für eine dringende Notwendigkeit

Von Stuttgart kommend bildet das Entwurfsgebiet Schwäbisch Gmünds westlichen Stadteingang. Es besteht größtenteils aus Gewerbehallen sowie Brachflächen und weist einen hohen Versiegelungsgrad auf. Jedoch birgt das Areal erhebliche Potenziale dank des bewaldeten Talhangs im Norden, der Rems im Süden, einiger historisch bedeutsamer Gebäude sowie der Nähe zum ÖPNV und zur Altstadt. Zur Schaffung eines lebendigen Quartiers und würdigen Stadteingangs knüpft der Entwurf an diese Potenziale an.

Der Aufbau orientiert sich an der Stadtstruktur: im Osten ein dichter Kern mit einem Längsplatz, begrenzt durch einen Freiraum, gefolgt von Großstrukturen und einer Randzone mit geringerer Dichte. Herzstück ist der Freiraum, welcher als Querzäsur zu den Talparallelen die Hänge im Norden und Süden verbindet. Mit der dreifachen Baumreihe, durchbrochen durch einen Turm, der den neuen Stadteingang markiert, zitiert er als *Grüner Wall* die Reste der Befestigungen der Altstadt und legt als produktiver Raum den Grundstein für eine lokale Kreislaufwirtschaft. In Fortführung der Landesgartenschau 2014 wird die Rems weiter zugänglich gemacht. Über eine Promenade verbindet sie Innenstadt und westliche Vororte. Der Mühlbach wird reaktiviert und bringt Grün in die neuen Innenhöfe. Beide Wasserläufe dienen auch als Retentionsflächen. Rad- und Fußverkehr werden u. a. durch zwei Radschnellwege gestärkt. In Kombination mit einer Quartiersgarage und besserer Vernetzung wird das neue Quartier so autofrei. Produktive Betriebe entlang der Bahnstrecke ergeben zusammen mit Wohnen, Geschäften, Büroflächen, sozialen und kulturellen Angeboten eine bunte Nutzungsmischung.

Die Umsetzung in Phasen soll in enger Zusammenarbeit mit den Anwohnerinnen und Anwohnern und unter Berücksichtigung des Bestandes und zirkulärer Strategien erfolgen.

Team

Um Erfahrungen zu sammeln und eine gemeinsame zukünftige Selbstständigkeit zu testen, beschlossen wir – Kriss Edouard Gabriel, Falk Jähnig, Tom Macht, Hong Trang Mai, Simona Rošer –, am Europan teilzunehmen. Angesichts der komplexen Aufgabenstellung suchten wir unter unseren ehemaligen Kommilitonen nach Mitstreitern, und so entstand unser slowenisch-belgisch-deutsches Team, in dem wir von Landschaftsarchitektur über Städtebau und Denkmalpflege bis hin zu Projektmanagement verschiedene Disziplinen zusammenbringen konnten. Uns vereint, dass wir alle in Dresden studiert haben. Zwei leben und arbeiten mittlerweile in Berlin, die anderen drei in Dresden bzw. Leipzig. Trotz der Distanz haben wir eng zusammengearbeitet und konnten die Studienzeit ein bisschen wiederaufleben lassen.

Project

viriditas (Latin) = greenness; vitality
ante portas (Latin) = before the gates; also an expression for an urgent necessity

When approached from Stuttgart, the design area forms the western gateway to the city of Schwäbisch Gmünd. It consists for the most part of commercial halls and derelict land and has a high degree of soil sealing. The site nevertheless holds considerable potential thanks to the forested slope of the valley in the north, the Rems River in the south, a few historically significant buildings, and its proximity to the public transport network and the old town. The design taps these potentials to create a lively district and dignified entrance to the city.

The development is oriented towards the urban structure: a dense core with an elongated square in the east, bordered by an open space, followed by large structures and a peripheral zone with more limited density. The centrepiece is the open space as a turning point situated obliquely to the valley parallels that link the slopes in the north and south. With the threefold row of trees, broken up by a tower that marks the new gateway to the city, it cites the remnants of the fortifications of the old town as a 'green wall' and lays the foundation for a circular local economy as a productive space. The Rems is made further accessible in a continuation of the Landesgartenschau (State Horticultural Show) of 2014. Via a promenade, it links the city centre and western suburbs. The Mühlbach will be reactivated and bring green into the new interior courtyards. The two waterways also serve as retention areas. Bicycle and pedestrian traffic are improved et al. by means of two fast bicycle paths. In combination with a district garage and more optimal cross-linking, the new district is thus car-free. Productive enterprises along the railway line, along with housing, businesses, office areas, and social and cultural offerings give rise to a diverse mix of uses.

The realization in phases is intended to take place in close cooperation with the residents and take the existing inventory and circular strategies into account.

Team

We – Kriss Edouard Gabriel, Falk Jähnig, Tom Macht, Hong Trang Mai, Simona Rošer – decided to participate in the Europan competition in order to gain experience and try out shared self-employment in future. Due to the complex task, we looked for comrades-in-arms among our former classmates, which thus led to the creation of our Slovenian-Belgian-German team, in which we have been able to bring together landscape architecture, urban planning, monument conservation, and project management in various disciplines. What unites us is the fact that we all once studied in Dresden. Two of us meanwhile live and work in Berlin and the other three in Dresden respectively Leipzig. Despite the distance, we worked together closely and were able to resurrect our time as students.

Schwäbisch Gmünd (DE)

VIRIDITAS ANTE PORTAS

EIN NEUES TOR FÜR SCHWÄBISCH GMÜND

viriditas (lat.)
das Grün; Lebhaftigkeit, (Jugend-)Frische, Munterkeit

ante portas (lat.)
vor den Toren, im Anmarsch;
auch ein Ausdruck für eine dringende Notwendigkeit

Die Stadt Schwäbisch Gmünd hat eine lange Geschichte, die bis zum Limes, dem Grenzwall des Römischen Reiches, zurückreicht. Ihre heutige Erscheinung stammt hauptsächlich aus dem Mittelalter mit Bauten wie dem gotischen Münster und den erhaltenen Türmen der Stadtmauer, die eine malerische Atmosphäre erzeugen.

Gmünds westlichem Stadteingang jedoch fehlt diese Qualität. Die Gegend besteht aus Brachen, Autohändlern, Industrie- und Gewerbeflächen sowie der sie durchschneidenden Bahnstrecke.
Allerdings hat das Gebiet auch einige Vorzüge: Die bewaldeten Hänge des Nepperberges, die grünen Ufer der Rems, die Nähe zur Altstadt, zum Bahnhof sowie zu einigen wichtigen Institutionen machen es zum idealen Ort für ein lebendiges Stadtviertel.

Dieser Entwurf nutzt die vorhandenen Potentiale und zielt darauf ab, ein Quartier zu schaffen, welches das Stadtzentrum nach Westen hin verlängert und dabei seine Charakteristiken aufnimmt. Er basiert auf fünf Punkten: 1. *Historisch und kontextuell inspirierte* **Struktur**, 2. *Grün-blaue* **Verbindungen**, 3. *Rad- und fußgängerzentrierte* **Mobilität**, 4. *Neue urbane* **Produktivität** und 5. **Nutzungsmischung** *für Vielfalt.*
Durch die Umsetzung dieser Punkte entsteht ein Stadtteil der grün, lebendig und produktiv ist, zur Entwicklung einer Kreislaufwirtschaft beiträgt und nachhaltige Formen von Mobilität fördert sowie das lokale Mikroklima verbessert.
Wie der Titel bereits andeutet, wird er außerdem als neues Tor nach Gmünd dienen, welches Besucher wie auch Anwohner begrüßt, indem die reiche Geschichte der Stadt mit der Gegenwart verbunden und Richtung Zukunft gewiesen wird.

  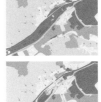

Fluss
Fluss, unzugänglich
Fluss, unterirdisch
Grünraum
Wald
unzugängliches Grün
intensive Dachbegrünung
Grünraum, geplant
Versiegelung bis 50 %
Versiegelung bis 75 %, warm
Versiegelung bis 100 %, heiß
Kaltluftstrom talwärts

Karten zum aktuellen Zustand (oben) und den angestrebten Zielen (unten), v. l. n. r.: Gewässer, Grünräume, Klimaanalyse

Radschnellweg
Mobilitätspunkt
Radweg
Radspur
Fußweg, bestehend
Fußweg, geplant
Fußweg, mögliche Erweiterung
Bundesstraße 29
viel Verkehr
mäßiger Verkehr
wenig Verkehr
verkehrsberuhigt

Karten zum aktuellen Zustand (oben) und den angestrebten Zielen (unten), v. l. n. r.: Radnetz, Fußwegenetz, Straßennetz

historischer Verlauf des römischen Limes
historischer Verlauf der Stadtmauern
neuer Grüner Wall

Karte mit dem Verlauf von Gmünds Mauern, eine Inspiration für das Entwurfskonzept

Grün- und Freiräume

Das Entwurfsgebiet wird durch die Rems im Süden und den bewaldeten Hang des Nepperberges im Norden begrenzt. Der Großteil des Flussufers ist unzugänglich, eine Ausnahme bildet der Remspark weiter östlich. Der fast verschwundene Mühlbach durchquert das Gebiet.
Der Ort zeichnet sich durch große Brachflächen, teils Überbleibsel des Tunnelbaus für die B29, und einen hohen Versiegelungsgrad aus. Dadurch hat die Gegend ein sehr schlechtes Mikroklima.
Unser Entwurf sieht die Öffnung des Mühlbaches und die Erschließung der Rems vor. Die bestehenden Grünflächen werden verbunden und bilden ein Band zwischen dem nördlichen und südlichen Talhang. Die Rems und der Mühlbach bringen ebenfalls Grün in das neue Quartier. Durch die große Freifläche vom Hang zum Fluss wird das Mikroklima wesentlich verbessert.

Infrastruktur

Das Gebiet liegt neben dem Bahnhof und dem ZOB, also direkt an Gmünds ÖPNV-Knoten. Es gibt einige Radwege, die ans regionale Netz angeschlossen sind, in der Regel als Spuren auf Straßen oder Bürgersteigen. Wenige Fußwege verbinden das Gebiet mit der anderen Flussseite, es gibt jedoch keine direkte Verbindung über die Bahnstrecke nach Norden oder zum Remspark.
Die Lorcher Straße ist für den Pendler-, Anwohner und Besucherverkehr sehr wichtig. Sie führt direkt von der B29 ins Stadtzentrum.
Der Entwurf sieht eine Reihe neuer eigenständiger Radwege vor, zwei davon Radschnellwege. Ein Netz neuer Fußwege verzahnt das Gebiet mit den angrenzenden Stadtteilen. Die Lorcher Straße soll für Pendler unattraktiv gemacht werden. Durch verbesserte Umsteigemöglichkeiten sollen Anwohner und Besucher motiviert werden, alternative Transportmittel zu verwenden.

1 HISTORISCH UND KONTEXTUELL INSPIRIERTE STRUKTUR

Auf der Suche nach Gmünds Charakter bemerkten wir ihre sehr gut erhaltene historische Struktur: ein mittelalterlicher Stadtkern, umschlossen von einem grünen Ring, gefolgt von Villen und Wohngebieten. Diese Ordnung wird nur durch einige größere Gebäude wie das Kongresszentrum gestört. Die Struktur des Entwurfs basiert auf dieser Beobachtung.
Nahe des ZOB ist ein Cluster von Blöcken, der die hohe Dichte des Stadtzentrums aufnimmt. Westlich folgt ein Freiraum, der *Grüne Wall*, der den ersten Cluster vom Rest trennt so wie einst die Stadtmauern. Dieser bildet das neue Tor und führt zum *Westtorplatz*.
Eine Schicht größerer Strukturen bildet die westliche Kante des Grünen Walls. Dahinter und nördlich der Bahnstrecke werden die Gebäude kleiner und weniger dicht, um so zum Maßstab der angrenzenden Wohn- und Industriegebiete zu vermitteln.

Schwarzplan mit Entwurf in Grün
1 : 10.000

Schwäbisch Gmünd (DE)

VIRIDITAS ANTE PORTAS

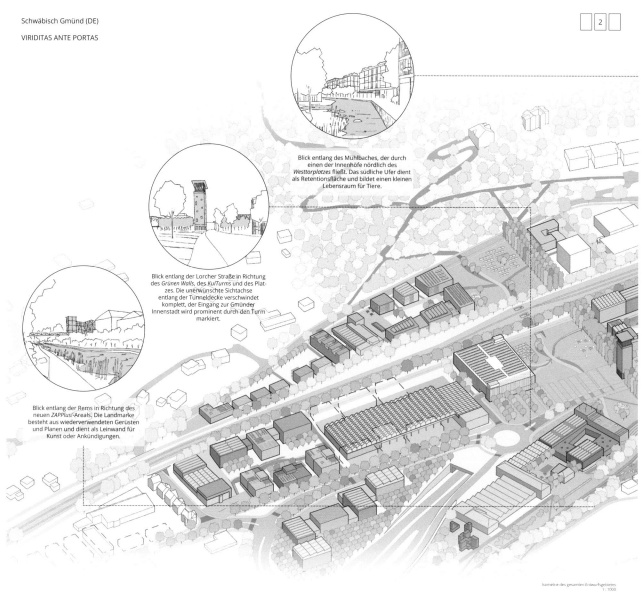

Blick entlang des Mühlbaches, der durch einen der Innenhöfe nördlich des *Westtorplatzes* fließt. Das südliche Ufer dient als Retentionsfläche und bildet einen kleinen Lebensraum für Tiere.

Blick entlang der Lorcher Straße in Richtung des *Grünen Walls*, des *KulTurms* und des Platzes. Die unerwünschte Sichtachse entlang der Tunneldecke verschwindet komplett, der Eingang zur Gmünder Innenstadt wird prominent durch den Turm markiert.

Blick entlang der Rems in Richtung des neuen *ZAPPlus!*-Areals. Die Landmarke besteht aus wiederverwendeten Gerüsten und Planen und dient als Leinwand für Kunst oder Ankündigungen.

Isometrie des gesamten Entwurfsgebietes
1 : 1000

UMSETZUNG

Phase 1 - Beginn

- Bifora-Halle als urbaner Katalysator
- *KulTurm* und *Grüner Wall* als Landmarken
- Radschnellwege als neue Zugänge zum Gebiet
- Bifora-Gebäude und nördliche Blockrandbebauung als produktives Rückgrat entlang Radschnellweg

Phase 2 - Gerüst

- Ausformulierung der Kanten von Grünraum und Platz
- Schaffung des *Westtorplatzes* und Implementierung des neuen Verkehrsschemas
- Quartiersgarage
- Grundgerüst von *ZAPPlus!* und *Zeitwerkquartier*
- Beginn der urbanen Landwirtschaft

Phase 3 - Erweiterung

- Erschließung der Rems
- Öffnung des ersten Teils des Mühlbaches
- Erweiterung der Blöcke Richtung Rems und Mühlbach
- Erweiterung von *ZAPPlus!* und *Zeitwerkquartier*
- Errichtung des Kulturpfades entlang der Rems

Phase 4 - Konsolidierung

- Südwestliche Erweiterung der Remspromenade (Verbindung nach Schirenhof)
- Errichtung von *Kreuzmühlenquartier* und *Hainquartier*
- Fertigstellung *Zeitwerkquartier*
- Zukünftige Erweiterung nach Westen vorstellbar

2 GRÜN-BLAUE VERBINDUNGEN

- Kulturpfad
- Wald/Bäume
- Platz
- Gewächshäuser/produktive Dächer

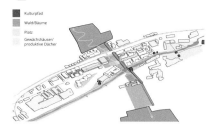

Der *Grüne Wall* verbindet die Wälder des Nepperberges im Norden und des Siechenberges im Süden unter Einbeziehung der bestehenden Sportplätze. Eine breite, natürlich belichtete Unterführung überwindet die Bahnstrecke. Es gibt Platz für Urban Farming, Sport und Erholung.
Neue Brücken und zusätzliche Wege, die Rems zu überqueren, werden installiert. Der Fluss wird durch einen Steg am Wasser und eine Promenade oberhalb der Uferböschung zugänglich gemacht. Diese Wege verbinden verschiedene kulturelle Orte miteinander.
Der reaktivierte Mühlbach definiert ein sekundäres Freiraumband und bringt Grün in die verschiedenen Quartiere. Er dient auch als Retentionsfläche für Regenwasser und potenzielle Energiequelle.

3 RAD- UND FUSSGÄNGERZENTRIERTE MOBILITÄT

- Mobilitätspunkte
- MIV-Infrastruktur
- Rad-Infrastruktur
- Öffentlicher Verkehr

Um den Autoverkehr zu reduzieren, wird die Lorcher Straße zwischen Zapp und ZOB zu einem verkehrsberuhigten Bereich und „shared space". Am Westrand des *Grünen Walls* entsteht eine Quartiersgarage, wodurch das gesamte Quartier autofrei gestaltet werden kann. P+R-Parkplätze werden weiter westlich etabliert.
Der Radverkehr wird durch zwei Radschnellwege gestärkt, einer nördlich der Bahnstrecke (von Stuttgart nach Aalen) und einer südlich (entlang der ehemaligen Hohenstaufenbahn von Gmünd nach Böppingen). Diese werden durch Radwege ins Stadtzentrum ergänzt.
Mobilitätspunkte bieten Parkmöglichkeiten für Autos und Fahrräder, Bike-Sharing-Stationen, Reparaturstationen und Zugang zum ÖPNV.

VIRIDITAS ANTE PORTAS

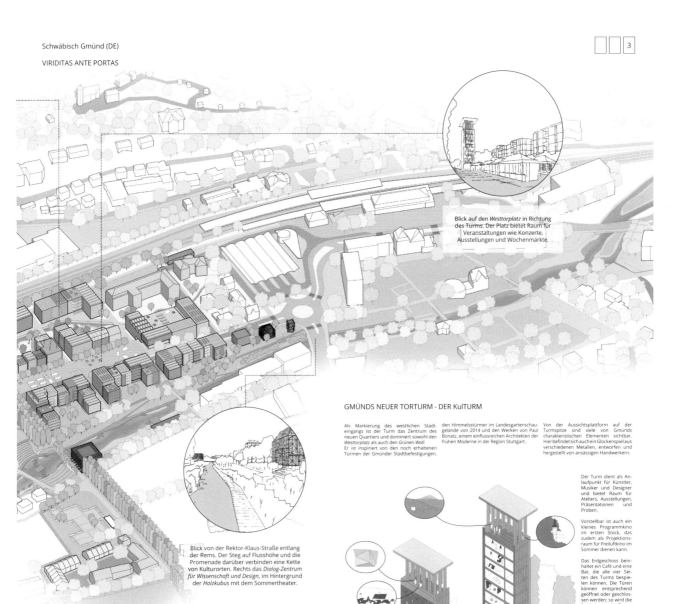

Blick auf den *Westtorplatz* in Richtung des Turms. Der Platz bietet Raum für Veranstaltungen wie Konzerte, Ausstellungen und Wochenmärkte.

Blick von der Rektor-Klaus-Straße entlang der Rems. Der Steg auf Flusshöhe und die Promenade darüber verbinden eine Kette von Kulturorten. Rechts das *Dialog-Zentrum für Wissenschaft und Design*, im Hintergrund der *Holzkubus* mit dem Sommertheater.

Isometrie des gesamten Entwurfsgebietes
1 : 1000

GMÜNDS NEUER TORTURM - DER KulTURM

Als Markierung des westlichen Stadteingangs ist der Turm das Zentrum des neuen Quartiers und dominiert sowohl den *Westtorplatz* als auch den *Grünen Wall*. Er ist inspiriert von den noch erhaltenen Türmen der Gmünder Stadtbefestigungen, den Himmelsstürmern im Landesgartenschaugelände von 2014 und den Werken von Paul Bonatz, einem einflussreichen Architekten der frühen Moderne in der Region Stuttgart.

Von der Aussichtsplattform auf der Turmspitze sind viele von Gmünds charakteristischen Elementen sichtbar. Hier befindet sich auch ein Glockenspiel aus verschiedenen Metallen, entworfen und hergestellt von ansässigen Handwerkern.

Der Turm dient als Anlaufpunkt für Künstler, Musiker und Designer und bietet Raum für Ateliers, Ausstellungen, Präsentationen und Proben.

Vorstellbar ist auch ein kleines Programmkino im ersten Stock, das zudem als Projektionsraum für Freiluftkino im Sommer dienen kann.

Das Erdgeschoss beinhaltet ein Café und eine Bar, die alle vier Seiten des Turms bespielen können. Die Türen können entsprechend geöffnet oder geschlossen werden; so wird die Erscheinung des Turms verändert.

Die drei Seiten Richtung Grünraum sind massiv konstruiert, während das Innenleben aus einer Holzkonstruktion besteht, die zum Platz hin sichtbar ist. Die massiven Fassaden sind mit Solarziegeln verkleidet und mit bunten Dachziegeln verschiedenen Farben gesprenkelt, so wie die Türme der Stadt.

Die Position des Turms innerhalb der dreifachen Baumreihe und die Tatsache, dass man ihn von Westen kommend umrunden muss, um auf den Platz zu gelangen, beziehen sich auf die bestehenden Türme, vor allem den Fünfknopfturm.

Isometrie des KulTURMs
1 : 250

ZIRKULÄRE STRATEGIE

Die ehemalige Bifora-Halle wird als urbaner Katalysator dienen. Sie beherbergt eine Organisation, die das Quartier zusammen mit relevanten Akteuren durch Workshops und Diskussionen entwickelt.

Sie bewerten den Bestand aufgrund nachhaltiger Kriterien wie graue Energie und verbauter Ressourcen.

Geeignete Gebäude werden umgebaut und Teil des neuen Quartiers. Ungeeignete werden rückgebaut. Die entnommenen Materialien kommen in die Halle, welche zum Experimentierfeld für Wiederverwendung, Recycling und Upcycling wird. Die Materialien werden bei der Planung der neuen Gebäude berücksichtigt.

Die entnommenen Materialien werden in den neuen Gebäuden wiederverwendet oder z. B. zu Stadtmobiliar. Dabei gesammeltes Wissen kann anderen Projekten zugutekommen oder zur Gründung von Start-ups führen. Das Projekt könnte so zum Vorreiter für die Implementierung zirkulären Bauens werden.

4 NEUE URBANE PRODUKTIVITÄT

- Urban Farming
- Manufakturen
- Markt
- Konsument
- Recyclingpunkt
- bestehende Industrie
- Strom
- Wärme

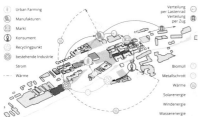

Verteilung per Lastenrad
Verteilung per Zug
Biomüll
Metallschrott
Wärme
Solarenergie
Windenergie
Wasserenergie

Die Stadt wird wieder produktiv! Der *Grüne Wall* bietet Platz für Urban Gardening und Urban Farming; Dachflächen werden durch die Nutzung als Dachgärten und Gewächshäuser oder zur Energiegewinnung aktiviert.

Auch Bestandsgebäude werden angepasst (z. B. wird das Dach des Busdepots zu einem aquaponischen Gewächshaus). Die Ernte wird in Manufakturen weiterverarbeitet, die Produkte werden per Lastenrad an die lokalen bzw. per Zug an die regionalen Märkte verteilt. Abfall wird lokal gesammelt, Biomüll kommt als Dünger wieder in den Kreislauf. Schrott kann dagegen im angrenzenden Industriegebiet verwertet werden. Entstehende Abwärme heizt die Gewächs- und Wohnhäuser. Alle Gebäude produzieren Strom, der vor Ort genutzt oder ins städtische Netz gespeist wird.

5 NUTZUNGSMISCHUNG FÜR VIELFALT

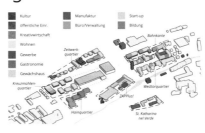

- Kultur
- öffentliche Einr.
- Kreativwirtschaft
- Wohnen
- Gewerbe
- Gastronomie
- Gewächshaus
- Manufaktur
- Büro/Verwaltung
- Start-up
- Bildung

Die Rückkehr der Produktion bedeutet auch die Rückkehr von Arbeitsplätzen ins Stadtzentrum. Damit einher geht eine Durchmischung der Nutzungen, um monofunktionale Bereiche zu verhindern. Synergien und Kontraste sollen eine lebendige Atmosphäre kreieren. Die Verteilung der Nutzungen erzeugt Wege zwischen den Clustern und damit Begegnungen im öffentlichen Raum.

Die Cluster haben Schwerpunkte:
Westtorquartier - Wohnen, Gewerbe
Bahnkante - Produktion, Büros
Zeitwerkquartier - Produktion, Wohnen
Kreuzmühlenquartier - Verwaltung, Bildung, Ateliers
ZAPPlus! - Start-ups, Bildung, Wohnen
St. Katharina nel Verde - Nachbarschaftszentrum

Gmünder Talfinger

Projekt

Unser Projekt geht von der territorialen Ebene des Tals aus und interpretiert die Stadt Schwäbisch Gmünd als Teil der neuen „Rems-Tal-Metropole" neu. Der westliche Stadteingang wird in ein widerstandsfähiges Netzwerk verwandelt, das mit dem Tal, seiner Geschichte, Geologie, Infrastruktur und Landschaft verflochten ist. Die vorgeschlagenen „Talfinger" kommunizieren aktiv mit der Region und schaffen starke architektonische und landschaftliche Hybriden. Dabei belegen sie eine neue Art der ländlichen Urbanität und das Zelebrieren metabolischer Interaktionen innerhalb der Talmetropole. Durch die Integration der Flüsse und Strukturen des Remstals in eine langfristige Entwurfsstrategie konnten wir standortspezifische Antworten entwickeln, die den Stadteingang revitalisieren und ihn in ein unabhängiges, abfallfreies Gebiet verwandeln, in dem hybrides Leben und Produktionstypologien miteinander kombiniert werden.

Hin zu einer Talstadt: Wir schlagen eine schrittweise Entwicklung des Gebietes vor. Den Anfang machen Schlüsselprojekte, die erst räumliche Rahmenbedingungen schaffen und einen Modellcharakter für den weiteren Prozess darstellen. Das Ziel ist die Entwicklung einer flexiblen Struktur, in der sich später weitere Anlagen und Erweiterungen umsetzen lassen.

Die wichtigsten infrastrukturellen und landschaftsplanerischen Formate werden zuerst umgesetzt – der Rems-Allmende-Park, mit der ersten Rems-Farm (Gründung der Coop Rems), das Garten-Tor und die Hängenden Wassergärten, das Building Hub im zukünftigen Holz-Hof (um gleich von Anfang an mit dem Recycling von Abbruch- und Abfallmaterialien zu starten), aber auch Impulsstandorte wie das Gmünd-Wadi mit der Fischfarm sowie die Macher-Allee mit dem Macher-Hof im alten Bifora-Gebäude.

Alle weiteren Schritte intensivieren die Tal-Unternehmen und die ausgelösten Prozesse und werden Schwäbisch Gmünd in eine Talstadt verwandeln: Die Talfinger werden dabei ständig wachsen und breiter werden und in eine stabile und dynamische Zukunft für ein Leben in der Talmetropole führen.

Team

Michael Fay verfügt über Abschlüsse in Architektur und Stadtplanung, erworben in München, Porto und Berlin. In seiner wissenschaftlichen Forschung liegt der Schwerpunkt auf Siedlungsstrukturen, Kohabitationsprozessen und der Neuinterpretation des Berliner Blocks. Er machte Berufserfahrungen in zahlreichen Architekturbüros, aber auch mit eigenen Projekten und in Wettbewerben, wobei der Schwerpunkt auf Wohnbauprojekten und Innenausstattung liegt.

Marcel Tröger ist ein aufstrebender in Berlin lebender Landschaftsarchitekt und Stadtplaner, der an der Schnittstelle von Landschaftsarchitektur, Ökologie und Stadtplanung tätig ist. Seine Arbeitsschwerpunkte reichen von der Entwicklung territorialer Strategien und spekulativer Projekte bis hin zu räumlichen Umsetzungen und Installationen. Vor Kurzem gründete er die Designplattform *studio erde*, auf der er an einem intuitiven und hybriden Gestaltungsansatz für eine Landschaftsarchitektur im Anthropozän arbeitet.

Project

Our project is conceived based on the territorial scale of the valley and reinterprets the city of Schwabisch Gmünd as part of a new 'Rems valley metropolis'. The western entrance to the city is transformed into a resilient network that is interwoven with the valley, its history, geology, infrastructures, and landscapes. The proposed 'Talfinger' (valley fingers) communicate actively with the region and create strong architectural and landscape hybrids, demonstrating a new kind of rural urbanity and the celebration of metabolic interactions within the valley metropolis. By integrating the flows and structures of the Rems valley into a design strategy over time, we have developed site-specific responses that revitalize and turn the entrance to the city into a self-sufficient, zero-waste quarter, where hybrid living and production typologies are combined.

Towards a valley city: we propose a step-by-step development of the area, starting with key projects that formulate the initial spatial settings and will develop a model character for the ongoing process. The goal is to develop a flexible framework in which further settings and add-ons can subsequently be implemented.

The most important infrastructural and landscape settings are tackled first, such as the Rems-Allmende Park with the first Rems Farm (founding of the Rems Coop), the construction of a garden gate and hanging water gardens, a building hub in the future wood district (so as to start from the very beginning with the recycling of demolition and waste material), as well as trigger sites in the maker courtyards, such as the Gmünd Wadi with the fish farm and the maker boulevard with the maker house in the old Bifora building.

All further steps intensify the valley corporations and the processes initiated, and will transform Schwäbisch Gmünd into a valley city: The 'Talfinger' will thereby steadily grow and become denser, resulting in a resilient and dynamic future for living in the valley metropolis.

Team

Michael Fay completed degrees in architecture and urban design in Munich, Porto, and Berlin. His academic research focused on housing structures, cohabitation processes, and the reinterpretation of the Berlin block. He has obtained working experience in numerous architecture offices, and also as a self-employed architect with his own projects and competition submissions focusing on housing projects and interior design.

Marcel Tröger is an upcoming Berlin-based landscape architect and urban designer who works at the interface between landscape architecture, ecology and urban design. The focus of his work ranges from the development of territorial strategies and speculative projects to spatial implementations and installations. He recently founded the design platform *studio erde*, where he works on an intuitive and hybrid design approach to landscape architecture in the Anthropocene.

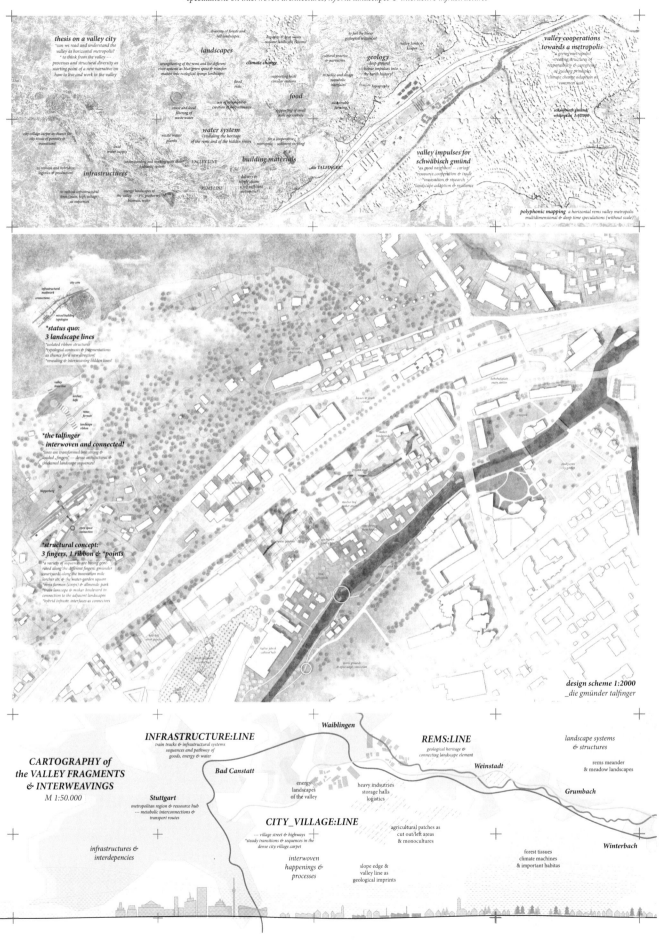

*gmünder talfinger_schwäbisch gmünd & the remstal metropolis
- speculations on interwoven architectures, hybrid landscapes & interactive infrastructures

*gmünder talfinger_schwäbisch gmünd & the remstal metropolis

- speculations on interwoven architectures, hybrid landscapes & interactive infrastructures

die rems.allmende und das garten.tor
the agricultural park & garden.gate
_living productively within metabolic flows!

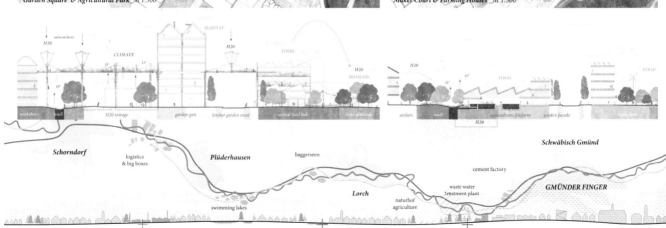

Zoom Gartenplatz & Rems.Allmende
Garden Square & Agricultural Park_M 1:500

Zoom Macher-Hof & Rems.Farmen
Maker Court & Farming Houses_M 1:500

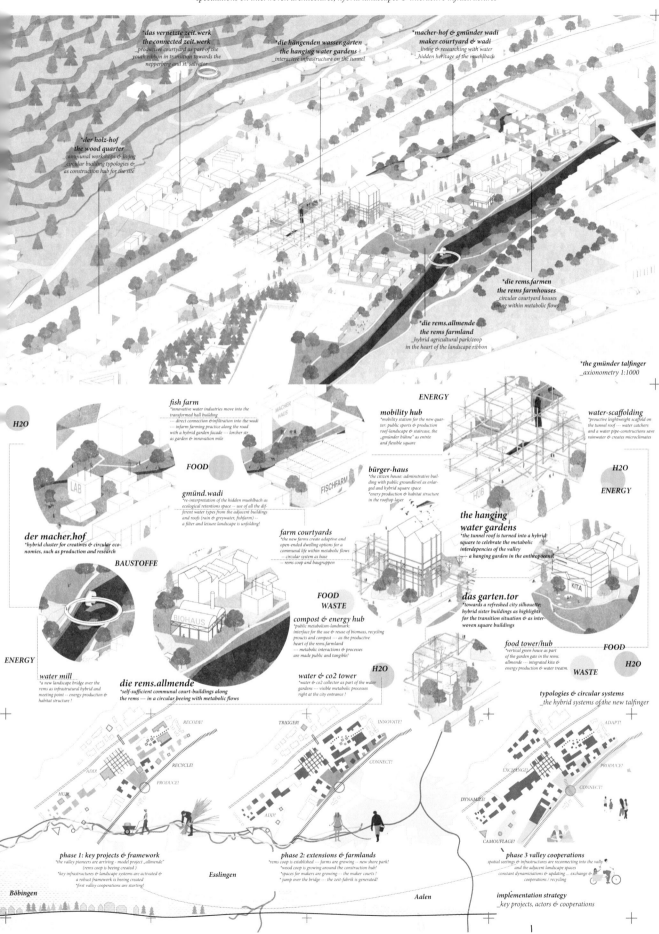

*gmünder talfinger_schwäbisch gmünd & the remstal metropolis
- speculations on interwoven architectures, hybrid landscapes & interactive infrastructures

RISE

Projekt

Der Entwurf RISE (Resilient, Innovativ, Sozial, Energetisch) nutzt die städtebaulichen Potenziale des Westeingangs Schwäbisch Gmünds und entwickelt das Areal zu einem aufstrebenden Quartier, das sich den Herausforderungen des Klimawandels stellt und verdeutlicht, wie in der Stadt von morgen gelebt, gearbeitet und gewohnt werden kann.

Das Industriegebiet ist geprägt von mangelnder Urbanität, inhomogener Baustruktur, monofunktionaler Nutzung und von Brachflächen. RISE durchmischt bewusst Wohnen, Dienstleistung und Gewerbe, Einzelhandel, Kultur und Bildung, um so urbane Vielfalt zu kreieren. Die Themen werden in der Baustruktur und im Freiraum charaktergebend und identitätsstiftend umgesetzt. Durch die konzeptionelle Einbindung eines innovativen Integrierten Wasser- und Ressourcenmanagements (iIWRM) und durch planerische Strategien der wassersensitiven Stadtgestaltung übernimmt RISE eine Vorreiterrolle zur zukunftsfähigen und damit auch klimagerechten Stadtentwicklung.

Die Einbindung von zukunftsorientierten Nutzungen und eine breite Funktionsmischung bilden die Grundlage für ein belebtes Quartier. Neue Gründerzentren machen Schwäbisch Gmünd als Arbeitsstandort attraktiv. Das Gemeinschaftsgefühl und die Solidarität der Bewohner werden durch ausgewiesene Flächen, Kultureinrichtungen und Freiräume gefördert und gestärkt. Clusterwohnen, Baugenossenschaften und Co-Housing bieten Variationen von Wohnformen an und fördern damit aktiv die soziale Durchmischung. Die Bewohnerinnen und Bewohner sollen ihr Viertel in partizipatorischen Prozessen aktiv mitgestalten, was durch Unterstützung des Quartierbüros am Einhornplatz begleitet wird.

In Zeiten erneuerbarer Energien werden Sharing-Konzepte, Solaranlagen, Gründächer und E-Mobilität gefördert sowie Experimentierfelder und autofreie Viertel ausgewiesen. Phasenweise entstehen so vier Teilquartiere mit unterschiedlichen Schwerpunkten – die Quartiersmitte mit Einhornplatz, die Werkhöfe, das Innovationsquartier und das Remsviertel.

Team

Wir – Huyen Trang Dao, Simon Gehrmann, Young Eun Ha, Mai Quynh Lai – sind eine Gruppe aus Architektinnen und Architekten sowie Absolventeninnen und Absolventen mit großem Interesse an Städtebau. Gleichzeitig sind wir durch das Architekturstudium an der TU Darmstadt eng miteinander befreundet. Während unseres Masterstudiums haben wir mehrere städtebauliche Projekte zusammen bearbeitet, sodass wir uns als ein gut eingespieltes Team für Europan 16 leicht zusammenfinden konnten.

Nun arbeiten wir in Architektur- und Städtebaubüros an drei unterschiedlichen Standorten. Neben der wöchentlichen Besprechung per Videocall haben wir zwei Wochen vor der Abgabe ein kleines, aber intensives *work camp* organisiert, um unsere Ideen final zu Papier zu bringen.

Unsere erste Europan-Teilnahme mit einer Anerkennung sehen wir als einen Auftakt und eine große Motivation für weitere Wettbewerbe in der Zukunft.

Project

The RISE (Resilient, Innovative, Social, Energetic) design utilizes the urban-development potential of the western entrance to the city of Schwäbisch Gmünd, and develops it into an aspiring district that addresses the challenges of climate change and shows how people can live and work in the city of tomorrow.

The industrial area is characterized by a lack of urbanity, an inhomogeneous building structure, monofunctional use, and derelict land.

RISE intentionally intermixes housing, services, and commerce, retail, culture, and education to generate urban diversity. The topics are implemented in the building structure and open space in a character-shaping and identity-forming manner. As a result of the conceptual integration of 'innovative Integrated Water and Resource Management' (iIWRM) and planning strategies for designing cities in a water-sensitive way, RISE takes on a pioneering role in achieving future-oriented and thus also climate-friendly urban development.

The integration of future-oriented uses and a broad mixture of functions form the basis for a lively district. New start-up centres make Schwäbisch Gmünd attractive as a place to work. The residents' sense of community (and solidarity) is promoted and fostered by designated areas, cultural institutions, and open spaces. Clusters of residences, cooperative building associations, and co-housing offer a variety of residential options and thus actively promote social intermixture. The residents are supposed to actively contribute to designing their district in participatory processes, which will be accompanied by the support of the district office on Einhornplatz.

In an era of renewable energies, sharing concepts, solar installations, green roofs, and e-mobility are promoted, and fields for experimentation and a car-free district are designated. Four sub-districts with different focuses are thus created: the district centre with Einhornplatz, the work yards, the innovation district, and the Rems district.

Team

We – Huyen Trang Dao, Simon Gehrmann, Young Eun Ha, Mai Quynh Lai – are a group of architects and graduates who have a great interest in urban development. At the same time, we became close friends while studying architecture at the TU Darmstadt and collaborated on several urban development projects during our master's studies, which means that it was easy to put together a smoothly functioning team for the Europan 16 competition.

We are now working at architecture and urban planning firms in three different locations. In addition to weekly discussions via video call, we organized a small, but intensive *work camp* three weeks prior to submitting our design in order to finally put our ideas down on paper.

We received recognition from our first participation in Europan, which we view as a promising beginning and great motivation for further competitions in the future.

RISE
SCHWÄBISCH GMÜND

The „RISE" design uses the urban development capabilities of Schwäbisch Gmünd's western entrance and develops it into an emergent quarter that meets the challenges of climate change and illustrates how people can live and work in the future.

Four sub-districts with different focus areas are being created in phases: The centre of the quarter with Einhornplatz, the hand-craft yard, the innovation centre, and the court yard.

RISE purposely mixes residential, service & commercial, retail, culture & education to create an urban diversity. The topics are implemented in the building structure and the open space in a character-forming and identity-creating way. Through the conceptual integration of an innovative Integrated Water and Resource Management (iIWRM), RISE takes on a leading role in sustainable and climate-friendly urban development.

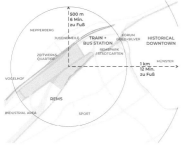

Location

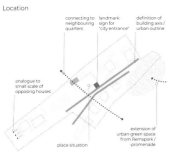

Building structure

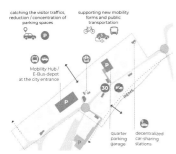

Mobility concept

existing buildings
culture / education
service / industry / gastronomy
quarter use (e.g. rentable common areas)
housing
mobility
department / administration

Utilization concept

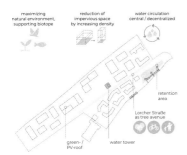

sustainability concept

Siteplan 1:2000

INNOVATION CENTER
(INNOVATIONSZENTRUM)

Pie chart:
- others 15%
- trade & commerce 8%
- service 16%
- culture & community 26%
- living 35%

roof terrace

Cluster 3 Pers.
Cluster 3 Pers.

floorplan 1:500
form of living:
- apartments for singles, families
- Cluster-apartments

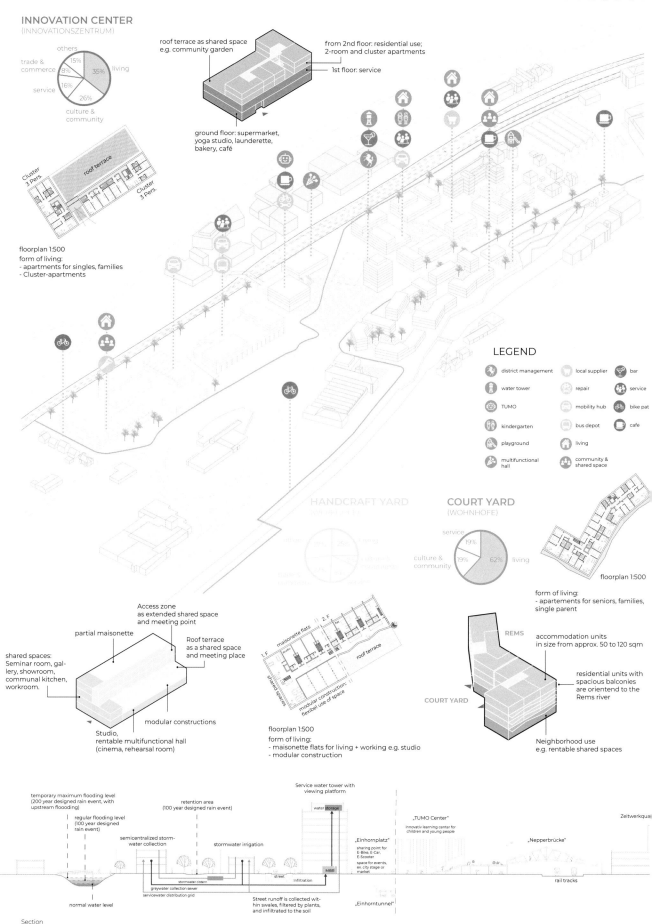

roof terrace as shared space
e.g. community garden

from 2nd floor: residential use;
2-room and cluster apartments

1st floor: service

ground floor: supermarket,
yoga studio, launderette,
bakery, café

LEGEND

district management	local supplier	bar
water tower	repair	service
TUMO	mobility hub	bike pat
kindergarten	bus depot	cafe
playground	living	
multifunctional hall	community & shared space	

HANDCRAFT YARD

Access zone
as extended shared space
and meeting point

partial maisonette

Roof terrace
as a shared space
and meeting place

shared spaces:
Seminar room, gal-
lery, showroom,
communal kitchen,
workroom.

modular constructions

Studio,
rentable multifunctional hall
(cinema, rehearsal room)

maisonette flats
2. F
1. F
shared spaces
roof terrace
modular construction:
flexibel use of space

floorplan 1:500
form of living:
- maisonette flats for living + working e.g. studio
- modular construction

COURT YARD
(WOHNHÖFE)

Pie chart:
- service 19%
- culture & community 19%
- living 62%

floorplan 1:500

form of living:
- apartements for seniors, families,
single parent

REMS

accommodation units
in size from approx. 50 to 120 sqm

residential units with
spacious balconies
are orientend to the
Rems river

COURT YARD

Neighborhood use
e.g. rentable shared spaces

Section

temporary maximum flooding level
(200 year designed rain event, with
upstream flooding)

regular flooding level
(100 year designed
rain event)

retention area
(100 year designed rain event)

Service water tower with
viewing platform

water storage

semicentralized storm-
water collection

stormwater irrigation

"Einhornplatz"
sharing point for
E-Bike, E-Car,
E-Scooter
space for events,
ex. city stage or
market

"TUMO Center"
innovativ learning center for
children and young people

"Nepperbrücke"

Zeitwerkqua

stormwater cistern
greywater collection sewer
servicewater distribution grid

street
Infiltration

MBR

normal water level

Street runoff is collected within swales, filtered by plants,
and infiltrated to the soil

"Einhorntunnel"

rail tracks

TUMO - center for
creative technologies

Nepper Bridge

Solar Power

Sharing station

Open air theatre

Urban games

Multifunctional Hall

Water Tower

Café

City Hall

„Quartiersbüro" -
district management

Sharing station

Aue im Sommer

Flooding situation

PHASE 1
INITIATING EINHORNPLATZ

The brownfield site above the Einhorn Tunnel, which is partly owned by the city, can be developed.
This is where Einhornplatz with the Water Tower, TUMO Centre and multifunctional hall portal buildings will be created. The Nepper Bridge creates a cross-connection through the area south of the Rems to the Nepperberg. Meanwhile, resettlement and negotiations on the use of existing buildings take place for the new „handcraft district". The planning of the Remsaue starts.

PHASE 2
MOVING INTO WERKHÖFE

The automobile-oriented existing uses require less space and have moved into showrooms in the Werkhöfe. Through co-housing and housing cooperatives, users can design and build their own living and working space. In this way, an experimental living environment is being created here.
The Stadtbus bus depot will be equipped with contemporary infrastructure for e-buses in the future and initial plans for mixed uses are taking place. The construction of the Remsaue, or the renaturation of the riverbank, can begin.
The preparations for the Innovation Quarter are in full progress, and calls for tenders for the intended users are taking place.

PHASE 3
START-UP CENTRE AND AUE

Since the existing businesses have moved to the Werkhöfe, the redevelopment can begin in the eastern area. The widening of the Rems as flood protection and accessible open space ties in with the design of the Remspark.
North of Lorcher Straße, the innovation quarter for new start-up centres begins.
The city bus mobility hub is being expanded.

PHASE 4
LIVING ON THE REMS

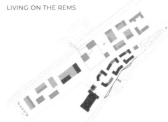

The new neighbourhoods create more jobs, the influx and population grows, the need for housing increases.
The open spaces and the educational & cultural opportunities increase the quality of life and make the area attractive for living.
The Remsviertel with its focus on housing can be developed after preparation by building cooperatives. Different sizes of housing allow for a social mix.

Selb (DE)

Standort

Die Stadt Selb liegt im Regierungsbezirk Oberfranken in Bayern. Aufgrund des demografischen und industriellen Strukturwandels in der bis dato traditionell von der Porzellanindustrie dominierten lokalen Wirtschaft, die ihre Produktion weitgehend eingestellt hat, schrumpfte die Stadt lange: Seit Ende der 1970er Jahre hat die Stadt Selb rund ein Viertel ihrer Einwohnerinnen und Einwohner verloren. In den letzten Jahren konnte jedoch durch veränderte Angebote der Wirtschaft und aktive städtebauliche Eingriffe, die zum Teil auf früheren Europan-Wettbewerbsergebnissen beruhen, eine Umkehr dieses Trends erreicht werden.

Das Projektgebiet liegt in unmittelbarer Nähe zum Stadtzentrum, ist aber mit einer Reihe von leer stehenden Gebäuden, einem undefinierten öffentlichen Raum und einer Straße, die keine Qualitäten für Fußgängerinnen oder Fahrradfahrende bietet, im Niedergang begriffen.

Neue Strategien auf allen Ebenen (Architektur, öffentlicher Raum, Mobilität) sind notwendig, um das Gebiet zu reaktivieren und die Bewohnerinnen und Bewohner in den Prozess zu integrieren. Für die Maßstabsebenen S, das konkrete Projekt, soll das Gebiet der östlichen Innenstadt von Selb neu definiert werden. Für die Maßstabsebene M sollen die Anbindungen an die angrenzenden Stadtgebiete hergestellt werden; es sind verkehrliche und freiraumplanerische Konzepte zur Integration und Aufwertung gefragt.

Dieses Projekt sucht nach Antworten zur Innenverdichtung auf städtebaulicher und architektonischer Ebene sowie nach einer Methode, wie ein zukünftiges Projekt entwickelt werden kann. Das Areal einer ehemaligen Brauerei könnte einer der Pilotstandorte für Transformationen sein, einschließlich sozialer Nutzungen und innovativer Wohnformen.

Das Projektgebiet, insbesondere die erwähnten sanierungsbedürftigen Gebäude, die aktuell durch Leerstand und Unternutzung charakterisiert sind, sollen neue Funktionen erhalten. Gesucht werden innovative sowie nachhaltige gemischte Wohnkonzepte, die generationsübergreifend und barrierefrei sind. Des Weiteren sollen diese Wohnkonzepte gleichzeitig zu einer Stärkung der Arbeitsfunktion im Quartier beitragen. Zusätzlich soll das Projektgebiet durch die Entwicklung attraktiver Verbindungen bestmöglich an die Innenstadt angebunden werden.

Den kleinstädtischen Charakter abseits der Metropolen gilt es in den Wettbewerbsbeiträgen zu beachten. Hier bietet sich die Chance, neuartige und vor allem auch veränderte Freiraumtypologien zu entwickeln, die für zukunftsfähige, flexible Nutzungen und vielfältiges kleinstädtisches Leben ausgelegt sind. Entsprechend der Europan-16-Aufgabenstellung „Living Cities – Lebendige Städte" werden Entwurfsbeiträge gesucht, die innovative Ideen und Prozesse aufzeigen und sich mit den Themenschwerpunkten Dynamiken der Kreislaufwirtschaft und Dynamiken der Integration befassen. Die sich aus dem Wettbewerb ergebenden Lösungsansätze sollen Bestandteil der formalen städtebaulichen Sanierungsziele für dieses Gebiet werden.

Location

The town of Selb is located in the administrative district of Upper Franconia in Bavaria. Due to demographic and industrial structural changes in the local economy – hitherto traditionally dominated by the porcelain industry, which has largely ceased production – the town has been shrinking continuously. Since the end of the 1970s it has lost about a quarter of its inhabitants.

In recent years, however, a reversal of this trend has been achieved through changes in the offerings of the business community and active urban planning interventions, some of them based on results of previous Europan competitions.

The project site is close to the town centre, but it is in decline, with a number of vacant buildings, a rather undefined public space, and a streetscape that has nothing to offer pedestrians or cyclists. New strategies on all levels (architecture, public space, mobility) are needed to reactivate the area and incorporate the residents into the process. For scale level S – the specific project – the area of the eastern town centre of Selb is to be redefined.

For scale level M, connections to neighbouring urban areas should be established, and ideas for integrating and upgrading traffic and open space planning are sought. This project is looking for answers on an urban planning and architectural level and seeking an approach to developing a future-oriented project. The site of a former brewery could be one pilot location for transformations, including social uses and innovative forms of housing. What else might give momentum to innovation?

The aim is to add new functions to the project site, and in particular to the buildings already mentioned, which require redevelopment and are currently vacant and underused.

Here, the focus is on developing innovative and sustainable mixed housing concepts suitable for all generations, and on taking the aspect of accessibility into account. Moreover, these housing concepts should simultaneously help to strengthen the role of employment in the district.

In addition, the project site needs to be linked to the town centre as optimally as possible by developing attractive connections. The competition entries should also take into account the small-town, non-metropolitan character.

There is an opportunity here to develop new and, above all, innovative typologies of open space, designed for sustainable, flexible uses and diverse (small-town) life.

In keeping with the Europan 16 task, 'Living Cities – Lebendige Städte', what are sought are design contributions that demonstrate innovative ideas and processes and deal with the main topics of the dynamics of the circular economy and the dynamics of integration.

Preparatory studies to examine the prevailing social, structural, and urban conditions on the project site will be carried out in 2021. The approaches to solutions that result from the competition will become part of the formal urban redevelopment goals for this area.

Bevölkerung   Inhabitants
ca. 15.000

Betrachtungsraum   Study Site
7,4 ha

Projektgebiet   Project Site
5,7 ha

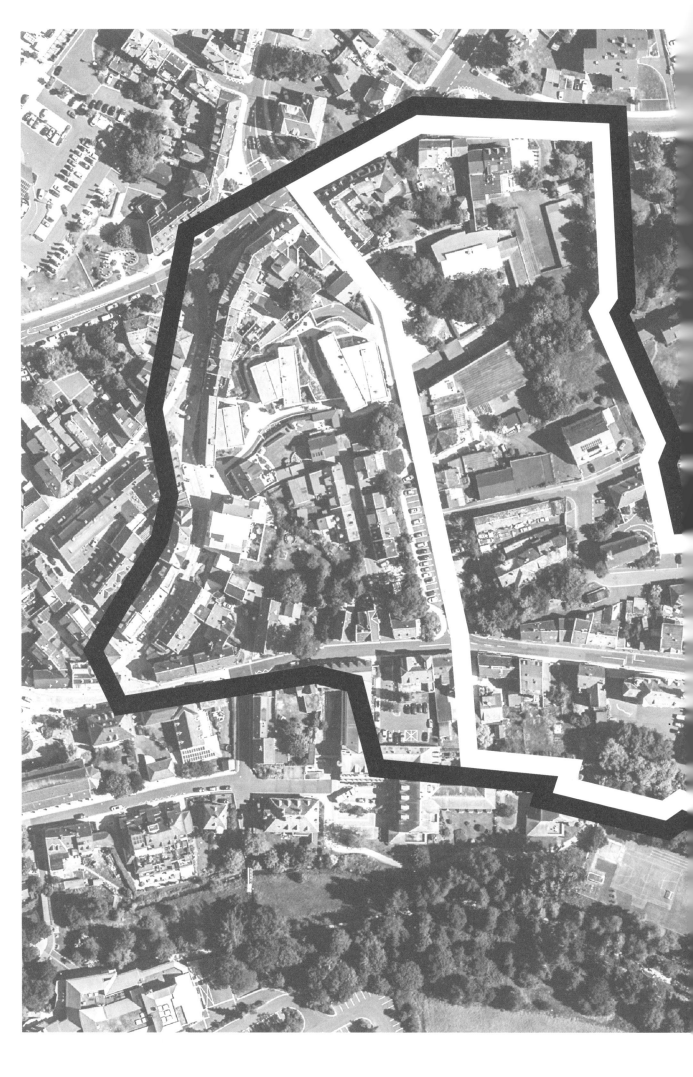

Selb Step by Step

Projekt

„Selb Step by Step" ist eine Anleitung, um Maßnahmen in der bebauten Umgebung zu ergreifen, die eine Vision für die kurz- und langfristige Zukunft von Selb bieten. Im aktuellen Kontext von Anthropozän und Klimakrise legt unser Projekt drei Richtungen für Selb dar, um bis 2050 zu einer sozial-inklusiven und klimaresistenten Stadt zu werden: Renaturierung, Diversifizierung und Dekarbonisierung. Um dies zu erreichen, schlägt es eine Liste konkreter Schritte vor, die im Laufe des nächsten Jahrzehnts in Richtung dieser Ziele führen. Dabei handelt es sich um unauffällige räumliche Eingriffe von unterschiedlichem Ausmaß und Umfang, die stufenweise umgesetzt werden können, entweder unabhängig voneinander oder in Kombination. Ihre Auswirkungen können mithilfe von Indikatoren bewertet werden, was wiederum Konsequenzen auf die nachfolgenden Schritte hat.

Critical Agents und Keystone Species: Da es unmöglich ist, die unendliche Vielfalt aller Arten und Akteurinnen und Akteuren in Betracht zu ziehen, empfiehlt die Anleitung, sich auf die Bedürfnisse einer eingeschränkten Zahl wesentlicher Akteurinnen und Akteure und grundlegender Arten zu konzentrieren, die im Hinblick auf ihre Präsenz und Häufigkeit überproportionale Auswirkungen auf ihre Umgebung haben. Ohne diese sähe die Stadtökologie von Selb grundlegend anders aus.

Nachbarschaft als integrativer, artübergreifender Lebensraum: Sollte adaptive Wiederbenutzung bestehender Gebäude nicht möglich sein, schlägt die Anleitung die Errichtung von Gebäuden vor, die inklusiv sind und die Prinzipien des offenen Bauens verfolgen. Gleiches gilt für neue öffentliche Räume. Dieser Ansatz bietet Strategien und Szenarien, um offene und dynamische Stadtviertel, zirkulare Konstruktionen sowie leistbares und integratives Wohnen zu verwirklichen.

Auf urbaner Ebene stärkt unser Vorschlag das bestehende Straßennetzwerk und schafft offene, grüne und gemeinschaftliche Plätze. Die Gebäude werden unter Einsatz von Trockenbauweise mit lokalem Sperrholz und geringem Energieaufwand errichtet. Ihre Grenzen sind durchlässig und dienen als thermische und programmatische Puffer, die von den Benutzerinnen und Benutzern kontrolliert werden können. Die Innenräume sind um mehrwertige Räume und flexible Gruppen angeordnet.

Die morphotypologischen, bioklimatischen und tektonischen Prinzipien schaffen Räume, die eine Bandbreite an unterschiedlichen Nutzungen umfassen können und eine ebenso breite Palette an Nutzungsarten, was eine Vielzahl unterschiedlicher Haushalte ansprechen wird. Zudem können sich Größe und Programm dieser Räume im Laufe der Zeit verändern, wobei sie wenig Abfall und Kohlenstoffemissionen produzieren.

Team

Íñigo Cornago und Claudia Sánchez entwickeln ihr professionelles Schaffen zwischen Architektur und Urbanismus. Ihre Arbeit, unabhängig oder in Zusammenarbeit mit verschiedenen Büros und Disziplinen, umfasst Wohnbau, Städteplanung, wissenschaftliche Forschung und Kunstschaffen. Gemeinsam führen sie ein Architekturbüro am Central Saint Martins College, University of the Arts (UAL), London.

Project

'Selb Step by Step' is a guide for taking action in the built environment that proposes a vision for the short- and long-term future of Selb. In the current context of the Anthropocene and the climate crisis, our project sets out three directions for Selb to pursue in order to become a socially inclusive and climate-resilient town by 2050: rewilding, diversifying, and decarbonizing. The project thus proposes a list of tangible steps towards achieving these objectives in the next decade. These steps are discreet spatial interventions with various scales and scopes that can be implemented progressively, either independently or in combination. Their impact can be assessed based on indicators, and thus informs the subsequent steps to be taken.

Critical Agents and Keystone Species: Since it is impossible to consider the entire diversity of species and agents, the guide proposes focusing on the needs and desires of a limited number of critical agents and keystone species that have a disproportionately large effect on their environment relative to their presence and abundance. Without critical agents and keystone species, the urban ecology of Selb would be dramatically different.

Neighbourhood as an Inclusive Multispecies Habitat: When adaptive reuse of existing buildings is not possible, this guide proposes constructing integrated buildings and public spaces that adhere to open building principles. This approach offers strategies and scenarios for working towards open and dynamic neighbourhoods, circular construction, and affordable and inclusive housing.

On an urban scale, our proposal strengthens the existing network of streets and creates open green communal courtyards. The buildings are erected with dry techniques in local CLT and low embodied energy. Their perimeters are permeable and serve as a thermal and programmatic buffer that can be controlled by users. The interior spaces are organized around polyvalent rooms and flexible bands.

The morpho-typological, bioclimatic, and tectonic principles result in spaces that can accommodate a wide range of different uses and an equally broad range of types within those uses, which will thus attract a large diversity of households. Furthermore, the size and program of these spaces can change over time, thus generating little waste or carbon emissions.

Team

Íñigo Cornago and Claudia Sánchez develop their professional practice between architecture and urbanism. Their work, independently and in collaboration with various studios and disciplines, encompasses housing, academic urban design research, and art production. They jointly run an architectural design studio at Central Saint Martins College, University of the Arts (UAL), London.

1

SELB STEP BY STEP

A guide for a more inclusive and resilient city

Towards an ecological urbanism

In the current geological epoch of the Anthropocene, the boundaries between artificial and natural, the built and unbuilt environment, have blurred to become indistinguishable. Far from implying the rule of man over nature, we confront the paradox of dominating a planet beyond our control. The effects of climate change and its global scope are increasingly becoming undeniable. The floods that hit central Europe in the summer of 2021, especially Germany, are just one example of how urgent taking action is. As often happens with crises, those already vulnerable due to other factors (age, race, social and economic class, in the case of humans and endangered in terms of biodiversity) will suffer disproportionately the effects of climate change.

In this context, our proposal turns to ecological systems theory and landscape urbanism perspective to develop the spatial intervention tools to tackle this challenge. If social and environmental aspects are so closely interconnected, we need to learn from ecology about which conditions increase biodiversity and how habitats become resilient and thrive.

'Selb Step by Step' is a guide to take action in the built environment that proposes a vision for the short and long term future of Selb in relation to broader policies. The European Commission aims to achieve climate neutrality by 2050; it has set key targets to be met by 2030: 55% greenhouse gas emissions cut, 32% share for renewable energy, and 32.5% improvement in energy efficiency. Working in synchrony with the EU framework, this guide sets out three directions for Selb to follow in order to become a social-inclusive and climate-resilient town by 2050: Rewilding, Diversifying, and Decarbonising. To achieve them, it proposes and describes a list of tangible steps towards those objectives in the next decade. These steps are discreet spatial interventions with different scales and scopes that can be implemented progressively, both independently or in combination. Their impact can be measured and assessed through indicators, informing the following steps to achieve the targets best.

Selb's Horizon 2050

steps towards
REWILDERING

Rewilding is defined as a progressive approach to conserving, restoring and managing natural processes and wilderness areas. It implies "enabling natural processes to shape land and sea, repair damaged ecosystems and restore degraded landscapes. Through rewilding, wildlife's natural rhythms create wilder, more biodiverse habitats."

As such, rewilding is one of the methods identified by the UN to achieve massive scale restoration of natural ecosystems and meet climate targets. The steps proposed by this guide in this direction focus on creating the right conditions for nature's self-management (by uncovering the Erkersreuther Bächlein river, by reducing active management of wildlife populations and by allowing natural forest regeneration), providing connectivity between natural areas (Selbbach riparian areas or the forest northeast of the cemetery) and protecting and reintroducing keystone species. Furthermore, rewilding contributes to individual and collective well-being -as the current pandemic has demonstrated- connecting with wild nature positively impacts mental and physical health.

steps towards
DIVERSIFYING

Diversity refers to all the variety of life found in Selb, including the communities they form and the habitats in which they live. Biodiversity is essential for the resiliency of ecosystems for their intrinsic value and the ecosystem services and benefits it provides. However, diversity in our built environment needs to foster not only the diversity of natural species and habitats but also of different people in terms of age, socio-economic status, culture and race. The steps proposed in this guide attract heterogenous dwellers and visitors and keep those already established in these ways. First, by mixing various uses of ranging sizes within buildings and in neighbourhoods. Secondly, by ensuring affordability of housing, commercial, and cultural spaces. Finally, by contributing to a more welcoming public realm for as many agents and species as possible.

Diversity and complexity are vital factors for urban resilience. Thus, the proposed spatial interventions are meant to be future proof by ensuring flexibility and adaptability to tomorrow's uncertain challenges, uses, and users.

steps towards
DECARBONISING

Decarbonisation refers "to the process of reducing 'carbon intensity', lowering the amount of greenhouse gas emissions produced by the burning of fossil fuels." The built environment contributes to nearly 40% of carbon emissions globally. The three primary sources of these emissions are mobility, operating buildings, and building materials; therefore, the steps proposed to focus on these three aspects. First, promoting non-polluting mobility such as pedestrian or active travel (like cycling) and operating energy-efficient electric public (and private) transport. Secondly, reducing energy consumption by making buildings more efficient (retrofit and newly built) and producing more clean energy that they consume through carbon-negative buildings. Finally, by using building materials with low embodied energy and tectonics that allow for demounting, and thus, reusing components, recycling materials, and reducing waste.

By working towards decarbonising our built environment, we can not only decrease emissions but also contribute to healthier and fairer communities.

The Erkersreuther Bächlein riverside path meets Obere Bergstrasse

Vision for Lorenz-Hutschenreuther-Straße as a slow street

New access to Gottesackerkirche from Lorenz-Hutschenreuther-Straße

Selb's urban ecological networks *People and wildlife*

A Nolli plan for the Anthropocene

Key
- Proposed pedestrian connection
- Proposed pedestrian crossing
- Proposed shared space
- Proposed new tree
- Proposed new tree
- Proposed sport recreational space
- Open accessible space
- Vehicular paved space
- Closed built space
- Closed open paved space
- Open green space
- Closed open green space
- Closed open green space
- River

1:1500   0 10   50   100   300

Territorial strategies
for enhancing spatiotemporal connectivity of habitats in dynamic urban landscapes

NODES

A range in size and types of nodes of urban networks is essential to attract a diversity of actors across time (daily, weekly, and seasonally). Selb's town centre is a linear commercial node of human activity for the area. Singular buildings with public functions like the youth centre, the school or the elderly home act as nodes for specific groups. Large green and blue areas work as critical nodes hosting numerous vegetal and animal species.

The project proposes to progressively expand the existing network of nodes in the area between Obere Bergstrasse and Friedhof splatz with a combination of linear commercial uses and singular cultural public uses. Multigenerational dwellings face communal courtyards with permeable grounds, vegetation and water ponds attract wildlife. Uncovering the Erkersreuther Bächlein river creates a fluvial linear park, acting as a new node for humans and non-humans alike.

Key
- ■ Proposed new nodes
- ■ Commercial node
- ■ Civic Community node
- Green node
- Blue Node

LINKS

Improving the connectivity between the various nodes is a crucial aspect that urban design can tackle to strengthen interaction and cohesion. Vehicular traffic and asphalt roads are the main current deterrents for people and species to dwell in or visit Selb. Therefore, all the steps proposed univocally promote walkability and low emissions mobility, such as cycling and public transport, resulting in a safer, barrier-free and pedestrian-friendly environment.

The proposal strengthens existing pedestrian, shared and permeable links in the town centre and proposes new ones connecting existing and new nodes. Pedestrian-only links traverse the proposed development in Obere Bergstrasse, and vehicular access is always through low speed, shared streets. The new fluvial park links the northeast neighbourhoods, and new pedestrian connections are opened between Lorenz-Hutschenreuther-Straße and the green and leisure infrastructure along Selbbach.

Key
- Proposed Pedestrian link
- Pedestrian link
- Shared link
- Natural trail link

STEPPING STONES

Linear connections are not the only way to link nodes, nor are they enough to ensure that certain citizens - such as the elderly or those with reduced mobility- and species - for example, insects- feel welcomed and be able to move between destinations in their journey. We define stepping stones in our guide for Selb as small pocket spaces with amenities that offer refuge and a place to pause for them to travel across. Their size, location, and number determine the distance that actors can travel and thus are vital for achieving an inclusive city.

Through multiple and complementary steps, the project proposes a range of stepping stones -commercial uses, benches, drinking water, trees and vegetation, etc.- along both Obere Bergstrasse and Lorenz-Hutschenreuther-Straße. Similarly, paths of stepping stones with public amenities are proposed along the green and blue corridors connecting Selb with other urban and landscape centres. For example, we propose placing a bench or ledge every 100m along urban links to provide pause points every 500 steps for those with short step-length like elderly people.

Key
- ◆ Stepping stones for humans
- Green trail of stepping stones

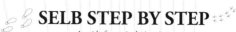

SELB STEP BY STEP
A guide for an inclusive city

a vision for
SELB 2030

The size and complexity of the site and the ambition of the competition brief cannot be responsibly and sensitively addressed with a monolithic architectural intervention or a closed urban masterplan. Quite the opposite, the **transition towards an ecological urbanism requires that a number of steps are progressively taken** towards the objectives stated: rewilding, diversifying, and decarbonising. In the following documents, we describe in detail our vision for Selb for the next decade.

Plate 2 enumerates the steps proposed for the next decade and identifies a limited number of key agents and species to keep in mind when designing and assessing the interventions. The extensive view of the site demonstrates **how some of these steps can be implemented and how the networks of people and wildlife will be strengthened**. As can be appreciated, these measures will improve the connectivity of their networks by developing nodes, links, and stepping stones.

Plate 3 zooms into the area delimited by Obere Bergstrasse in the West, Erkersreuther Bächlein to the North, the cemetery to the East and Lorenz-Hutschenreuther-Straße to the South. It describes the typologies of public realm and buildings proposed and presents the guiding principles and how they connect with the three long-term goals. Furthermore, this sample demonstrates how this **environment could be inhabited, becoming a thriving, inclusive and resilient urban ecosystem.**

List of
STEPS FORWARD

This list is open by definition, and we expect it to be developed in conversation with stakeholders and over time, reflecting in their monitoring and evaluation. The steps are organised according to their scope: Buildings (B), Uses (U), Urban furniture and amenities (A) and Street design and life (S).

CRITICAL AGENTS
and
KEYSTONE SPIECES

As it is impossible to consider the endless diversity of species and agents, the guide proposes to focus on the needs and desires of a limited number of critical agents and keystone species that **have a disproportionately large effect on their environment relative to their presence and abundance.** The selection has been made attending to two criteria. Either their vulnerability ensures that if they can thrive, everyone else can, or they play a critical role in maintaining the structure of an ecological community. Without critical agents and keystone species, Selb urban ecology would be dramatically different.

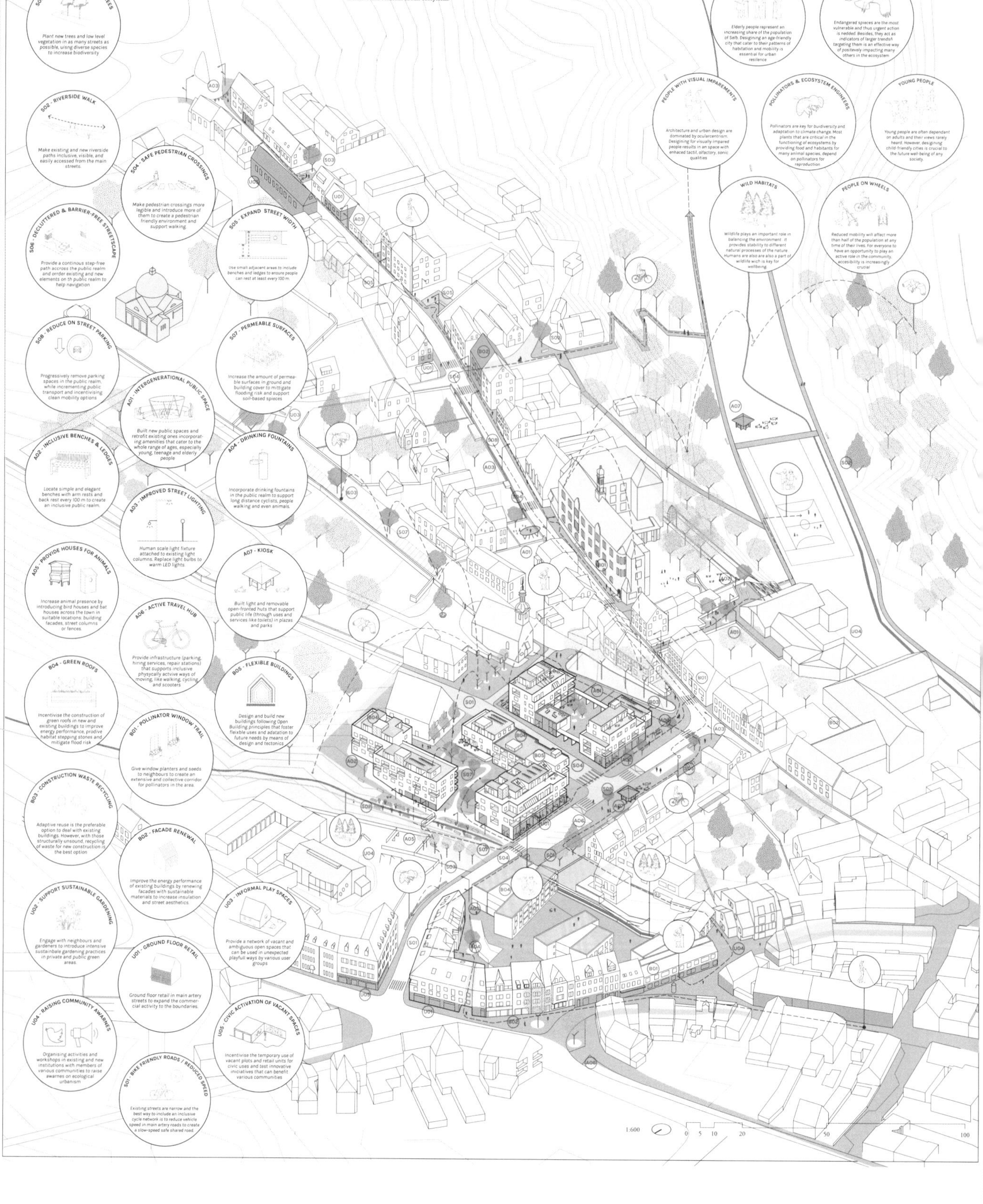

ELDERLY PEOPLE

Elderly people represent an increasing share of the population of Selb. Designing an age-friendly city that cater to their patterns of habitation and mobility is essential for urban resilience

ENGANGERED SPIECES

Endangered spieces are the most vulnerable and thus urgent action is needed. Besides, they act as indicators of larger trends; targeting them is an effective way of positively impacting many others in the ecosystem

PEOPLE WITH VISUAL IMPAIRMENTS

Architecture and urban design are dominated by ocularcentrism. Designing for visually impaired people results in an space with enhanced tactil, olfactory, sonic qualities

POLLINATORS & ECOSYSTEM ENGINEERS

Pollinators are key for biodiversity and adaptation to climate change. Most plants that are critical in the functioning of ecosystems by providing food and habitats for many animal species, depend on pollinators for reproduction

YOUNG PEOPLE

Young people are often dependant on adults and their views rarely heard. However designing child friendly cities is crucial to the future wel-being of any society.

WILD HABITATS

Wildlife plays an important role in balancing the environment. It provides stability to different natural processes of the nature. Humans are also a part of wildlife wich is key for wellbeing

PEOPLE ON WHEELS

Reduced mobility will affect more than half of the population at any time of their lives. For everyone to have an opportunity to play an active role in the community, accesibility is increasingly crutial

S03 - PLANTING NEW STREET TREES

Plant new trees and low level vegetation in as many streets as possible, using diverse species to increase biodiversity

S02 - RIVERSIDE WALK

Make existing and new riverside paths inclusive, visible, and easily accessed from the main streets.

S04 - SAFE PEDESTRIAN CROSSINGS

Make pedestrian crossings more legible and introduce more of them to create a pedestrian friendly environment and support walking.

S06 - DECLUTTERED & BARRIER-FREE STREETSCAPE

Provide a continous step-free path across the public realm and order existing and new elements on th public realm to help navigation

S05 - EXPAND STREET WIDTH

Use small adjacent areas to include benches and ledges to ensure people can rest at least every 100 m

S08 - REDUCE ON STREET PARKING

Progressively remove parking spaces in the public realm, while incrementing public transport and incentivising clean mobility options

A01 - INTERGENERATIONAL PUBLIC SPACE

Built new public spaces and retrofit existing ones incorporating amenities that cater to the whole range of ages, especially young, teenage and elderly people

S07 - PERMEABLE SURFACES

Increase the amount of permeable surfaces in ground and building cover to mitigate flooding risk and support soil-based spieces

A02 - INCLUSIVE BENCHES & LEDGES

Locate simple and elegant benches with arm rests and back rest every 100 m to create an inclusive public realm.

A03 - IMPROVED STREET LIGHTING

Human scale light fixture attached to existing light columns. Replace light bulbs to warm LED lights

A04 - DRINKING FOUNTAINS

Incorporate drinking fountains in the public realm to support long distance cyclists, people walking and even animals

A05 - PROVIDE HOUSES FOR ANIMALS

Increase animal presence by introducing bird houses and bat houses across the town in suitable locations: building facades, street columns or fences.

A07 - KIOSK

Built light and removable open-fronted huts that support public life (through uses and services like toilets) in plazas and parks.

S04 - GREEN ROOFS

Incentivisse the construction of green roofs in new and existing buildings to improve energy performance, prodive habitat stepping stones and mitigate flood risk

A06 - ACTIVE TRAVEL HUB

Provide infrastructure (parking, hiring services, repair stations) that supports inclusive physically active ways of moving, like walking, cycling and scooters

B05 - FLEXIBLE BUILDINGS

Design and build new buildings following Open Building principles that foster flexible uses and adaptation to future needs by means of design and tectonics

B01 - POLLINATOR WINDOW TRAIL

Give window planters and seeds to neighbours to create an extensive and collective corridor for pollinators in the area.

B03 - CONSTRUCTION WASTE RECYCLING

Adaptive reuse is the preferable option to deal with existing buildings. However, with those structurally unsound, recycling of waste for new construction is the best option

B02 - FACADE RENEWAL

Improve the energy performance of existing buildings by renewing with sustainable materials to increase insulation and street aesthetics

U02 - SUPPORT SUSTAINABLE GARDENING

Engage with neighbours and gardeners to introduce intensive sustainable gardening practices in private and public green areas.

U03 - INFORMAL PLAY SPACES

Provide a network of vacant and ambiguous open spaces that can be used in unexpected playful ways by various user groups

U01 - GROUND FLOOR RETAIL

Ground floor retail in main artery streets to expand the commercial activity to the boundaries.

U05 - CIVIC ACTIVATION OF VACANT SPACES

Incentivise the temporary use of vacant plots and retail units for civic uses and test innovative initiatives that can benefit various communities

U04 - RAISING COMMUNITY AWARENESS

Organising activities and workshops in existing and new institutions with members of various communities to raise awarnes on ecological urbanism

S01 - BIKE FRIENDLY ROADS / REDUCED SPEED

Existing streets are narrow and the best way to include an inclusive cycle network is to reduce vehicle speed in main artey roads to create a slow-speed safe shared road

1:600   0 5 10   20   50   100

SELB STEP BY STEP
A guide for a more inclusive and resilient city

1:100
0 1   3   5

List of steps taken

(S01) Bike-friendly roads
(S02) Riverside walk
(S03) Planting new street trees
(S04) Safe pedestrian crossings
(S05) Expand street width
(S06) Decluttered streetscape
(S07) Permeable surfaces
(S08) Reduce on street parking
(A01) Intergenerational public space
(A02) Inclusive benches and ledges
(A03) Improved street lightning
(A04) Drinking Fountains

(A05) Provide houses for animals
(A06) Active travel hub
(A07) Kiosk
(B01) Pollinator window trail
(B02) Façade renewal
(B03) Construction waste recycling
(B04) Green roofs
(U01) Ground floor retail
(U02) Support sustainable gardening
(U03) Informal play spaces
(U04) Raising community awareness
(U05) Civic activation of spaces

Neighbourhood as
Inclusive Multispecies Habitat

1:300
0   5   10   20   50

the ecological performance of
Open Building

Open Buildings are flexible, adaptable, circular and resilient. With distinct architecture, they contribute to a dynamic urban context. Drawing on principles advanced by J. Habraken in the 1960s and developed over the years by visionary and pioneer designers, their principles offer strategies and scenario to work towards open and dynamic neighbourhoods, affordable and inclusive housing , and building innovation and circularity.

When adaptive-reuse and retrofit of existing buildings is not possible, this guide proposes to build buildings and public realm that are integrated and follow Open Building principles. Below, we outline the main features of the proposed urban and building typologies.

Morpho-typological principles

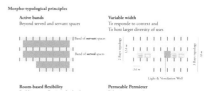

Active bands
Beyond served and servant spaces

Variable width
To responde to context and
To host larger diversity of uses

Room-based flexibility
Building as a collection of polyvalent rooms
Louis Khan meets Hertzberger

Permeable Perimeter
Balconies, terraces & passages
The importance of in-between space

Passive Bioclimatic principles

Performance principles that reduce energy consumption by increasing efficiency and increase energy production through clean energy and harvesting resources

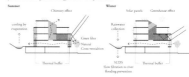

CLT Industrialised timber tectonic

Tectonic principles
towards Decarbonising

- Materials with low embodied energy
- Locally sourced timber > Circular economy
  + Reduce emissions from transport
- Demountable dry construction
  > Reuse components
  > Recycle material
  > Reduce Waste
- Optimisation of lifespan of each component

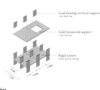

Inclusivity through a flexible mix of uses and sizes

The morpho typological, bioclimatic and tectonic principles result in spaces that can host a wide range of different uses (housing, commercial, office, workshop, cultural centre) and an equally broad range of types within those uses (studios, 1-4 bed apartments, cluster homes for communal living of up to 14 bedrooms) that will attract a large diversity of households (in terms of age, lifestyle, socioeconomic status, race, culture, household structure, etc.). Furthermore, the size and program of this spaces can change over time, generating few waste and carbon emissions.

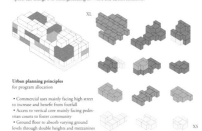

Urban planning principles
for program allocation

- Commercial uses mainly facing high street to increase and benefit from footfall
- Access to vertical core mainly facing pedestrian courts to foster community
- Ground floor to absorb varying ground levels through double heights and mezzanines

Wernigerode (DE)

Standort

Die Stadt Wernigerode im Harz liegt in Sachsen-Anhalt und ist überregional als touristisches Ziel bekannt. Die Bevölkerungszahlen sind stabil, mit einem leichten Abnahmetrend in den letzten Jahren. Freie Mietwohnungen für junge Familien sind in der Stadt kaum vorhanden. Die meisten Familien weichen deshalb auf die umliegenden Gemeinden aus. Die GWW Gebäude- und Wohnungsbaugesellschaft Wernigerode mbH möchte dies mit neu zu entwickelnden Arealen im Stadtraum ändern.

Der Betrachtungsraum ist von der historischen Innenstadt durch die Bahnlinie Hannover-Halle getrennt. Die Bebauung ist sehr heterogen und bildet eine gemischte Struktur aus großflächigen Gewerbebetrieben, zwei- bis viergeschossigen Wohnbauten (Einfamilienhäuser, Mehrfamilienhäuser, Reihenhäuser) sowie Gartengrundstücken. Im Norden des Areals schließt der Bürgerpark, ein ehemaliges Gartenschaugelände, mit großzügigen Wiesen und Wasserflächen und unterschiedlichen Freizeitnutzungen an. Der Hauptbahnhof befindet sich in unmittelbarer Nähe und ist mit dem Fahrrad in fünf Minuten zu erreichen. Der Siedlungsbau an der nordwestlichen Ecke ist aus den Jahren 1890 bis 1930 und wurde als Werkswohnungsbau bzw. Siedlungsbau konzipiert, Gartenanlagen waren Selbstversorgergärten.

Ziel des Verfahrens ist, einen nachhaltigen und gemischten Rahmenplan für den größeren Betrachtungsraum zu entwickeln, der in kleineren und sinnvollen Bau- und Erschließungsabschnitten entwickelt werden kann. Als Auftakt sollen die beiden Projektgebiete 1 und 2 als Rahmensetzung und Initiationsprojekte entstehen. Die Aufgabe besteht in der Weiterentwicklung einer Gartenstadt und der Entwicklung passgenauer neuer Wohntypologien für zwei Projektstandorte.

Gesucht werden Ideen zur Nutzungsvielfalt und Wohnungsmischung mit integrativem Charakter, welche die Konzepte der traditionellen Gartenstadt- und Siedlungsbewegungen der Vergangenheit zeitgenössisch interpretieren und besondere Rücksicht auf die wachsende Bedeutung von Grünräumen als soziale und ökologische Orte nehmen. Die Innenentwicklung der Städte, die aus ökologischer Sicht sinnvoll ist – Reduktion von Flächeninanspruchnahme, Versiegelung, Verkehrserfordernisse –, führt dazu, dass auch Freiräume heute mehr sein müssen als Orte der Kontemplation oder Ökosystemdienstleistung. Sie können sowohl als Gemeinschaftsgärten als auch als Standorte lokaler Lebensmittelproduktion einen Beitrag zu einer sozialökologisch nachhaltigen Stadtentwicklung leisten. Zwar ist eine Bebauung des Betrachtungsraums nicht zeitnah geplant, doch sollten hier Vorschläge gemacht werden, wie die „Living City" der Zukunft aussehen kann. Aktuelle Debatten – wie zum Beispiel die populistische Polarisierung zwischen Einfamilienhaus einerseits und Plattenbau andererseits – zeigen, dass hier dringend differenziertere Vorschläge und neue Vorstellungen vom städtischen Leben („urban imaginaries") benötigt werden, die über Wernigerode hinaus Vorbildfunktion haben können.

Location

The town of Wernigerode, in Saxony-Anhalt in the Harz Mountains, is known nationwide as a tourist destination. Population figures are stable, with a slightly downward trend in recent years. There are hardly any vacant apartments available for young families to rent in the city. Most families thus move to surrounding municipalities. The GWW Gebäude- und Wohnungsbaugesellschaft Wernigerode mbH wants to change this situation by developing new areas in the city. The area under consideration (including both competition sites) is close to the historic centre, but separated from it by the Hanover-Halle railway line.

The development in the study site is heterogeneous: large-scale commercial enterprises, two- to four-storey residential buildings (single-family homes, apartment buildings, terraced houses), and garden plots. To the north is the Bürgerpark, the site of a former garden show, with extensive grassy areas, lakes, and various recreational uses.

The residential development surrounding the site dates from ca. 1890 to 1930 and was designed as housing for factory workers. The large gardens were envisaged to provide self-support. Other green areas are now used as allotments and growers' gardens or are derelict.

The two project sites mark the corners of a space that is today largely garden land with some small-scale development (former growers' gardens). From an urban planning point of view, it would be interesting to link traditional concepts from the garden city and settlement movements with the increased attention now being given to green spaces in the town for social and ecological reasons. The internal development of cities, which makes sense from an ecological perspective (reductions in land use and sealed-surface areas, and traffic requirements), means that today's open spaces must be more than places for contemplation or ecosystem services. They can make an important contribution to socio-ecologically sustainable urban development, both as community gardens and as sites where food is produced locally.

There are no plans to build on the study site in the near future, but ideas about what the future 'Living City' could look like should be offered. Current debates – such as the populist polarization between 'single-family homes' on the one hand and 'prefabricated housing' on the other – show the urgent need for more differentiated proposals and new ideas of urban living ('urban imaginaries'), which can serve as models far beyond Wernigerode.

Ideas for a continuing diversity of use and mixture of housing with an integrative character are desired. Propositions that address sustainability and the circular economy are also welcome. A mobility and energy concept that is adaptable to the future would also be appropriate. The process aims to develop a sustainable and ecological mixed-use framework plan, with a view to practicable development in smaller construction and development phases. As a prelude, the two project sites 1 and 2 should be understood as framework and initiation projects.

Bevölkerung   Inhabitants
ca. 32.810

Betrachtungsraum   Study Site
22,37 ha

Projektgebiet   Project Site
8 ha

Duet

Projekt

Heute ist der Standort in ein Industriegebiet eingegliedertes Wohngebiet; zu seinem Zentrum hin ist das Areal durch Gruppen von Einfamilienhäusern mit Privatgärten charakterisiert. In dem Entwurf ist das Gebiet als grünes Band zwischen Fluss und Bürgerpark konzipiert, aber auch als Brücke zum historischen Zentrum.

Der Fokus liegt auf der Öffnung und Stärkung des urbanen Potenzials des Standorts, um diesen mit einer neuen Mikroinfrastruktur einzubinden und eine neue nachhaltige Mobilität zu fördern. An den Rändern werden Geh- und Radwege angelegt, im Gebiet ein Netzwerk interner Wege. Die wichtigsten Schnittpunkte sind als neue Grundlage für gesellschaftliches Leben vorgesehen. In diesen Nischen wird eine Reihe kollektiver Plattformen und Pavillons eingesetzt, in deren Prozess der Umsetzung und Positionierung die Bürgerinnen und Bürger einbezogen werden. Die Pavillons werden nicht nur von gesellschaftlichem Nutzen sein, sondern auch eine energetische Funktion erfüllen, da jeder mit Systemen zur Energieproduktion und -speicherung versehen werden kann.

Zwei Ecken des Projektgebietes sind für die Verdichtung vorgesehen. Wenn auch unterschiedlich in Morphologie und Typologie, sind die Gebäude doch ähnlich, was Sprache und Bauprozess anbelangt. Die Gebäude, mit Ausnahme der Erdgeschossbuchten und -erker, bestehen aus vorgefertigten Elementen. Das nördliche Areal hat einen extrovertierten Charakter, was für eine wirtschaftliche Basis und einen öffentlichen Raum in Richtung Bürgerpark sorgt. Der introvertiertere Süden überblickt einen Hofgarten, der mit den offenen Bereichen des Kindergartens und des Hügels verbunden ist.

Das nördliche Gebäude spiegelt die Entscheidung wider, Wohnen mit hoher Dichte zu fördern. Die Wohnbauten sind eine Abfolge gleichartiger Buchten, gerahmt durch dicke Mauern, die alle notwendigen Versorgungseinrichtungen enthalten. Die Gestaltung bietet verschiedene Wohnarten und umfasst klassische Familienwohnungen ebenso wie individuelle Strukturen für Ältere und Jüngere. Die Rhythmik von Struktur und Raum ermöglicht bei Bedarf eine weitere kollegiale Aufteilung der Buchten.

Im südlichen Teil des Areals basiert das angebotene Lebensmodell auf Wohnen mit niedriger Dichte (der Typologie des Reihenhauses entsprechend) mit gemeinsamem Innenhof.

Team

Francesco Baggio studierte an der Università Iuav di Venezia und der Accademia di Architettura di Mendrisio. Er arbeitete im AMAA Office und dann bei Flaim Prunster Architekten.

Erasmo Bitetti studierte an der Università Iuav di Venezia und an der Accademia di Architettura di Mendrisio. Er war im AMAA Office und bei Herzog & de Meuron tätig.

Clara Faccio studierte am Politecnico di Milano und an der ETSAV. Sie arbeitete für FLOS Milan, dann im AMAA Office und später bei Piovenefabi.

Federico Giorgio studierte Architektur am Politecnico di Milano und an der Accademia di Architettura di Mendrisio. Er war bei Baserga Mozzetti tätig, arbeitete mit Bartke Pedrazzini Architetti zusammen und ist Mitbegründer des Künstlerkollektivs COSE in Mailand.

Project

Today the site is a residential location embedded in a larger industrial area and its edges are defined by transport infrastructures. Towards its interior, the neighbourhood is characterized by a constellation of single-family houses and their private gardens. In the proposal, the area is envisioned as a green hinge between the river and the Bürgerpark and as a bridge to the historic centre.

The project focuses on the idea of opening up and strengthening the urban potential of the strategic site, integrating it by means of a new micro-infrastructure, and encouraging sustainable mobility. New pedestrian and cycling paths are laid out along the edges, and a network of internal paths is derived from the reclamation of interstitial areas. The main points of intersection are imagined as new assets for civic life. A series of collective platforms and pavilions is implemented in these slots. These pavilions will have not only social value but also an energy-related function with systems for energy production and storage.

The corners of the study area are intended for densification. Though different in morphology and typology, the buildings are alike in language and construction processes. The buildings, except for the ground floor bays, consist of prefabricated elements. The proposal develops the northern area with an extroverted character, thus facilitating a commercial base and a large public space with a view of the Bürgerpark. The more introverted southern area overlooks a courtyard garden linked to the open spaces of the kindergarten and the hill.

The northern building reflects the decision to encourage a condition of high-density living. The housing consists of a sequence of bays framed by thick walls containing all the fixed utilities. The design offers a diverse number of housing types and includes conventional family apartments as well as individual dwellings for older and younger users.

Team

Francesco Baggio studied at the Università Iuav di Venezia and at the Accademia di Architettura di Mendrisio. He worked at AMAA Office and Flaim Prunster Architekten. Erasmo Bitetti studied at Università Iuav di Venezia and at Accademia di Architettura di Mendrisio. He worked at AMAA Office and Herzog & deMeuron.

Clara Faccio studied at the Politecnico di Milano and ESTAV in Barcelona. She worked for FLOS Milan, AMAA Office and Piovenefabi.

Federico Giorgio studied architecture at the Politecnico di Milano and at the Accademia di Architettura di Mendrisio. He worked at Baserga Mozzetti and Bartke Pedrazzini Architetti, he is a co-founder of COSE, an artistic collective in Milan.

DUET

Duet focuses on the idea of opening and strengthening the urban potential of the strategic site, integrating it with a new micro-infrastructure.

Today the site is a residential area embedded in a larger industrial one. Its edges are defined by vehicular infrastructures: the railway to the south and the main access roads to the city on the other three sides. Towards its interior, the neighborhood is characterized by the constellation of single-family houses and their private gardens drawing the urban image.

In the proposal the area is envisioned as a green hinge between the river and the Bürgerpark as well as a bridge to the historic center of Wernigerode.

It takes place in stages.
First, pedestrian and cycling paths are laid out along the edges, then a network of internal paths is derived from the reclamation of interstitial areas.
A second phase involves a private land shrinkage (acquisition of thin strips between properties) creating a greater porosity of the neighborhood. The system is then connected to the roads that pass through the site which are converted to slow mobility. At the points of main intersection of the internal paths a series of collective platforms and pavilions is implemented.

The two left corners of the study area are intended for densification. However different in morphology and typology, the buildings are alike in language and construction processes.
The proposal develops the north area with an extroverted character granting a commercial base and a large public space looking Bürgerpark. The south, more introverted, overlooks a courtyard garden linked to the open spaces of the close kindergarten and the green dune in the vicinity.

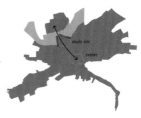

MORPHOLOGY

The study site slots in the middle of an etherogeneous area of the city Wernigerode. Due to its intermediate position, it acts as a cushion between the main urban development and the residential expansion in the north, the industrial area and the natural system of Bürgerpark.

- urban area   - industrial area   - Bürgerpark

GREEN MORPHOLOGY

A rich system of natural elements faces the northern part of the study site. A necklace of water basins alternates with green spaces and marks a gap between two parts of the city. Considering our study area as a green appendix of Bürgerpark, we imagined it in dialogue with a territorial system of landscape elements.

- parks   - lakes

MOBILITY

The existing mobility develops along the edges of the 'green pocket'. Slow mobility is basically non existent. The lack of permeability, the presence of the infrastructure and a weak connection with the urban center results in a condition of isolation and introversion.

train line   ● bus stop   — bus line   pedestrian path

STRATEGY

Encouraging a sustainable mobility is intended as a basic concept for the future development of the area. Porosity is increased thanks to the allotment of new bus stops and the reorganization of pedestrian paths. Proximity with the city beyond the railway is improved by a restructured system of connections along the tracks.

new bus stop   ▲ new accesses   new pedestrian path

STUDY SITE STRATEGY
TIME LINE

N   0   50   100m

Study site in 2027 - Axonometry

Today
An extreme parcellization of the soil and the hegemony of the single-family house are peculiar for the site. One of its most remarkable aspects is the lack of civic spaces: shared infrastructure is scarce and underdeveloped.

Tomorrow
A short-term scenario proposes punctual actions focused on public facilities. Interstitial spaces and residual voids are imagined as new assets for civic life. In these slots a technological infrastructure is envisioned and access to energy and water is granted.

2025
The construction of the two housings starts and 'civic pavilions' are scattered in the site. Simoultaneously, the beginning of a process of private land shrinkage is imagined. Landowners are asked to give the community a minimum part of their private land in order to enhance quality of movement and daily life.

2035
Permeability keeps improving and space occupied by dismissed bad deposit is returned to the community. New vegetation is planted. Residential densifications towards the south can be imagined.

1. PLAYGROUND
Swing
Slide

2. CONDENSER
Concert stage
Dance floor
Plaza

3. SPORT FIELD
Football
Basket
Tennis

4. SHELTER
Co-working space
Study space
Workshop

5. HUB
Car parking
bike parking
bus stop

6. HALL
Local market
Shops
Space for event

PAVILIONS
AUTO-CONSTRUCTION

 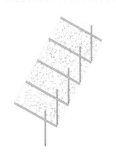  

The process of implementation of the strategic site is carried out by the co-existence of a technological and a social component.
A set of tools is provided to the citizens to allow them to occupy the new infrastructured 'open platforms' with 'civic pavilions'.
While the 'platforms' require specialized planning and realization, the organization of the 'pavilions' relies on self construction. The citizens are imagined to directly involved with their placement and the process of assembly.
A metallic support, a wooden strut, a steel cable, panels for flooring, dividing and roofing: the kit of tools is shrunk to its minimum. Maximum variety, instead, is gained in their manipulation. Citizens can, in fact, use their shared toolkit in order to build a sheltered canopy (for aggregation or parking), a fenced playground, a platform for assemblies and many other devices.

Being intended as shared devices of communal domain, the 'civic pavilions' will carry not only a social value but also bear an energetic function. In particular, each on them could be integrated with systems for energy production and storage. Photovoltaic panels will provide thermic and electrical energy for pavilions' self-dependence. Rainwater will be saved, collected in tanks and reused for irrigation and small domestic uses (draining, laundering, washing …). The kinetic energy generated by the wind will be collected by flying kites and stored by accumulators. Each of the devices will sit as an abstract object on top of the pavilions' roof or be integrated with one of their elements.

Sun

Water

Wind

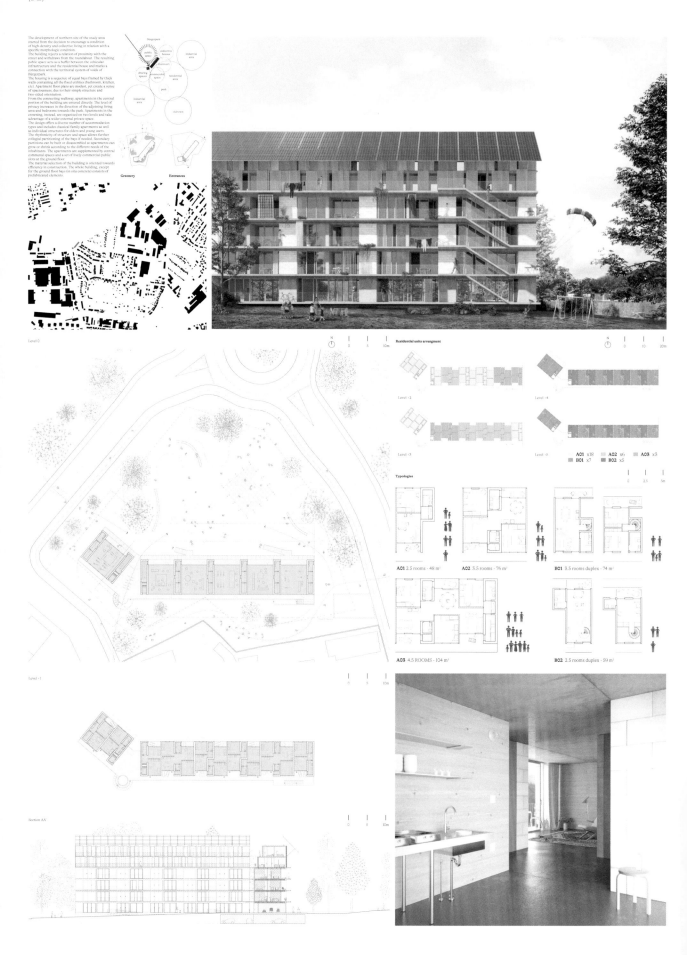

United Gardens
of Wernigerode

Projekt

Zusammenhängende Landschaften reaktivieren die Vision einer gemeinschaftlich orientierten Gartenstadt als grüne, durchlässige Umgebung in einer Walking City; mit einer selbstverwalteten Gemeinschaft und landwirtschaftlicher Aktivität, die Menschen miteinander verbindet.

Huts Seeding Community: Die lokale Kultur von Hütten unterschiedlicher Größe aus unterschiedlichen Materialien und mit verschiedenen Funktionen strebt die Entwicklung an von: Phase 1 als Nachbarschaftszentrale mit sozialen und landwirtschaftlichen Aktivitäten, und Phase 2 als kontemplativem Gemeinschaftsgarten für alle Altersstufen sowie einer Kultur des Teilens und der lokalen Wirtschaftskreisläufe.

Soft Dwelling: Die Architektur bietet Verkehrsflächen, die aktives Gemeinschaftsleben fördern. Eine Kombination von Wohnungen ist an sich verändernde Lebensweisen angepasst. Eine lokale strukturelle Logik stellt Wirtschaftlichkeit und nachhaltige Bauweise sowie die Entwicklung einheimischer Elemente sicher.

Team

Wir – Moritz Ahlers, Patxi Martín Domínguez, Paul Schaeger, Josep Garriga Tarres, Natalia Vera Vigaray – glauben an das Unternehmen Europan und an dessen interdisziplinären Gestaltungsansatz. Wir sind vier Architektinnen und Architekten und ein Anwalt, alte Erasmus-Freunde.

Mit reichlich Berufserfahrung und verschiedenen Architekturpreisen aus vorherigen Europan-Wettbewerben haben wir den Standort Wernigerode wegen unseres Anspruchs gewählt, die Europan-Ideen zu gebauter Realität werden zu lassen. Wir hoffen, dass die United Gardens of Wernigerode in diesem Prozess eine Chance erhalten.

Project

Connective landscapes reactivate the vision of a community-oriented garden city as a green, porous neighbourhood in a city of short distances, with a self-governing community and agricultural activities that connect people.

Huts Seeding Community: The local culture of huts of various size, material, and functionality will develop in two phases: In phase 1 as a neighbourhood centre, with social and agricultural activities; in phase 2 as a contemplative community garden for all ages, with a culture of sharing and a circular local economy.

Soft Dwellings: The architecture will offer circulation areas that foster active community life, a combination of various apartment typologies corresponding to changing lifestyles, and a structural logic of local sources that ensures economic viability and sustainable construction and facilitates vernacularity.

Team

We – Moritz Ahlers, Patxi Martín Domínguez, Paul Schaeger, Josep Garriga Tarres, Natalia Vera Vigaray – believe in the Europan endeavour and its interdisciplinary approach to planning. We are four architects and one lawyer – old Erasmus buddies.

With a diverse range of professional experience and having won awards in previous Europan competitions, we chose the Wernigerode site in particular because of its ambitions to make Europan ideas a built reality. We hope the United Gardens of Wernigerode will be able to contribute to this process.

United Gardens of Wernigerode

Connective Landscapes

Reactivate the vision of a community-oriented Garden city
_as a green, porous neighborhood in a walking city,
_with a self-governing community and
_agricultural activity that connects people.

A walking City

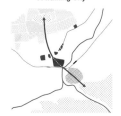

Neighborhood Club

United Gardens

Building up a walkable city path network by
_Closing off unnecessary car road connections
_Slow down car traffic
_encourage walking and cycling with better infrastructure and information campaigns
_Strengthen and extend shared mobility services
_Open up gates and fences of public space i.e. at Zaunwiese
_Free up land for trespassing
(City buys land with right of preemption / gives incentives for ensuring passageway)

With the help of the GWW and the city, the local community could set up a Neighbourhood Club to esta-blish forms of local self-governance. The City and GWW would have to define a contact person, create an internal and external communication structure for workshops with the community and local stakehol-ders, allocate and adapt funds and spaces in the site and the new building accordingly.
The Neighbourhood Club foundation and establishment would have to be community based, its roles, articles of association (=Satzung), tasks, spaces, communication are rooted in the ideas of the old and new residents of the Galgenberg Neighbourhood, but i.e. circle around the 4 topics of gardening and agriculture, community, shared mobility and intergenerational cooperation.

+To strengthen an active community we propose to:
_Introduce activity with public community furniture
_Enlarge and enrich streetscapes
_Temporary use of underutilized spaces for common agricultural activity by the Neighbourhood Club
_Shared spaces in the new buildings
_Funds for the Neighbourhood Club to start a system of sharing mobility, tools, amenities, crops and helping hands
_To develop an interconnected ecosystem and a diverse flora and fauna we propose:
_An ecosystem refuge on parts of the Galgenberg
_Development of underutilized spaces for community based agriculture
_Potential green space management through the Neighbourhood Club
_Pathways and resting spots to contemplate nature and viewpoints
_Local fruit trees to form an the edible city and a urban Garden Eden
_

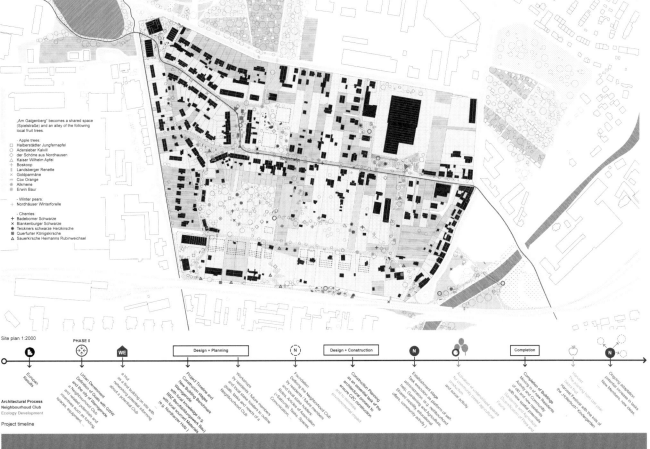

"Am Galgenberg" becomes a shared space (Spielstraße) and an alley of the following local fruit trees.

- Apple trees:
□ Halberstädter Jungfernapfel
○ Adersleber Kalvill
◇ der Schöne aus Nordhausen
△ Kaiser Wilhem Apfel
+ Boskoop
‖ Landsberger Renette
× Goldparmäne
= Cox Orange
✳ Alkmene
⊞ Erwin Baur

- Winter pears:
+ Nordhäuser Winterforelle

- Cherries:
✛ Badeborner Schwarze
✕ Blankenburger Schwarze
✳ Teickners schwarze Herzkirsche
⊞ Querfurter Königskirsche
△ Sauerkirche Heimanns Rubinweichsel

Site plan 1:2000

Site panorama

United Gardens of Wernigerode

Huts Seeding Community

The local culture of huts of various size, material and functionality will develop
_P1 as neighborhood central, with social and agricultural activities.
_P2 as contemplative community garden for all ages,
_and a culture of sharing and local economic circles.

Already a Hut Summer

New Neighborhood Central

Garden am Südhang

Sharing economic cycles

The neighborhood is full of huts. They came as boxes, garages, sheds, ..
They are bought, build, tinkered, unseen by architects and legal planning processes,
and full of activity and functional recycling. They work as an extension to home, as hob-
by rooms, a storage, etc. and activate their spatial surrounding.
Their easy construction, deconstruction, and functional flexibility is a great potential.
While most huts seem to be privatized for individual or nuclear family use, a new hut generation can further develop the neighbourhood's social life and its multifaceted activity.

Site P1 will be a meeting place for residents of all ages and people from the neighbourhood. They can join a community based on agriculture, community, logistics and mobility
located in external huts on site and „huts" as flexible rooms within or at the facades or
roofs of buildings.
_Outside huts
agro workshop and community room, chicken coop, recycling infrastructure, bee hives
_Garden Oriented
tool shed, sharing and logistic box, event space,
_Within the building
co-working room / shared office as an extension to the house
guest room for tourists, friends and relative, storage, community rooms

Site P2 will be a contemplative community garden that makes use of its wonderful orien-
tation with great views. It connects local, especially older residents with the kindergarten,
kids with local agriculture and garden knowledge and activity and therefore their families
into a healthy neighbourhood community.
Its implementation at the northern side of the plot will set the benchmarks for the future
urban densification of the southern quarter, to become an urban mixed-use development
that embrace the existing facilities (kindergarten) found on the site with a green buffer to
the train tracks. Its activated by the following

A wide functional and structural diversity of buildings, public space, social institutions,
just like a local circular economy, value creation and helping hands shall be stimulated
by
_Juxtapositions of apartments for elderly with the kindergarten, family apartments, com-
munity spaces, agricultural gardens that stimulate the involvement of the old into community, activity and local economy
_Vice versa, the community can more easily take care of elders.
_Local agricultural production stimulates community, and local, transport free food pro-
duction of unmatched quality
_Solar panels produce energy for local value creation and district heating improves local
energy efficiency .

P1 Axonometric 1:400

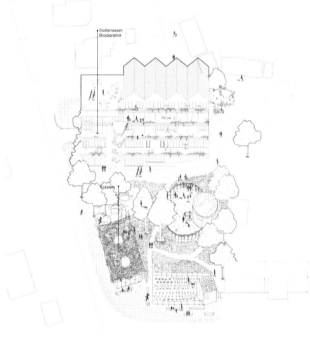

P2 Axonometric 1:400

P1 N-S Section 1:400

P2 N-S Section 1:400

P1 Apfelerntefest in the yard

P2. Perspective. Gardening activities on a Sunny day

United Gardens of Wernigerode

Soft Dwelling

The architecture will offer
_Circulation areas that foster active community life.
_A combination of apartments correspond to changing lifestyles.
_A locally sourced structural logic ensures economic viability, sustainable construction and develops vernacularity.

Inside - Outside

Residential Units and Cluster Living

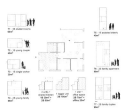

Intergenerational life

Wernigerode weiter bauen
Contemporary vernacularity

Circulation areas are enlarged, functionally enriched and leave empty spots for functional appropriation, spontaneous meetings and act as a community activator. Planting beds induce a first community activity and improve well-being. They are oriented towards the interior of the cluster, enhancing the visual connections and interactions among the residents.

3 degrees of sociability are defined with different bioclimatic conditions:
1- Outdoor circulation and terraces
2- Common living rooms
3- Domestic thresholds

A catalogue of different apartment typologies respond to different needs and can respond to various changes. The apartment type juxtaposition creates a diverse community of tenants: classical nuclear families, elderly, youngsters, single parents and patch–work families, shared house communities, temporary guests, refugees, apprentices, students, tourists and business travelers.

The combination of different apartments and flexible rooms can help to live through the change of different phases of life in an accustomed spatial and social surrounding: A couple moves in. They get a child, use an attached small apartment as an extension, to rest at night, to work, etc. In the teenage times, the kids move to the extended room, still close by, but far enough for some autonomy. Maybe later, the parents need less space and the grown up child gets a partner, so the swap of apartments happens again and the story begins all over again.

We want to combine the provision of age-appropriate living space for older and affordable living space in the city for young families

Creating good age-appropriate apartments and a low-threshold offer with the city administration and the Neighbourhood Club, the GWW housing association can establish future-oriented intergenerational communities and free up close by single-family houses for young families.

On the one hand, GWW should attract and prioritize elders from the neighbourhood who cannot or don't want to live in their previous homes anymore to move into vacant age-appropriate apartments. Thereby elders receive suitable living space and community connection without having to leave their neighbourhood. On the other hand, young families from the GWW apartments can, in return, use the living space that becomes available. The GWW can act as an intermediary together with the Neighbourhood Club, or take over the management of the elder's housing (Hausverwaltung) or even buy the houses in suitable cases. In every case, a „swap" of housing within the neighbourhood takes place, to provide the right housing to suitable tenants.

The building follows a contemporary and sustainable constructive logic of elements that are rooted in the vernacular architectural history of Wernigerode.

_The stone podium is a long-lasting humidity resilient foundation of the building already found in old buildings from Wernigerode downtown.

_A wooden structural skeleton, that uses local material from the Harz, reinterprets vernacular architecture (Fachwerkbau), allows easy future adaptations and construction recycling, while reducing the CO_2 footprint.

_Cladding closes of more private facade types, protects construction from atmospheric conditions and introverted spaces from views and sounds.

South Elevation 1:300
Plot 01 - We live building

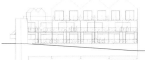

East elevation 1:300
Plot 01 - Veckenstedter Rücken building

West elevation 1:300
Plot 01 - Garden City Families building

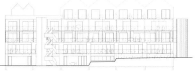

South elevation 1:300
Plot 02 - Südterrasse n / Brockenblick building

Typical floorplan 1:300
Plot 01 - We live building

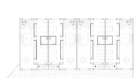

Family Units 1F 1:300
Plot 01 - Veckenstedter Rücken building

Family Duplex Units GF+1F 1:300
Plot 01 - Garden City Families building

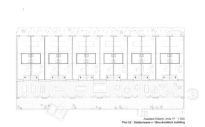

Assisted Elderly Units 1F 1:300
Plot 02 - Südterrasse n / Brockenblick building

1F floorplan 1:500
Plot 01 - We live building

4F floorplan 1:500
Plot 01 - We live building

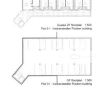

GF floorplan 1:500
Plot 01 - We live building

2F coworking floorplan 1:500
Plot 01 - We live building

Duplex 3F floorplan 1:500
Plot 01 - Veckenstedter Rücken building

Duplex 2F floorplan 1:500
Plot 01 - Veckenstedter Rücken building

GF floorplan 1:500
Plot 01 - Veckenstedter Rücken building

2F floorplan 1:500
Plot 02 - Südterrasse n / Brockenblick building

GF floorplan 1:500
Plot 02 - Südterrasse n / Brockenblick building

4F floorplan 1:500
Plot 02 - Südterrasse n / Brockenblick building

3F floorplan 1:500
Plot 02 - Südterrasse n / Brockenblick building

PLOT 01 - NEW NEIGHBOURHOOD C.		PLOT 02 - GARTEN AM SÜDHANG	
Total Units	37u	**Total Units**	28u
Parking	40p	**Parking**	35p
We live building	28u	**Südterrasse n / Brockenblick**	28u
T1 1B 60m²	3u	T5 1B 45m²	12u
T2 1B 40m²	9u	T6 2B 90m²	8u
T3 1B 30m²	3u	T7 2B 90m²	8u
T4 2B 55m²	5u	Parking	35p
Co-working Space 80m²	1u		
Common Meeting Room 20m²	3u		
Common GF facilities 25m²	4u		
Parking	18p		
Veckenstedter Rücken	11u		
T6 2B 90m²	5u		
T7 2B 90m²	6u		
Parking	22p		
Garden City Families	8u		
T7 2B 90m²	8u		
Outdoor parking			

P1 - We building. Flexible shared spaces hosting unexpected events.

P1 - Veckenstedter Rücken. Sharing domestic habits

P1 - Garden city families. Living thresholds

P2 - Südterrassen Brockenblick. Piano lessons during the morning.

Domestic Machines

Projekt

„Domestic Machines" ist ein Projekt, bei dem es darum geht, die traditionelle deutsche Stadt zu überdenken und diese in ein zeitgenössisches Paradigma zu übertragen.

Es aktualisiert das Modell der Gartenstadt in eine „Techno-Gartenstadt", die einen neuen Rahmen eröffnet, in dem ländlicher und städtischer Raum – ebenso wenig wie privat und öffentlich, arbeiten und leben – keine entgegengesetzten Bereiche mehr sind, sondern unterschiedliche temporäre Zustände des gleichen Kontexts. In der Folge sind Einfamilienhäuser oder Gemeinschaftsunterkünfte nicht länger entgegengesetzte Typen oder unvereinbaren Situationen.

Wir haben eine Reihe von Artefakt-Aktivatoren für urbanes häusliches Leben entworfen. Sie erweitern das Ethos des Zuhauses, ausgehend von den aus Wänden bestehenden Grenzen des konventionellen Hauses. Sie erlauben das Ausweiten häuslicher Elemente auf den städtischen Raum und damit die Entstehung einer urbanen Häuslichkeit, die gemeinschaftlich gelebt wird.

Diese „sozialen Mikro-Kondensatoren" sind keine isolierten Inseln häuslicher Programme im urbanen Kontext, sondern ein echtes Netzwerk ähnlicher Nutzungen.

Durch zwei unterschiedliche Typologien der Formalisierung erlaubt die Kombination von „Domestic Machines" das Erschaffen einer neuen Art von Häuslichkeit, in der Unabhängigkeit und Gemeinschaft nicht inkompatibel sind, sondern vielmehr in der gleichen Architektur koexistieren, innerhalb der beiden neuen, für diesen Standort vorgeschlagenen Modelle.

Die strikte Begrenzung urbaner Programme, die jahrzehntelang das Design der modernen Stadt geprägt hat, führte zu einer territorialen Ungleichheit zwischen großen Wohngebieten am Stadtrand und dichten Arbeitszentren in der Stadtmitte. Angesichts dieser Ungleichheit wurde eine Hybridisierung von Leben und Arbeiten vorgeschlagen. Ein neues Paradigma, das nicht einfach nur urban, sondern auch sozial ist, in dem neue Modelle ausgewogene Koexistenz von Leben und Arbeiten ermöglichen. Eine gemischte territoriale Struktur, die neue urbane Instrumente wie Telearbeit, Co-Working und Co-Living integriert, um innovative, heterogenere Formen von großstädtischem Leben hervorzubringen.

Team

Pedro Pitarch ist Architekt (ETSAM, UPM) und Musiker (COM Cáceres). Er ist aktuell Lehrbeauftragter am Fachbereich Architektur der Polytechnischen Universität Madrid. Er lehrte im Bereich Architekturdesign an der Bartlett School of Architecture (UCL) und war Steedman Fellow (Washington University in St. Louis). Seine Arbeiten wurden im Rahmen der Architekturbiennale von Venedig, der Triennale in Mailand, von SBAU, der Lissabonner Architekturtriennale und der Vienna Design Week ausgestellt.

2015 gründete er Pedro Pitarch Architectures & Urbanisms, ein Architekturbüro, dessen Projekte unter anderem mit dem ersten Platz für die Restaurierung des Central Cinema, dem fünften Platz für Berlin-Brandenburg 2070, dem zweiten Platz in der Dom Competition, dem zweiten Platz für das New Cyprus Museum und dem ersten Platz für die Restaurierung der CLESA-Fabrik ausgezeichnet wurden.

Project

'Domestic Machines' is designed as a project that rethinks the traditional German city and updates it as a contemporary paradigm.

It upgrades the model of the 'garden city' into the 'techno-garden city', which opens up a new framework in which the rural and the urban are no longer opposing realms but instead different temporal states of the same context, in which the private and the public, work and life come together. Single-family homes and collective housing are thus no longer contrasting types or irreconcilable situations.

What we have designed is a series of artefacts as activators of urban domesticity. They expand the ethos of the home beyond the wall-framed boundaries of the conventional house. They make it possible to extend features of domesticity into the urban realm, thus generating an urban domesticity that is lived together.

These 'social micro-condensers' are not isolated islands of domestic programs within the urban context, but rather a real network of related uses.

Based on two different formal typologies, the combination of 'domestic machines' facilitates the creation of a new type of domesticity, in which independence and community are no longer incompatible, but instead coexist in the same architecture within the two new models proposed for the sites.

The strict zoning of urban programs that has governed the design of the modern city for decades has resulted in a territorial inequality between large residential suburbs on the periphery and dense work areas in city centres.

In view of this inequality, a hybridization of life and work is proposed: a new paradigm that is not simply urban, but also social, in which new models for combining life and work facilitate a balanced coexistence of both; a mixed territorial structure that integrates new urban tools such as teleworking, co-working, and co-living to generate innovative and more heterogeneous forms of metropolitanism.

Team

Pedro Pitarch is architect (ETSAM, UPM) and musician (COM Cáceres). He is currently Associate Teacher at the Architecture Faculty of the Polytechnic University of Madrid. He has been Teaching Fellow in Architectural Design at the Bartlett School of Architecture (UCL) and Steedman Fellow (Washington University in St Louis). His work has been exhibited at the Venice Architecture Biennale, Triennale of Milan, SBAU, Lisbon Architecture Triennale and Vienna Design Week.

In 2015 he founded Pedro Pitarch Architectures & Urbanisms, an architectural office whose projects have been awarded prizes such as First Prize for the Restoration of Central Cinema, Fifth Prize for Berlin-Brandenburg 2070, Second Prize in Dom Competition, Second Prize for New Cyprus Museum and First Prize for the Restoration of CLESA Factory.

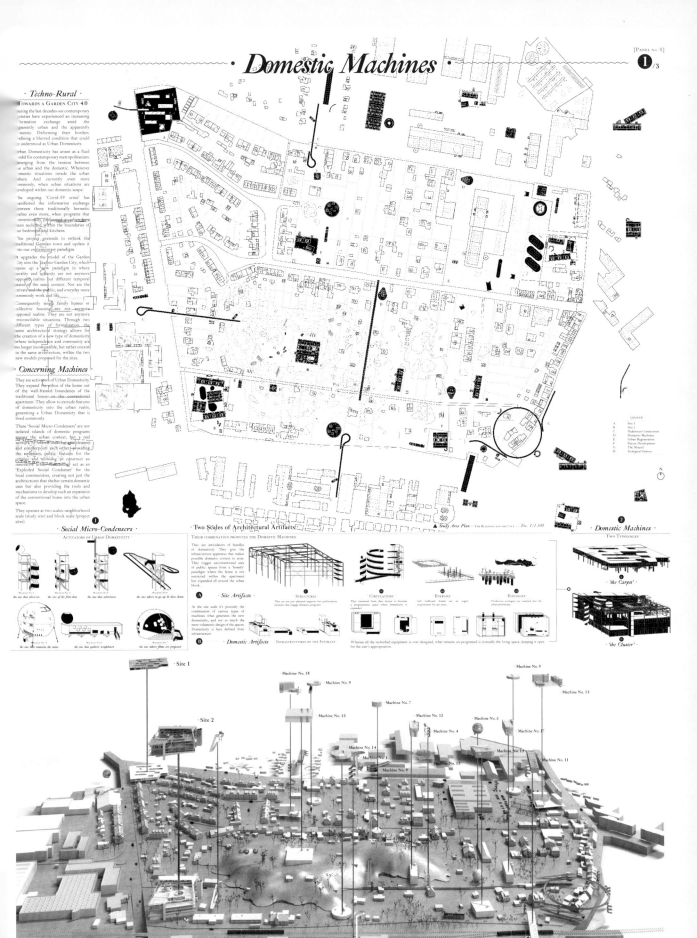

· Domestic Machines ·

[PANEL No. 1] **1** /3

· Techno-Rural ·

Towards a Garden City 4.0

During the last decades our contemporary societies have experienced an increasing information exchange amid the apparently urban and the apparently domestic. Deforming their borders, defining a blurred condition that could be understood as Urban Domesticity.

Urban Domesticity has arisen as a fluid model for contemporary metropolitanism, emerging from the tension between the urban and the domestic. Whenever domestic situations invade the urban sphere. And currently even more commonly, when urban situations are developed within our domestic-scape.

The ongoing 'Covid-19 crisis' has manifested the information exchange between those traditionally hermetic realms even more, when programs that conventionally performed in urban have been secluded within the boundaries of our bedrooms and kitchens.

This project pretends to rethink the traditional German town and update it into our contemporary paradigm.

It upgrades the model of the Garden City into the Techno-Garden City, which opens up a new paradigm in where rurality and urbanity are not anymore opposed realms but different temporal states of the same context. Nor are the private and the public, and everyday more commonly work and life.

Consequently single family homes or collective housing are not anymore opposed realms. They are not anymore irreconcilable situations. Through two different types of formalization, the same architectural strategy allows for the creation of a new type of domesticity where independence and community are no longer incompatible, but rather coexist in the same architecture, within the two new models proposed for the sites.

· Concerning Machines ·

They are activators of Urban Domesticity. They expand the ethos of the home out of the wall-framed boundaries of the traditional house or the conventional apartment. They allow to extrude features of domesticity into the urban realm, generating a Urban Domesticity that is lived commonly.

These 'Social Micro-Condensers' are not isolated islands of domestic programs among the urban context, but a real network of related uses that complement and counterpoint each other, providing the necessary public features for the citizens and allowing to construct an innovative urban fabric that act as an 'Exploded Social Condenser' for the local communities, creating not just the architectures that shelter certain domestic uses but also providing the tools and mechanisms to develop such an expansion of the conventional home into the urban space.

They operate at two scales: neighborhood scale (study site) and block scale (project sites).

· Social Micro-Condensers ·

Activators of Urban Domesticity

the one that advertises · *the one of the first line* · *the one that advertises* · *the one where to go up & down*

the one that contains the noise · *the one that gathers neighbours* · *the one where films are projected*

Two Scales of Architectural Artifacts

Their combination produces the Domestic Machines

They are articulators of bundles of domesticity. They give the infrastructure apparatus that makes possible domestic context to arise. They trigger unconventional uses of public spaces from a 'homify' paradigm where the home is not restricted within the apartment but expanded all around the urban block.

A · *Site Artifacts*

At the site scale it's precisely the combination of various types of machines what generates the new domesticity, and not so much the mere volumetric design of the spaces. Domesticity is here defined from infrastructure.

B · *Domestic Artifacts* — Infrastructures of the Intimate

Structures — They are not just physical supports but performative elements that engage domestic programs

Circulations — They transcend from their fuction to become a programmatic space where domesticity is expanded

Energies — Self-sufficient homes are an urgent requirement for our cities

Ecologies — Productive ecologies are inserted into the urban prototypes

Whereas all the technified equipment is over-designed, what remains un-programed is ironically the living space, keeping it open for the user's appropriation.

▲ *Study Area Plan* — The Buildings and the City — *Esc. 1/1.500*

LEGEND
A Site 1
B Site 2
C Pedestrian Connections
D Domestic Machines
E Urban Regeneration
F Future Development
G The Mound
H Ecological Pathway

· Domestic Machines ·
Two Typologies
'the Carpet'
'the Cluster'

Site 1 · Site 2 · Machine No. 18 · Machine No. 9 · Machine No. 9 · Machine No. 13 · Machine No. 15 · Machine No. 7 · Machine No. 12 · Machine No. 5 · Machine No. 17 · Machine No. 14 · Machine No. 4 · Machine No. 1 · Machine No. 13 · Machine No. 9 · Machine No. 13 · Machine No. 11

Panel · 1: *Study Site & General Concept*

Europan 16 · Germany · Wernigerode

E16   Ergebnisse Results DE   Wernigerode Runner Up   83

an X-ray of our Societies

Our cities defined from the spaces where we live in. Both domestic and urban realms are the spatialization of our societies, of their citizens' lives and of their social behavior.

This proposal establishes a series of different Typologies of apartments that correspond to different models of users and groups of users. Each Typology materializes social features by means of architectural conditions: double floors with double entrance for independence, common spaces for socializing and sharing, bathrooms that become circulations, kitchens that behave as living rooms, etc. Those architectural conditions have been arranged in various combinations in order to achieve a contemporary, complex and real model for our societies requirements. And also for the upcoming needs, for those futurable situations that cannot be predicted but for which we can provide tools for adaptation.

For that purpose, we have worked with Models of users. Both these Models of Users and the Architectural Typology that corresponds them are not just defined in terms of quantities (number of users, age range, square meters, number of specific rooms, services, etc) but in terms of conditions and qualities that define them as citizens of our society. For example, such a Qualification of our Users would establish different models according to the grade labor stability, to the grade of compromise of a partnership, to the grade of independence within a family, or even to the possibility of growth or shirk of a family. The qualities of these groups of users are the ones that construct the daily bases that establish the rules for the definition of our urban an domestic realms.

· the Carpet ·

FROM DISPERSION TO CONGESTION

It solves this dichotomy though a very basic architectural operation: whereas the traditional semi-rural villa of the garden city works in plan (a patio or garden is confronting a home) the carpet villa works in section (the garden does not confront the home anymore, but is the home that is elevated over a commonly shares patio that extends its public ethos to the site and neighbor).

HOME VS. LABOR VS. LEISURE

In the contemporary city, Home and Labor are not anymore opposed realms but merged realities. They are just radicalized terms of a much more blurred reality. Work has been merged with domestic activities as well as domesticity has been released from the home in order to take place within labor spaces.

That primary division of labor space and domestic space that sustained the triumph of modernity during decades has been dismantled by the subsequent releases of the personal computer, the world wide web and the smartphone, among others. The technologies that those devices and systems involve have constructed a change in the medium by which publicness is constructed in the contemporary society.

While work and home have been opposite spheres in the modern life, in the contemporary city, digital technologies have generated a medium that constantly mediates between both, establishing much more complex situations and conditions where new publicness is achieved and performed.

Labor is not anymore developed uniquely within work spaces. As consequence, domesticity is not anymore solely rendered within the home, nor urbanism is exclusively developed in the streets. Both of them have escaped the restricted boundaries that Modernity gave them in order to define a whole series of in-between spaces that are shaping the economical, political and cultural spheres of our societies.

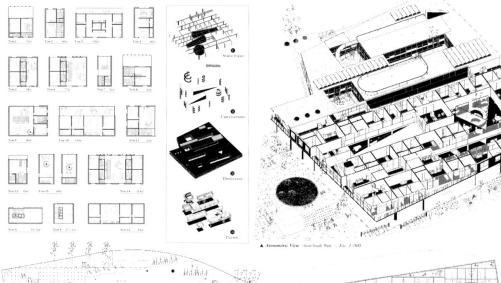

STRUCTURES

CIRCULATIONS

DWELLINGS

PATIOS

▲ *Axonometric View* -from South West .. *Esc. 1/300*

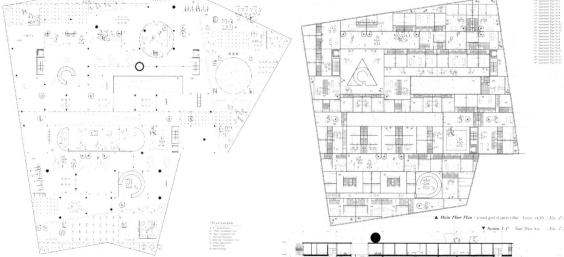

▲ *Ground Floor Plan* - a Public Plaza under the Dwellings LEVEL +0,00 .. *Esc. 1/300*

▲ *Main Floor Plan* - a raised grid of patio villas LEVEL +4,30 .. *Esc. 1/300*

▼ *Section 1-1'* - East-West Axe *Esc. 1/200*

PANEL 2: *Project Site 1* - Domestic Machine Typology: 'The Carpet'

EUROPAN 16 - GERMANY - WERNIGERODE

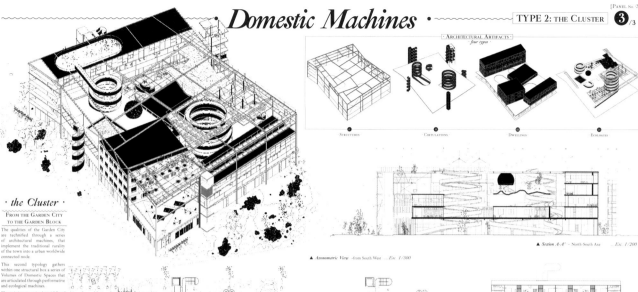

· ARCHITECTURAL ARTIFACTS ·
four types

STRUCTURES   CIRCULATIONS   DWELLINGS   ECOLOGIES

▲ *Axonometric View* -from South West   *Esc. 1/300*

▲ *Section A-A'* - North-South Axe   *Esc. 1/200*

· the Cluster ·

FROM THE GARDEN CITY TO THE GARDEN BLOCK

The qualities of the Garden City are technified through a series of architectural machines, that implement the traditional rurality of the town into an urban worldwide connected node.

This second typology gathers within one structural box a series of Volumes of Domestic Spaces that are articulated through performative and ecological machines.

The existing trees in the middle of the site are kept and the spiral turns around them generating a vegetal patio.

FROM FORM TO PERFORM

For centuries, the way that we have lived our cities has been defined by an univocal assignment of a program to a particular form, establishing a series of architectural typologies that dictated 'what' should be done 'where'.

However, situations such as Urban Domesticity prove that the bilateral relationship between program and form is no longer stable. Everyday it becomes more evident that our bedrooms are not used exclusively for resting. Nor our kitchens to cook. Nor our bathrooms to wash ourselves up. Consequently, stable urban typologies, just as auditoriums, libraries, hospitals, stations or parks also suffer permutations that question whether their designs should be driven by a decrepit relationship between form and use.

Both the fugue of programs outside of the architectures where they were conceived and their appropriation for unexpected uses, are leading towards a new metropolitan paradigm.

The domain of the urban is no longer built in the streets of the city, but spread intermittently inhabiting the domestic interiors of existing architectures. As a consequence, the practice of architecture requires a mediation between conditions that perform at a particular moment, generating the resources and requirements that allow something to happen, something to "take place". There are no architectural typologies anymore, but 'architectural performances'. Performance, and not program, is nowadays the driver of architecture.

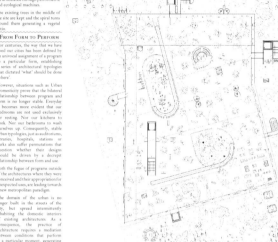

▲ *Ground Floor Plan* - a Public Living Room under the Dwellings Blocks   Level +0,00   *Esc. 1/300*

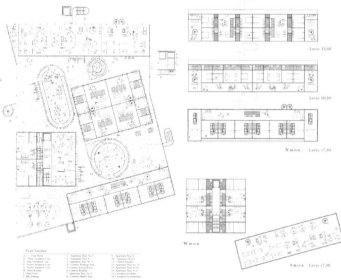

PLAN LEGEND

▲ *Main Floor Plan* - Four Blocks connected by infrastructural machines   Level +4,50   *Esc. 1/300*

LEVEL 13,50
LEVEL 10,50
N BLOCK   LEVEL +7,50
W BLOCK
S BLOCK   LEVEL +7,50

▲ *Upper Floor Plans of each block*   *Esc. 1/300*

PANEL ·3: *Project Site 2 - Domestic Machine Typology: 'The Cluster'*   EUROPAN 16 - GERMANY - WERNIGERODE

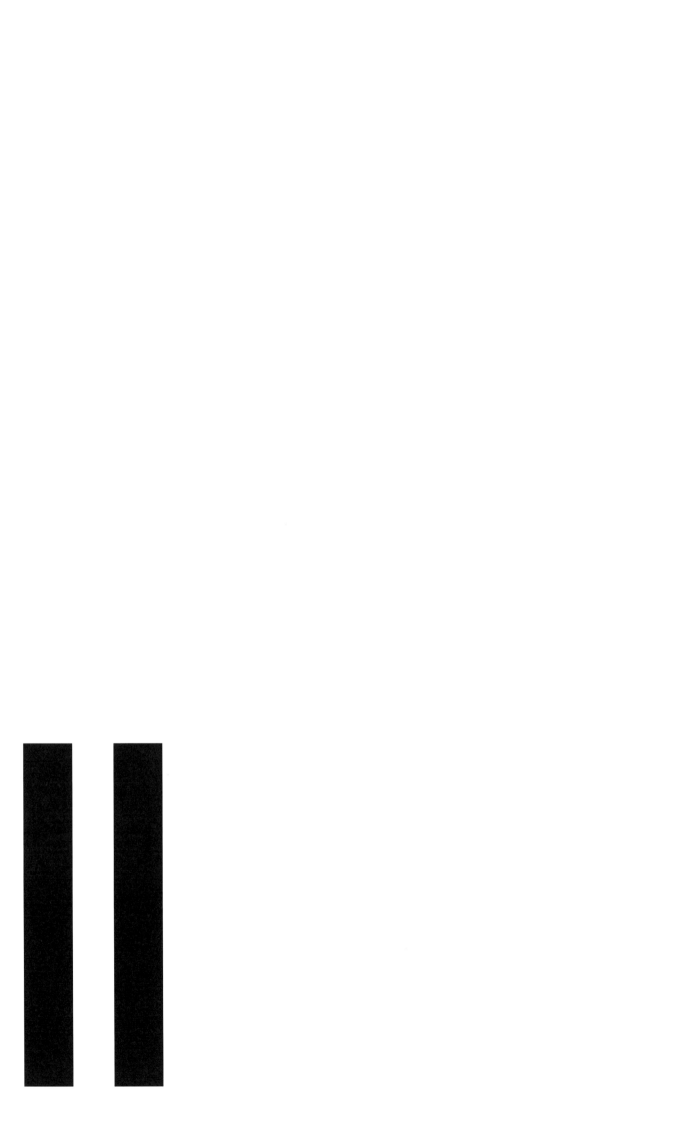

Thema 2
Inklusive Städte

Topic 2
Inclusive Cities

Eine inklusive Stadt ist eine Stadt, in der sich unterschiedliche Menschen begegnen

„Lebendige Stadt" ist das Thema von Europan 16, und Eigenschaften der lebendigen Stadt werden unter anderem mit *inclusive vitalities* (inklusive Lebendigkeit) beschrieben. Diese Tatsache veranlasst dazu, darüber nachzudenken, was eine inklusive Stadt ist und wie inklusive Lebendigkeit entstehen kann.

Interessant ist in diesem Zusammenhang das Konzept der Inklusion, das von der UN-Behindertenrechtskonvention entwickelt wurde. Hier wird „das Recht jedes Menschen" eingefordert, „in sozialen Bezügen leben zu können, also in allen Lebensbereichen dabei sein zu können … Nur wer in einem Lebensbereich dabei ist, kann dort seine Freiheit leben – sich bilden, arbeiten, kreativ sein, politisch mitentscheiden – und so seine Persönlichkeit entfalten."[1] Doch nicht nur Menschen mit Behinderungen droht Exklusion; es gibt viele Gründe, ausgeschlossen zu werden. Inklusion muss sich auf alle beziehen, die an den Rand gedrängt werden.

Konzeptionell bedeutet Inklusion, dass die Gesellschaft nicht länger aus den „Normalen" und den „Anderen" besteht, die integriert werden müssen. Inklusion setzt radikal an und definiert die Verschiedenheit der Menschen als Grundlage der Gesellschaft. „Vergesellschaftung bedeutet nicht mehr Einpassung in einen Rahmen und Ausrichtung auf einen Wert, sondern Aushandlung in einem Kontext und Verständigung über Prinzipien."[2] Daher ist Inklusion auch kein Endzustand, sondern ein Prozess, in dem Unterschiede aufeinandertreffen und Lösungen ausgehandelt werden müssen.

Andere in ihrer Verschiedenheit zu akzeptieren und gemeinsam handeln zu können, braucht Schulung. Zuerst müssen Gelegenheiten entstehen, auf unterschiedliche Menschen zu treffen und sich gegenseitig wahrzunehmen. Nur so kann die Fähigkeit erlangt werden, sich in andere hineinzuversetzen und dadurch mit sehr unterschiedlichen Menschen feinfühlig und respektvoll umzugehen. In einer Gesellschaft, die durch zunehmende Diversifizierung gekennzeichnet ist, aber auch dadurch, dass die Menschen immer mehr unter ihresgleichen bleiben,[3] ist die Forderung nach Begegnung nicht trivial. Eine Stadt mit Orten für Begegnungen zu entwerfen, wird ein äußerst schwieriges Unterfangen. Hierzu gehören bezahlbare Wohnungen genauso wie öffentliche Räume oder Institutionen, an denen alle teilhaben können.

Architektur kann weder Gemeinschaft noch Begegnung hervorrufen. Dennoch gibt es eine schwer zu fassende Abhängigkeit zwischen sozialen Handlungen, die an einem Ort entstehen, und den baulich-räumlichen Möglichkeiten, die dieser bietet. Früher ging man die Aufgabe, einen Ort für Begegnung zu schaffen, beherzt an. Der niederländische Bauingenieur und Architekt im Selbststudium Frank van Klingeren kann 1967 mit dem Kulturzentrum De Meerpaal in Dronten, für die auf Poldern neu geschaffenen Siedlungen, seine Idee einer multifunktional bespielbaren Agora, an der sich alle treffen, umsetzen. Als Vorbild für seine Vorstellung von einem offenen (inklusiven) Raum dienen Plätze in südeuropäischen Städten. Dort spielt sich ein großer Teil des alltäglichen Lebens der Bevölkerung ab. Um ihn an die Witterung in den Niederlanden anzupassen, hauste van

Klingeren den Platz ein.[4] In einer großen, von Parkplätzen umgebenen offenen Halle bot er unterschiedlichsten Aktivitäten einen Ort – Theater, Volkskonzerte, ein Restaurant mit Sitzplätzen und einer Bar, Markt, Bowling, gemeinsames Fernsehen, Vereinstreffen, Bürgerversammlungen, Schulungen, Tanz oder auch nur Herumlungern und Gucken, was passiert. Mit einer unperfekten, preiswerten Architektur wollte van Klingeren Raum für Unerwartetes schaffen, durch die offene Architektur ein „ontklonteren" (Entklumpen) unterstützen. Darunter versteht er, der Tendenz entgegenzuwirken, unterschiedliche gesellschaftliche Gruppen in „Klumpen" zusammenzufassen, die keinen Kontakt zu anderen ermöglichen.[5]

Das Erstaunlichste an dem Projekt ist aus heutiger Sicht, dass es eine ganze Zeit lang sehr gut funktioniert hat. Die Halle wurde über Jahre von der Nachbarschaft genutzt, und Frank van Klingeren erhielt Folgeaufträge für zwei weitere Agoragebäude. Erst nach einigen Jahren wurde das Konzept des offenen Raums durch nachträgliche Trennwände immer weiter aufgegeben. Anfang des 21. Jahrhunderts wurde De Meerpaal generalsaniert und umgebaut – immerhin nicht abgerissen –, um veränderten Anforderungen gerecht zu werden.

Heute besteht wieder großes Interesse an Orten, an denen sich unterschiedliche Menschen begegnen, doch man ist zurückhaltender damit, diese mit großer Geste als einzelner Entwerfender zu planen. Hinzu kommt, dass sich bestehende öffentliche Institutionen legitimieren und wandeln müssen. Wer braucht eine Bibliothek, wenn weniger gelesen wird? Ist das Theater das Herz der Stadt?

Der Druck ist so stark, dass Institutionen sich fragen, wie sie Orte für alle sein können, und Ideen entwickeln, die wiederum den architektonischen Diskurs bereichern. Inklusion und Diversität spielen hierbei eine große Rolle. Es kann nicht nur baulich und in Abstimmung mit dem Brandschutz darum gehen, das Theaterfoyer tagsüber für Bürgerinnen und Bürger zu öffnen und Bibliotheken in Aufenthaltsorte zu verwandeln. Inklusion bezieht sich auch auf Fragen der Repräsentation und der Partizipation. Wer wird repräsentiert? Welche Medien sind im Magazin, welche Stücke werden von wem aufgeführt? Wer bestimmt, wer repräsentiert wird? Welche Formen der Aneignung werden ermöglicht? In De Meerpaal kümmerten sich teilweise Bewohner um die Bespielung der Räume, und es gab ein Programm, das dem Leben des „durchschnittlichen Niederländers"[6] entsprach. In einer inklusiven Stadt lautet die Frage ganz anders: Wie ist es möglich, alle zu repräsentieren, und wie ist es möglich, viele unterschiedliche Menschen an den erforderlichen Entscheidungen zu beteiligen?

Das Theater beispielsweise entwickelt neue Formen, die den Stadtraum und seine Bewohnerinnen und Bewohner ins Geschehen einbeziehen. Es wird so zu einem Ort, an dem Lebenswirklichkeiten der Stadt, ihre politischen, sozialen und medialen Realitäten öffentlich verhandelt werden, in Form von Interventionen, Versuchsanordnungen und Plattformen, die das Theater gewissermaßen in die Stadt verlagern.[7] Aus der Perspektive der Architektur ist es nicht unerheblich, dass zu diesem Zweck meist das Gebäude verlassen wird. Offenbar müssen bekannte Typologien völlig neu gedacht und weiterentwickelt werden, sowohl baulich wie auch bezogen auf Organisationsformen und Inhalte, um einer inklusiven Lebendigkeit in der Stadt gerecht zu werden. Nicht zuletzt stellt sich die Frage, wie viel geplant und geregelt werden muss oder ob es hauptsächlich darum geht, Freiräume zu erhalten?

Das Isarufer in München ist zum Beispiel ein Ort, an dem viele teilhaben können und sich unterschiedliche Menschen begegnen. In dem Abschnitt auf Bild 1 ist es nicht barrierefrei zugänglich – bei renaturierten Räumen kann es allerdings auch nicht das Ziel sein, sie komplett barrierefrei auszubilden. Hier kann weitestgehend jeder und jede tun, was er oder sie gerade möchte. Bild 2 zeigt einen Abschnitt, der urbaner wirkt, obwohl er eigentlich weiter vom Stadtzentrum entfernt ist. Die Atmosphäre unter der Brücke ist ähnlich rau wie die auf einem riesigen Parkplatz. Wie zufällig spielt dort eine Band, und Leute lassen sich zum Zuhören nieder. So zufällig ist es aber gar nicht: In München gibt es Kulturinstitutionen, die technisches Outdoor-Equipment verleihen – die kleinste Einheit lässt sich mit einem Lastenfahrrad transportieren –, und es gibt Fördergelder, die Musiker für solche Vorhaben beantragen können.

Andrea Benze
Prof. Dr.-Ing., Architektin, Stadtforscherin und Professorin für Städtebau und Theorie der Stadt an der Hochschule München. Sie ist Mitgründerin von offsea (office for socially engaged architecture), London, München.

1   Vgl. Rudolf, Beate (26. September 2012): „Inklusion ist Bestandteil jedes Menschenrechts". www.institut-fuer-menschenrechte.de/aktuell/news/meldung/article/inklusion-ist-bestandteil-jedes-menschenrechts (letzter Zugriff: 2019)
2   Bude, Heinz: „Was für eine Gesellschaft wäre eine ‚inklusive Gesellschaft'?" In: Inklusion. Wege in die Teilhabegesellschaft. Heinrich-Böll-Stiftung (Hg.), Frankfurt, New York, 2015, S. 37–43, hier S. 40
3   Vgl. Allmendinger, Jutta: Das Land, in dem wir leben wollen. München 2017
4   Vgl. van Klingeren, Frank: „Multifunktionale Raumnutzung. Gemeinschaftszentrum in Dronten".
    In: Bauen + Wohnen, Band 22, 1968, Heft 9, S. 337–340; Bohning, Ingo: „Die Agora-Bauten der 70er-Jahre."
    In: Bauwelt, 1987, Heft 36, Stadtbauwelt 95, S. 1350–1353; Slawik, Han: „Agonie der Agora". In: db 8/88, S. 84–88
5   Vgl. van den Bergen, Marina/Vollaard, Piet: „The Biggest Living Room in the Netherlands: Frank van Klingerens Karregat in Eindhoven, 1970–1973".
    In: Maaike Lauwaert und Francien van Westrenien (Hg.): Facing Value: Radical Perspectives from the Arts.
    Den Haag 2017, S. 419–25, hier: S. 420
    Oder dieselben: „Participation and Development: Frank van Klingerens Jeugdgebouw Noord".
    In: Susanne Pietsch und Andreas Müller (Hg.): Walls That Teach. On the Architecture of Youth Centres. Prinsenbeek, 2015. S. 157–167, hier S. 158 f
6   van den Bergen/Vollaard: „The Biggest Living Room in the Netherlands", S. 421
7   Informationen aus dem Gespräch mit Roman Leonhartsberger, Architekt, Elke Bauer und Martín Valdés-Stauber (letzterer über Zoom zugeschaltet), Münchner Kammerspiele, ebendort am 12. April 2022

An Inclusive City Is a City in which Different People Come into Contact with Each Other

Living cities is the topic of Europan 16 and delineates characteristics of the living city with the term 'inclusive vitalities', among others. This fact prompts contemplation of what an inclusive city is and how 'inclusive vitalities' can be produced.

The concept of inclusion developed by the UN Convention on the Rights of Persons with Disabilities is interesting in this context. It calls for the 'right of every person' to 'be able to live in social contexts, and thus to be able to participate in all areas of life… Only persons who are part of an area of life can live out their freedom there – get an education, work, be creative, and participate in political decision-making – and thus develop their personality.'[1] But not only individuals with disabilities are threatened with exclusion. There are many reasons for being excluded. Inclusion must therefore apply to every excluded individual.

Conceptually, 'inclusion' means that society no longer consists of 'normal' persons and 'others' who need to be integrated; it instead starts radically and defines the diversity of individuals as the basis of society. 'Socialization no longer means adapting to a framework and being oriented toward one value, but instead negotiating within a context and arriving at an understanding of principles.'[2] Inclusion is thus also not an end state, but a process in which differences come together and solutions have to be negotiated.

Accepting the diversity of others and being able to take joint action requires training. Providing opportunities to meet and perceive different individuals is the very first step. It is only in this way that it is possible to put oneself in other people's shoes and thus deal with very different individuals in a sensitive and respectful way. In a society that is characterized by more and more diversification, but also by the fact that people are increasingly spending their time with individuals who are similar to them,[3] the call for encounters with others is not trivial. Designing a city with places for encounters is thus becoming an extremely difficult undertaking. It includes not only affordable housing, but also public spaces or institutions in which everyone is able to participate.

While architecture is unable to generate community or encounters, there is nonetheless a difficult-to-grasp dependency between the social activities that take place in a location and the structural-spatial possibilities that this location offers. In the past, the task of creating a location for encounters was tackled with determination. Frank van Klingeren, a Dutch structural engineer and self-taught architect, succeeded in 1967 in realizing his idea of an agora that could be used in a multifunctional way as a place where all people could come into contact with one another with the De Meerpaal cultural centre in Dronten, for settlements newly created on polders. Public squares in southern European cities served as a model for his idea of an open (inclusive) space. A large part of the day-to-day life of the population takes place there. To adapt this concept to the weather in the Netherlands, the public square was enclosed in the agora project.[4] In a large hall surrounded by a car park, diverse things took place without any delimitation from one another, including theatre, concerts, a restaurant with seats and a bar, a market, bowling, public television, club meetings, town meetings, training, dancing, or also simply hanging out and watching the goings-on. With an imperfect, inexpensive architecture, Klingeren wanted to create space for the unexpected. By means of the open architecture, he wanted to support an 'ontklonteren' (de-clumping). He understood this as countering the tendency to summarize different groups in society in 'clumps', which facilitates no contact with others.[5]

The most astonishing aspect of this project from the perspective of today is that it functioned very well for a very long time. The neighbourhood used the hall for years and Frank van Klingeren received subsequent commissions for two additional agora buildings. It was first after a few years that the concept of open space was increasingly carved up by means of partition walls added retrospectively. At the beginning of the twenty-first century, the De Meerpaal centre was at least not demolished, but completely renovated and converted to meet changed needs.

Today, there is once again a lot of interest in designing places where different individuals can come into contact with one another, but rather than attempting to do so with a grand gesture as an individual designer, this is being approached in a more reserved way. Moreover, existing public institutions have to legitimize and transform themselves. Who needs a library if people are reading less? Is the theatre really the heart of the city?

The pressure is so intense that institutions are asking themselves how they can be places for everyone, and are in turn developing ideas that can enrich the architectural discourse. Inclusion and diversity play a big role in this. It cannot only be about dealing with this question structurally and in compliance with fire protection regulations, or opening the theatre foyer to citizens during the day, or transforming libraries into places to spend time. Inclusion instead also pertains to questions of representation and participation. Who is represented? What media are in the depot, what theatre pieces are performed by whom? Who decides who is represented? What forms of appropriation are facilitated? In De Meerpaal, local citizens were partially responsible for how the spaces were used and there was a program that corresponded to the life of the 'average Netherlander'.[6] In an inclusive city, the question looks quite different. How is it possible to represent everyone and how is it possible to involve many different people in the decisions required?

Theatres, for instance, are developing new theatrical forms that incorporate the urban space and its residents. The theatre thus becomes a place where the realities of life in the city, its political, social, and medial realities, are negotiated publically, in the form of interventions, experimental setups, and platforms that shift the theatre to the city to some extent.[7] From the perspective of architecture, it is not insignificant that the theatre building generally has to be left for this purpose. Familiar typologies apparently have to be completely rethought and developed anew, but with respect to their design and forms of organization and contents so as to meet the requirement of 'inclusive vitalities' in the city. What arises not least is the question of how much has to be planned and regulated, or whether it is mainly about preserving open spaces.

The bank of the Isar River in Munich, for instance, is a place where many can participate and where diverse individuals encounter one another. In the section in figure 1, it is not accessible without barriers – while, at the same time, in the case of renatured spaces the aim can also not be developing them completely without barriers. As far as possible, everyone can do what he or she wants here. In figure 2 is a different section that seems more urban, even though it is located farther away from the city centre. Under the bridge, a roughness similar to that on a huge parking lot prevails. A band is playing there as if by chance and people have sat down to listen. But it is not that random at all, because there are cultural institutions in Munich that lend mobile outdoor equipment – the smallest unit of which can be transported with a delivery bike – and funding for such projects for which musicians can apply.

Andrea Benze
Prof. Dr.-Ing., architect, urban researcher, and professor of urban design and urban theory at the Munich University of Applied Sciences. She is a co-founder of offsea (office for socially engaged architecture), London, Munich.

1   See Rudolf, Beate (26 September 2012): 'Inklusion ist Bestandteil jedes Menschenrechts', www.institut-fuer-menschenrechte.de/aktuell/news/meldung/article/inklusion-ist-bestandteil-jedes-menschenrechts/ (accessed in 2019)
2   Bude, Heinz: 'Was für eine Gesellschaft wäre eine "inklusive Gesellschaft"?' In: Inklusion. Wege in die Teilhabegesellschaft. Heinrich Böll Foundation (Ed.), Frankfurt and New York, 2015, pp. 37–43, esp. p. 40
3   See Allmendinger, Jutta: Das Land, in dem wir leben wollen. Munich, 2017
4   See van Klingeren, Frank; 'Multifunktionale Raumnutzung. Gemeinschaftszentrum in Dronten'. In: Bauen + Wohnen 22, no. 9 (1968), pp. 337–340; Bohning, Ingo: 'Die Agora-Bauten der 70er Jahre', Bauwelt 36 (1987), Stadtbauwelt 95, pp. 1350–1353; Slawik, Han: 'Agonie der Agora', db 8, no. 88, pp. 84–88
5   See van den Bergen, Marina/Vollaard, Piet: 'The Biggest Living Room in the Netherlands: Frank van Klingerens Karregat in Eindhoven, 1970–1973'. In: Facing Value. Radical Perspectives from the Arts, Maaike Lauwaert and Francien van Westrenien (Eds), Den Haag, 2017, pp. 419–425, esp. p. 420 Or idem: 'Partizipation and Development: Frank van Klingeren's Jeugdgebouw Noord'. In: Walls That Teach. On the Architecture of Youth Centres, Susanne Pietsch and Andreas Müller (Eds), Prinsenbeek, 2015, pp. 157–167, esp. pp. 158 f
6   van den Bergen/Vollaard: 'The Biggest Living Room in the Netherlands', p. 421
7   Information from the conversation with the architect Roman Leonhartsberger, Elke Bauer, and Martín Valdés-Stauber (the latter participated via Zoom) at the Münchner Kammerspiele, 12 April 2022

1

2

1   München Isarufer zwischen
    Wittelsbacher- und Brudermühl-
    brücke
2   Themenfeld Arbeits- und
    Wissenschaftsstadt, Masterplan
    Darmstadt 2030+

1   Bank of the Isar River in Munich
    between the Wittelsbacher and
    Brudermühl bridges
2   Thematic field: city of work
    and science, Master Plan Darm-
    stadt 2030+

Eine lebendige Stadt für alle

Wenn man die Teilnehmerinnen und Teilnehmer des Europan-Wettbewerbs, die Auslobenden und die Gemeindevertreter und -vertreterinnen fragen würde, was sie unter einer lebendigen Stadt verstehen, würden die meisten ein sich ähnelndes Bild zeichnen: Die 15-Minuten-Stadt, grün und mit kurzen Wegen, gemischt und multimodal, sicher und nachhaltig – schlicht eine Stadt für Menschen, auch für Kinder und Ältere. Wir sind uns also mehr oder weniger einig in unseren Fachrunden und Podiumsdiskussionen.

Einig sind wir uns auch, dass die Realität in vielen europäischen Städten eine andere ist. Es gibt durchaus Quartiere, die eine hohe Lebensqualität haben und viele der oben genannten Kriterien erfüllen, aber der Großteil der urbanisierten Flächen sieht anders aus. Vor allem die Quartiere an der Peripherie, die Großraumsiedlungen in den Banlieues haben wenig mit diesem Idealbild zu tun. Die soziale Herkunft und das Einkommen entscheiden mehr denn je darüber, wo man lebt. In einer Stadt – auch in Kleinstädten – gibt es parallele Lebenswelten, deren Gegensätze härter nicht sein könnten.

Dabei sind die Grundbedürfnisse der meisten Menschen gleich. Mit der Stiftung Berliner Leben führen wir in einigen Berliner Quartieren Beteiligungsprojekte mit Kindern und Jugendlichen durch. Wünsche für das eigene Lebensumfeld sind immer dieselben: „mehr Grün", „mehr Wasser", „mehr Spielplätze", „mehr Orte zum Abhängen" und „weniger Autos" – egal, wo die Befragten leben und welchen sozialen oder migrantischen Background sie haben. Einige Quartiere mögen in ihrer städtebaulichen Struktur schon mehr Qualität bieten als andere, aber überall lässt sich durch die Aufwertung der öffentlichen Räume etwas tun: städtisches Grün, grüne und blaue Infrastruktur, offene Nutzungsangebote, gut gestaltete Plätze und nutzbare Räume für alle Generationen.

Denn in Zeiten aufbrechender Familienstrukturen, beengter Wohnsituationen und von Armut gezeichneter städtischer Milieus werden Kinder und Jugendliche weitgehend im öffentlichen Raum geprägt und erzogen. Öffentliche Räume sind Lebens- und Bildungsorte, gerade für Menschen mit geringem Einkommen. Ihre Aufwertung ist vergleichsweise preisgünstig und kann einen großen Effekt auf die Umgebung haben. Eine angemessene Beteiligung derer, die vor Ort leben, sollte dabei eine Selbstverständlichkeit sein. Partizipation ermöglicht passendere Lösungen für räumliche Herausforderungen, ist gelebte Demokratie und Bildung zu mehr Verantwortung. Aber auch die Pflege und Instandhaltung des öffentlichen Raums hat eine enorme Auswirkung auf ihre Aufenthaltsqualität und Lebendigkeit.

Zukunftsfähig sind unsere Städte nur, wenn wir alle in die Produktion einer lebendigen Stadt einbeziehen. Auf die eine oder andere Art. Überlebensfähig sind wir nur gemeinsam. Fangen wir an, zu fragen, zuzuhören, miteinander zu reden und mit vielen kleinen und großen Projekten zu handeln. Für eine lebendige Stadt für alle.

Anne Schmedding
Dr. phil., seit 2020 Leitung Stiftungsprojekte der Stiftung Berliner Leben, davor u. a. stellvertretende Vorstandsvorsitzende der Bundesstiftung Baukultur, wiss. Mitarbeiterin der TU Braunschweig, Redakteurin und freie Autorin.

A Living City for Everyone

If one were to ask the participants in the Europan competition, the organizers, and the municipal representatives what they understand under the term 'living city', the vast majority of them would provide a similar picture: a fifteen-minute city, a green city, a city of short distances, mixed districts, multimodality, cities for people, for children and older individuals, a safe city, a sustainable city, et cetera, to mention only a few of the common key terms. We thus more or less agree in our specialist circles and podium discussions.

We also see a different reality in many European cities. While there are certainly districts that have a high quality of life and satisfy many of the aforementioned criteria, the majority of urbanized areas look different. Particularly districts on the periphery, such as large housing estates in the banlieues, have little to do with the ideal picture sketched. Whether one lives in a district with a high quality of life is related in particular to social origins and incomes. There are parallel life worlds in one and the same city – also in small towns – whose contrasts could hardly be more severe.

The basic needs of most people are nonetheless the same. With the Stiftung Berliner Leben we realize participatory projects with children and young people in various districts in Berlin. When what is concerned are wishes connected with one's own living environment, the responses are always the same: 'more green', 'more water', 'more playgrounds', 'more places to hang out', and 'fewer cars' – no matter where the individuals surveyed come from or what social or migrant background they have. While the urban development structure of some districts is able to provide more inherent quality of life for people than others, it is nonetheless possible to do something in every location by upgrading open spaces: urban greenery, green and blue infrastructure, offerings for public use, well-designed public squares, and spaces that can be used by all generations.

At a time when family structures are breaking open and milieus are characterized by cramped living situations and poverty, children and young people are shaped to a significant extent by public space. Public spaces are places for living and learning, especially for people with a limited income. Upgrading them is comparatively cost-effective and can have a huge impact on the surroundings. The adequate participation of local residents should thus be self-explanatory. Participation facilitates more suitable solutions to local challenges, is lived democracy and education for bearing more responsibility. But the maintenance and upkeep of public spaces has an enormous effect on their liveliness and the quality of time spent there.

Our cities can only be suitable for the future if we involve everyone in producing the living city – in one way or another. Only together can we survive. When we begin to question, to listen, to talk with each other, and to take action with many small and large projects. For a living city for everyone.

Anne Schmedding
Dr. phil., head of the projects of the foundation Stiftung Berliner Leben since 2020, and previously, acting chairperson of the Bundesstiftung Baukultur, research associate at the TU Braunschweig, editor and writer.

1

2

3

4

1   Der Boxclub Isigym in Schöneberg-
    Nord bietet Kindern und Jugend-
    lichen eine Perspektive nicht
    nur im Sport, sondern betreut auch
    den schulischen Erfolg
2   Die Künstlerin Katrien Vanderlinden
    hat gemeinsam mit Kindern einen
    Basketballplatz in einer Groß-
    wohnsiedlung in Berlin-Spandau
    bunt gestaltet
3   Im Projekt My One Wall lädt der
    Künstler Markus Georg Kreuzberger
    Kinder dazu ein, inspiriert von
    künstlerisch gestalteten Wänden
    ihre eigene One Wall zu entwickeln

4   Das Pallasseum in Berlin-Schöne-
    berg ist eine Wohnmaschine;
    auf dessen Dach haben Kinder ge-
    meinsam mit dem Künstler
    Thomas Bratzke ein Modell ihrer
    eigenen Wohnmaschine gebaut

1   The Isigym boxing club in
    Schöneberg-Nord not only offers
    children and young people
    a future through sport, but also
    supervises success at school
2   The artist Katrien Vanderlinden
    gave a basketball court in a large
    housing estate in Berlin-Spandau

a colourful design in cooperation
with children
3   In the project 'My One Wall', the
    artist Markus Georg invites
    children in Kreuzberg to develop
    their own 'one wall' inspired walls
    designed by artists
4   The Pallasseum housing complex
    in Berlin-Schöneberg is a machine
    for living; on its roof, children
    constructed a model of their entire
    machine for living in cooperation
    with the artist Thomas Bratzke

EU

Deutsche Preisträger·innen in der EU

German Winners within the EU

Graz (AT)

Standort

Der Standort befindet sich an einem zentralen Punkt innerhalb eines Gebietes, das großen Umwandlungen unterworfen ist. Einerseits finden wir eine alte, gewachsene Stadtstruktur im Prozess der Verdichtung und andererseits ein großes Einkaufszentrum, das den Handel neu erfindet. Das aktuelle Einkaufszentrum ist nicht nur wirtschaftlich veraltet. Der Eigentümer ist bereit zu handeln, um für die Stadtbewohnerinnen und -bewohner weiter relevant zu bleiben, und malt sich einen neuen multifunktionalen Raum aus. Die Stadt unterstützt diesen Ansatz, während Pläne für eine neue Straßenbahnlinie, die den Standort und das Gebiet des Einkaufzentrums kreuzt, abgeschlossen sind. Trotz der unterschiedlichen Ausmaße, Funktionen und Ziele sollen beide Gebiete voneinander profitieren und zu einem sich ergänzenden Ganzen werden.

Das E16-Gebiet, ein kleines Juwel, liegt direkt im Zentrum und spielt eine ganz wesentliche Rolle bei der Verbindung.

Der Projektstandort bietet einzelne, jedoch versteckte Möglichkeiten. Seine vermittelnde Rolle wird von wesentlicher Bedeutung sein, um bestehende Werte zu stärken, zusammenzuführen und insbesondere neue Energien zu generieren. Er ist ein Angelpunkt, der dirigiert und verbindet. Geplant ist ein neues Ensemble, das eine offene und inklusive Mischung von Programmen beherbergt, inspiriert von Ergebnissen der verschiedenen Viertel: Welche Einsatzmöglichkeiten sollen angezogen werden und welcher Raum muss dafür geschaffen werden? Wie können alle Akteurinnen und Akteure, die das Gebiet bewohnen, besuchen und entdecken, miteinbezogen und integriert werden? Die anstehende Aufgabe lautet, einen integrativen Ort zu erschaffen, der das Areal bekannt macht und verankert.

Einkaufszentren finden sich normalerweise am Stadtrand. Untypischerweise befindet sich dieses, eine umfassende Einkaufsagglomeration mit Parkgaragen und einem dazugehörigen Straßenbild, an zentraler Stelle. Aufgrund der Ausdehnung und des Schwerpunkts auf Autos wirkt es fast wie ein „außerirdischer Riese", der in einem weitaus kleiner dimensionierten Umfeld sitzt. Das Gebiet des Einkaufszentrums soll innerhalb der nächsten Jahre in einen multifunktionalen lokalen Knotenpunkt verwandelt werden. Studien zum Programm schlagen eine Kombination von Einkaufen, Wohnen und Bildung vor.

Das Areal ist von markanten Grünräumen umgeben. Zudem kreuzt ein kleiner Bachlauf das Gebiet. Seine aktuell noch versiegelten Ufer haben das Potenzial, eines der wertvollsten Elemente einer Stadt für eine inklusive Nutzung zu aktivieren: eine resiliente Basis, welche die urbanen Eigenschaften für Menschen und nicht-menschliche Nutzer gleichermaßen verstärkt und zwischen verschiedenen urbanen Interessen vermittelt. Auch eine Straßenbahn kreuzt hier und bildet eine Achse öffentlicher Mobilität.

Eine Mischung verschiedener Ressourcen ist vorhanden und lässt sich zur Entwicklung eines kohärenten und inklusiven Konzepts einsetzen. Im Mittelpunkt steht der E16-Standort, dessen Aufgabe das Verhandeln und Bilden von Synergien sein wird, um alle Teile miteinander zu verbinden.

Location

The site is located on a pivotal spot within an area undergoing extensive transformation. On the one hand, we find a mature, old town structure experiencing a process of densification, and on the other hand a large shopping centre, which is reinventing commerce. The current mall is out-dated, not only in an economic sense. Its owner is thus prepared to take action in order to remain relevant for residents of the city, and is conceiving a new multifunctional space. The city is supporting this thinking with plans, which have already been finalized, for a new tramline running from the centre and crossing the site and the soon-to-be-transformed mall area. Even though differences in scale, functions, and objectives will be obvious, the goal is that both areas benefit from each other and become a self-supplementing whole. The E16 site, a small gem, is in the very centre, and thus plays a crucial role in weaving it all together.

The project site is positioned within a context of unique, yet hidden, potentials. Its mediating role will be key in order to strengthen existing values, bring them together and, more specifically, generate new energy. It is a central point in the area, a hinge that channels and merges. What is envisioned is a new ensemble that accommodates an open and inclusive mix of programs inspired by findings based on the various neighbourhoods: Which uses need to be attracted and have the necessary space created for them? How can all the actors and stakeholders that live in, visit, and discover the area be involved and integrated? The task at hand is thus to create an integrative location that announces and anchors the area.

Shopping malls are generally found on the outskirts of town. Atypically, this one, a substantial shopping agglomeration with parking garages and an accompanying streetscape, is in a central location. Due to its large volume and focus on car traffic, it seems to be something like an 'alien giant' sitting in a neighbourhood of much smaller scale. The shopping mall area will be transformed into a multi-functional local hub within the next couple of years. Studies dealing with its program suggest a combination of shopping, housing, and education.

The site is surrounded by noteworthy green spaces. Branching out from there, a patchy network of natural areas weaves into the area. A millstream, an agent for nature, in fact crosses the site. Its currently sealed banks hold potentials to activate one of the most precious elements for inclusive use a city may have: a resilient base that enhances the urban quality for humans and nonhumans alike and mediates between various urban interests. A tramline also crosses the area, thus anchoring a public mobility axis in the district.

A mix of resources is at hand and should be utilized so that a coherent and inclusive concept emerges. At the centre is the E16 site. Its role will be to negotiate and synergize, thereby weaving all the parts together. Its bridging function will not only be of a spatial sort. It will moreover need to mediate the social and the digital by interpreting future trade strategies and valorising local potentials.

Bevölkerung   Inhabitants
291.072

Betrachtungsraum   Study Site
15,1 ha

Projektgebiet   Project Site
0,737 ha

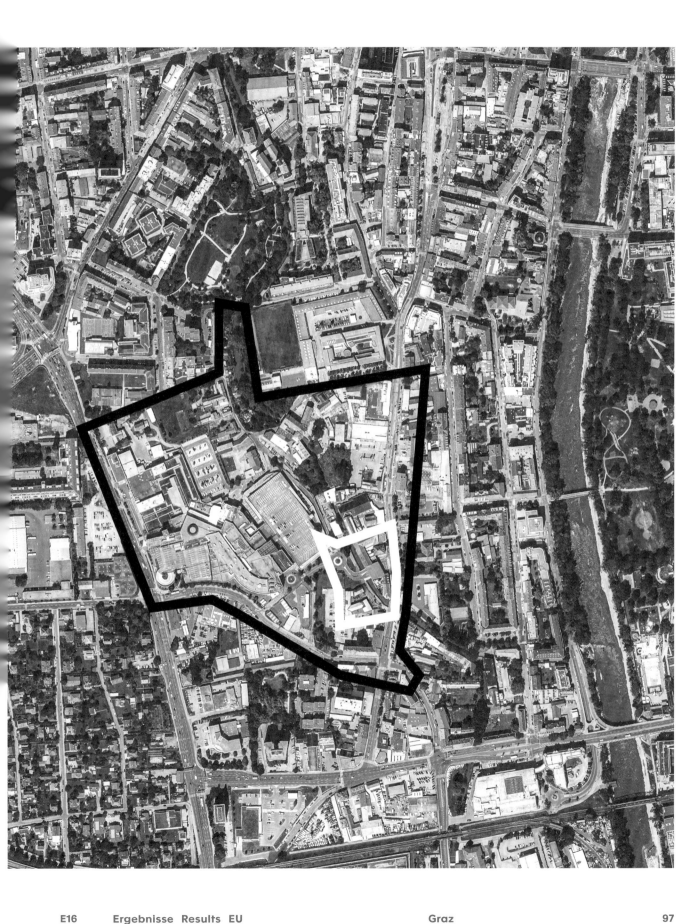

Superstructure
Urban Solution

Projekt

Die städtische Lebensweise steht vor einer massiven Transformation. Vieles muss sich verändern, damit der Lebensstandard trotz großer ökologischer und ökonomischer Transformation nicht abnimmt, sondern gesteigert werden kann. Die einzige Lösung hierfür liegt in Innovationen. Dies zeigt sich auch im Handelssystem, in dem Produkte von zentralen Lieferketten abhängig sind und fast ausschließlich über zentrale Vertriebssysteme von außen in die Stadt gelangen. Die Stadt ist reiner Konsument. Es braucht also ein dezentrales Produktions und Handelssystem, um die verfehlten Metabolismen der gescheiterten Lieferketten zu ersetzen.

Ein Lösungsansatz hierfür ist ein System aus sogenannten Superstructures. Diese setzen sich aus jeweils drei Paradigmen zusammen: Nahrung, Rohstoff und Handel. Diese Paradigmen stellen den größten Teil des Imports aus dem Um- und Ausland dar. Wer nachhaltigen Metabolismus in der Stadt generieren will, muss diese drei Paradigmen bereitstellen. Wir behandeln in diesem Superstructure-Netz, das an alte Handelsstandorte gekoppelt wird, einen Standort, der sich ortsspezifisch mit diesen Themen auseinandersetzt. Der Standort Superstructure Graz Süd 1 ist für den Vertrieb und die Herstellung von recycelten Produkten aus 3D-gedrucktem und urban-gemintem Kunststoff als Rohstoff verantwortlich.

Handel: Paradigma 1 stellt die Handelsstruktur dar. Sie ist die Grundvoraussetzung für eine funktionierende Eingliederung in das Superstructure-Netz. Hierzu gehört einerseits die direkte Anbindung an den ÖPNV der Stadt Graz, andererseits der regionale Vertrieb der produzierten Waren.

Rohstoffe: In unserem Superstructure-Netz werden die hier hergestellten Produkte wie FRP-Träger, Sitzschalen und an sich alles, was durch den 3D-Druck aus recyceltem Kunststoff hergestellt werden kann, vertrieben.

Nahrung: Für das Paradigma Nahrung steht eine Aquaponik-Anlage, die zwar automatisiert funktioniert, aber dennoch eng mit den Bewohnern der Superstructure verknüpft ist. Die Becken sind in die Tragstruktur des Gebäudes integriert, und die Hydroponik-Umgebung der Pflanzen bietet gleichzeitig einen paradiesischen Garten für die Bewohner.

Team

Mein Name ist René Dapperger. Ich lebe und arbeite in Stuttgart, Deutschland. Während meines Studiums an der Universität Stuttgart und in Mailand habe ich an verschiedenen Wettbewerben teilgenommen, um die Möglichkeiten der Architektur jenseits akademischer Grenzen auszuloten. Durch die Arbeit in verschiedenen Büros konnte ich verschiedene städtebauliche und architektonische Maßstäbe kennenlernen. Mir wurde bewusst, dass die Arbeit an Projekten, die eine Auswirkungen auf das tägliche Leben haben, ein wichtiger Bestandteil für mich ist. Vor einem Jahr habe ich zusammen mit Felix Hauff den Schinkel-Preis gewonnen. Seit meinem Masterabschluss arbeite ich bei se\arch in Stuttgart und entwickele neue Konzepte für zeitgenössische Architektur.

Project

The urban way of life is now facing a huge transformation. Many things must be changed so that the living standard does not decrease, but can instead be improved in spite of great ecological and economic change. The only possibility in this respect comprises innovation. This is also shown in the trading system, in which products are dependent on central supply chains and almost exclusively reach the city from the outside via central distribution systems. The city is purely a consumer. It thus requires a decentralized system of production and trade to replace the missing metabolism of failed supply chains. One approach to a solution to this is a system consisting of so-called Superstructures. They each consist of three individual paradigms: food, raw materials, and trade. These paradigms represent the largest share of imports from the surrounding region and abroad. These paradigms must be provided if one wants to generate sustainable metabolism in the city. In this network of Superstructures, which is coupled with old commercial locations, we deal with a location that examines these topics in a site-specific way. The site of Superstructure Graz Süd 1 is thus responsible for the production and distribution of recycled products made of 3D-printed and synthetic material minted in the urban surroundings as a raw material.

Trade: Paradigm 1 represents the trade structure. It is the fundamental requirement for functioning integration in the Superstructure network. It includes not only a direct connection to the public transport system of the city of Graz, but also the regional distribution of the goods produced.

Raw Materials: In our Superstructure network, the products produced here, such as FRP supported seats and everything that can be manufactured from recycled synthetic material by means of 3D printing are distributed.

Food: An aquaponics facility that functions in a fully automated way and is nonetheless closely connected with the residents of the Superstructure is responsible for food. The basins are integrated in the supporting structure of the building and the hydroponic surroundings of the plants offer residents a paradisiacal garden at the same time.

Team

My name is René Dapperger and I am based in Stuttgart, Germany. During my studies at the University of Stuttgart and in Milan, I participated in various competitions in order to explore architectural opportunities in addition to academic boundaries. Having worked in different offices during my student years, I have experienced the workflow of variable urbanistic and architectural scales. It also became clear that working on projects that have an impact on everyday life was an important component for me. One year ago, my colleague Felix Hauff and I won the Schinkel Prize. Since receiving my Master's degree, I started working at se/arch in Stuttgart, exploring new concepts for contemporary architecture.

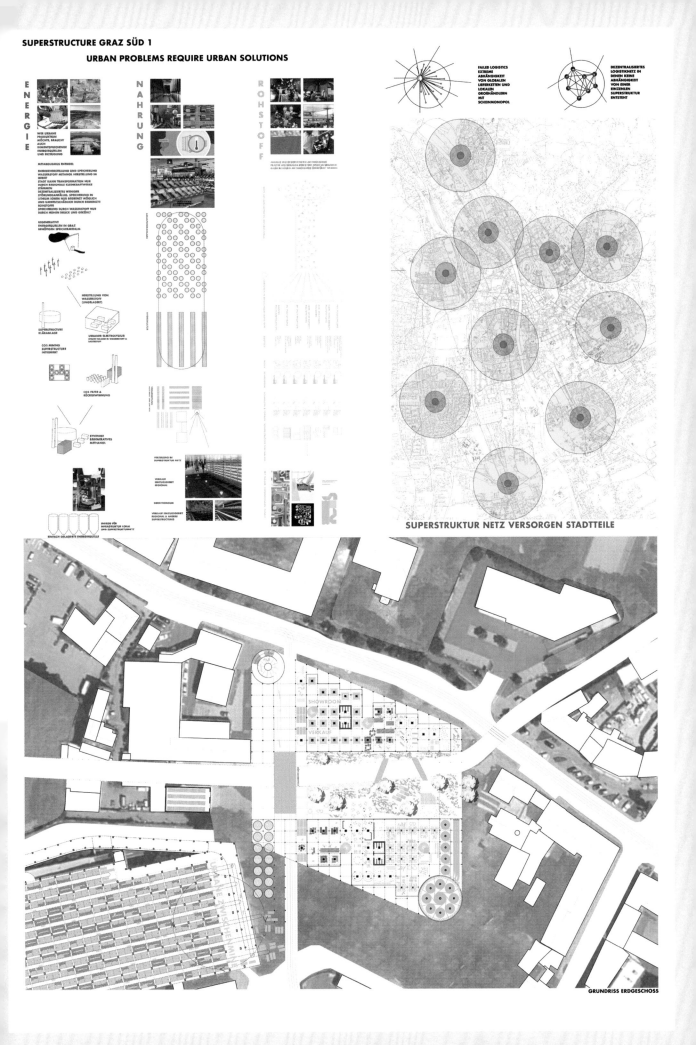

SUPERSTRUCTURE GRAZ SÜD 1

URBAN PROBLEMS REQUIRE URBAN SOLUTIONS

SUPERSTRUKTUR NETZ VERSORGEN STADTTEILE

GRUNDRISS ERDGESCHOSS

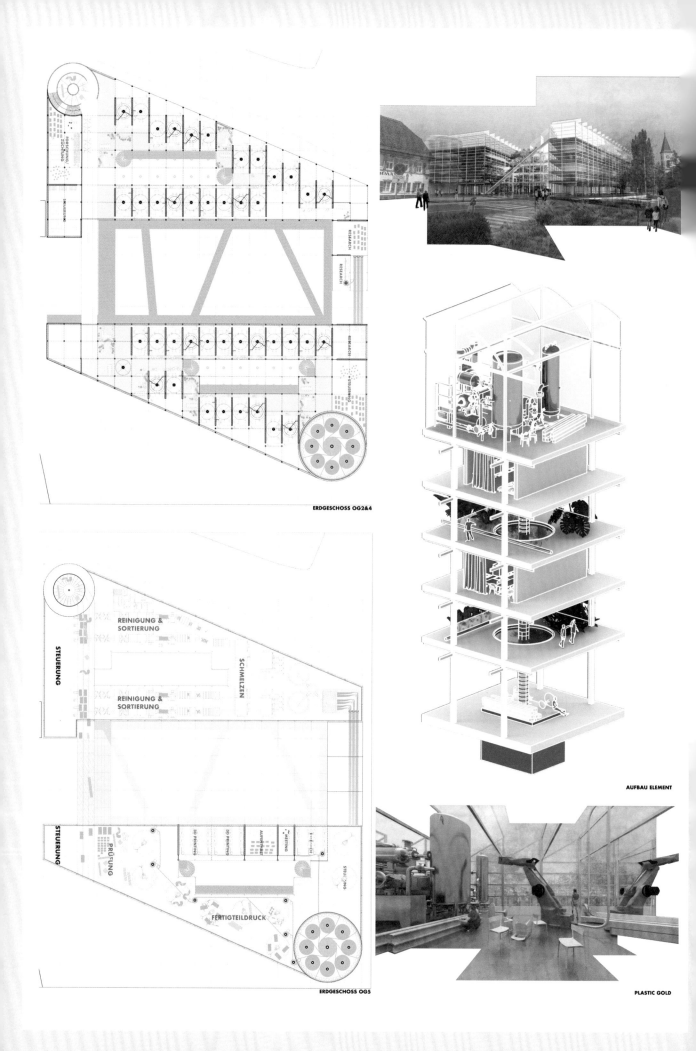

ERDGESCHOSS OG2&4

ERDGESCHOSS OG5

FORSCHUNG ZÜCHTUNG

STEUERUNG

RESEARCH

RESEARCH

RESEARCH

STEUERUNG

STEUERUNG

REINIGUNG & SORTIERUNG

SCHMELZEN

REINIGUNG & SORTIERUNG

STEUERUNG

PRÜFUNG

3D PRINTING

3D PRINTING

AUFBEREI...

MEETING

STEUERUNG

FERTIGTEILDRUCK

AUFBAU ELEMENT

PLASTIC GOLD

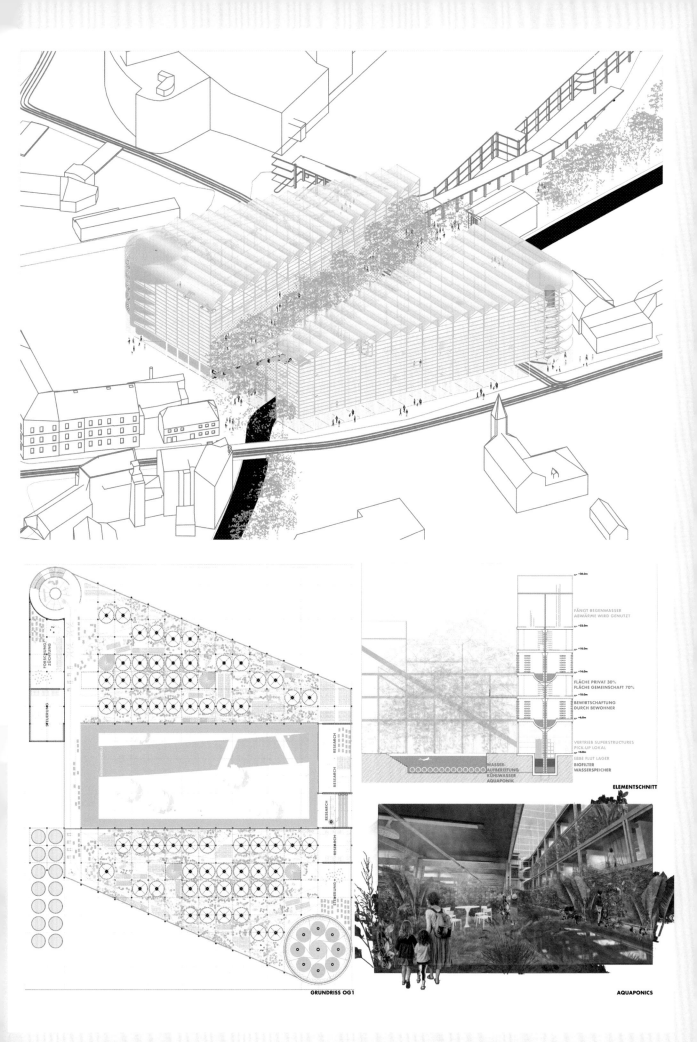

FÄNGT REGENWASSER
ABWÄRME WIRD GENUTZT

FLÄCHE PRIVAT 30%
FLÄCHE GEMEINSCHAFT 70%

BEWIRTSCHAFTUNG
DURCH BEWOHNER

VERTRIEB SUPERSTRUCTURES
PICK-UP LOKAL

EBBE FLUT LAGER
BIOFILTER
WASSERSPEICHER

WASSER-
AUFBEREITUNG
KÜHLWASSER
AQUAPONIK

ELEMENTSCHNITT

GRUNDRISS OG1

AQUAPONICS

Carouge (CH)

Standort

Das Projektareal ist durch ein gemischtes, fragmentiertes und sektorales Stadtgefüge gekennzeichnet, ohne definiertes Zentrum und ohne Durchlässigkeit für Fußgängerinnen und Fußgänger. Als Vorstadtgebiet spielt es dennoch eine bedeutende Rolle bei der Verbindung von Natur und urbanem Gefüge sowie als Einfallstor zur dichten städtischen Struktur von Carouge und Genf. Viele Projekte wurden kürzlich fertiggestellt, andere befinden sich in der Studienphase. Diese zeigen die Dynamik lokaler Entwicklungen auf, bei denen die Pläne keiner umfassenderen Vision unterliegen. Europan 16 ist eine Gelegenheit, diesem Territorium Bedeutung und Identität zu verleihen. Im Rahmen dieses Prozesses müssen die verschiedenen Komponenten in Betracht gezogen werden, die erhalten, verstärkt, abgeschwächt oder sogar gestrichen werden, um einen lebendigen Stadtteil zu erschaffen, der zum Fortschritt in Richtung einer „Ecological and Solidarity Based Transition" (TES) beitragen wird.

Der Standort Fontenette ist durch das Nebeneinander verschiedener Einheiten gekennzeichnet, denen es an allgemeiner Geschlossenheit und Identität fehlt. Aktuell gibt es keinen Masterplan für die Entwicklung dieses Standorts. Was die Planung betrifft, besteht hier also eine „Leerstelle", deren Zukunft von zahlreichen Herausforderungen geprägt sein wird, macht sie sich doch die vorhandene Natur nicht zunutze (der Fluss Arve, grüne Arterie), die eine wichtige Rolle spielen und die Grundlage einer neuen Identität bilden könnte. Die Aufgabe besteht darin, zukünftige Ausrichtungen für Veränderungen in diesem Gebiet anzuregen. Die Stadt ist auf der Suche nach einem globalen Projekt, das urbanen Bereich, Landschaft und Umgebung verbindet und das zu einem modellhaften Beispiel werden könnte.

Thema 1: Natur als gliederndes Rahmenwerk

Es ist von grundlegender Bedeutung, die Natur zu charakterisieren, Methoden hervorzuheben, um deren Funktionen zu identifizieren und sie als Netzwerk zu begreifen. Zudem sollen die natürlichen Eigenheiten dieses Gebietes aufgezeigt werden.

Thema 2: Dem Gebiet Identität verleihen

Die Gemeinde Carouge trat kürzlich dem „Conurbation Core" PACA bei und machte damit auf eine neue Facette in der Identität des Areals aufmerksam, das nun als eine Komponente des Ballungsraums Genf gilt. Diese veränderte Vision für Carouge unterstreicht ferner, wie wichtig es ist, den Charakter des Gebietes neu zu überdenken.

Thema 3: Öffnung

Zergliederung, Isolation und Heterogenität sind Hindernisse bei der Schaffung von Verbindungen zwischen bewohnten Gebieten (Stadt, Natur) und den Lebewesen, die darin leben (Biodiversität und soziale Vielfalt). Der Mangel an sozialem Engagement in diesem Gebiet wird auch durch das Fehlen von sozialer und urbaner Geschlossenheit deutlich. Es besteht ein echtes Problem, was die verschiedenen Arten von Öffnung in diesem Bereich betrifft: die Öffnung zwischen Vierteln, die Öffnung in die Natur, die Öffnung zwischen Menschen, die Öffnung zum Rest des Territoriums.

Location

The project area is characterised by a disparate, fragmented and sectoral urban fabric, with no defined centre and no permeability to pedestrians. As a suburban area, it nevertheless plays a major role in connecting the natural and urban fabrics and as a gateway to the dense urban fabric of Carouge and Geneva. Many projects have recently been completed and others are in the study phase. These reflect a dynamic of localised developments where the plans are not framed within any broader vision. Europan 16 is an opportunity to give meaning and identity to this territory. This process needs to be approached with consideration of its different components, which will be maintained, reinforced, attenuated or even removed in order to produce a living piece of city that will contribute to progress towards the Ecological and Solidarity Based Transition (TES) which has a similar purpose to living cities. The Fontenette site is characterised by the juxtaposition of entities that lack any overall coherence or identity. There is no masterplan currently developed for this site, by contrast with the rest of the municipal area. It is therefore a 'void' in terms of planning and its future presents numerous challenges and does not fully take advantage of the presence of nature (the Arve River, green artery, moraine), which could play a major role and form the basis of a new identity and a source of future meaning. The overall task is to propose future orientations for change in this inhabited zone and its embedded practices. The city is looking for a global project that combines the urban, landscape and the environment, which could become an example and a model.

Theme 1: Nature as the Structuring Framework

In this project, it is essential to characterise nature, to give it a meaning, to define ways of highlighting it, to identify its functions and envisage it as a network and the idea of revealing the natural specificities of this area.

Theme 2: Giving the Area an Identity

Carouge Municipality recently joined the 'Conurbation Core' PACA, revealing a new facet in the identity of the area, now considered to be a component of the core of the conurbation of Geneva. This shift in vision for Carouge further emphasises the importance of rethinking the character of the area. This process is underway in different neighbourhoods in Carouge, but the Fontenette sector is distinctive in that the process of reinventing its identity has yet to begin.

Theme 3: Opening Up

Fragmentation, isolation and heterogeneity are obstacles to the creation of links between inhabited milieus (urban, natural) and the beings that live in them (biodiversity and social diversity). The lack of social engagement in this area also reveals the absence of social and urban cohesion. There is a real issue of multiple kinds of opening in this zone: opening between neighbourhoods, opening onto nature, opening between people, opening to the rest of the territory.

Bevölkerung   Inhabitants
ca. 23.000

Betrachtungsraum   Study Site
200 ha

Projektgebiet   Project Site
2,7 ha

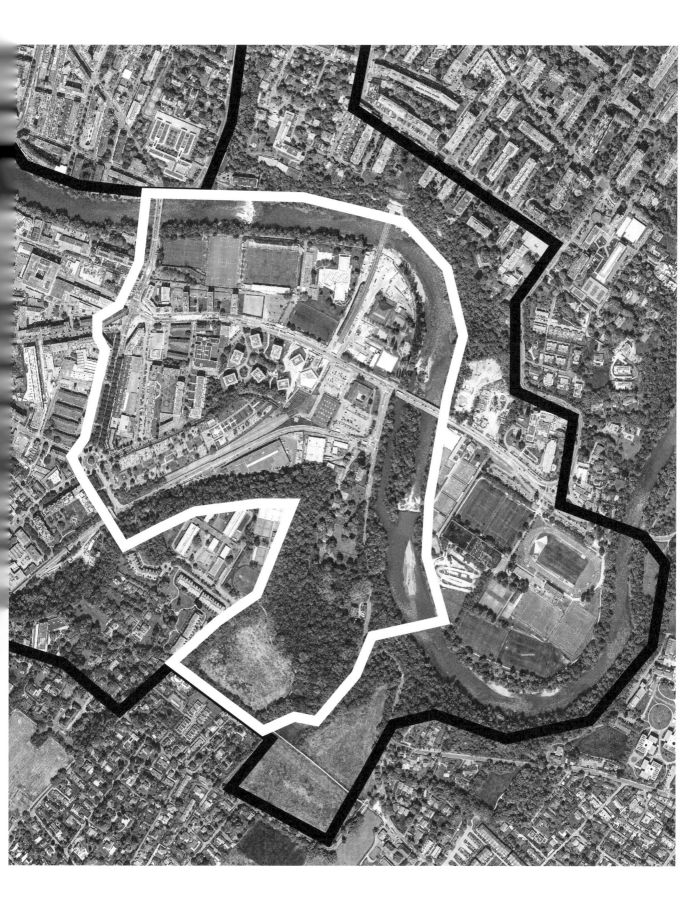

Au fil de l'or / Gold Line

Projekt

An den Ufern der Arve, zwischen Fischern und Badenden, durchkämmten Goldwäscher das Flussbett. Ehe sie in Jubel ausbrechen konnten, mussten sie die „goldene Linie" finden, einen Pfad, den das vom Strom gedrängte Gold genommen hatte. Fontenette neu zu denken, bedeutet in erster Linie, an seine Goldlinie zu denken: die Arve und ihre gliedernde Natur als grundlegendes Element, das die Umwandlung dieses Sektors lenkt.

„Au fil de l'or" (Goldlinie) räumt den Gewässern der Arve und ihrem Ufergebiet größeren Raum ein. Das Projekt verleiht dem Areal dank der umgebenden Natur neue Berechtigung und Aufwertung, während es die verschiedenen Landstriche darin wieder miteinander verbindet. Die Ufer der Arve werden zu einem neuen Raum für Leben, Freizeit, Erholung, Begegnungen und Spazierengehen in der Nähe des Wassers, auf Pontons oder Kiesstränden, an Beobachtungspunkten in den Auwäldern und in den neuen Parks zwischen der Uferzone und den ersten Gebäuden. Ein vergrößerter Auwald, neue Bäume, für Menschen vorgesehener Raum und ein neuer Seitenarm des Flusses – angelegt, um mit den immer häufiger werdenden Überschwemmungen umzugehen –, all das wird eine neue Umgebung schaffen, die Fauna und Flora zugutekommen wird.

Das neue Viertel Artisanes soll östlich des Bereiches Fontenette entstehen. Das Viertel, dessen Identität schon seit langer Zeit von (Kunst-)Handwerkern geprägt ist, wird neue Aktivitäten rund um Handwerk, Kunsthandwerk und Natur bieten. Der Platz wird Standort zahlreicher Veranstaltungen wie Handwerks- und Kunsthandwerksmärkten sein. Wasserelemente werden Kindern und Erwachsenen in Hitzeperioden Abkühlung bieten. Der Parc des Orpailleurs und die Place des Artisanes werden die beiden Seiten einer beruhigten Route de Veyrier vereinen und ein einziges Viertel bilden. Das Projekt fördert die Einbeziehung der gesamten Bevölkerung, verbindet aktuell getrennte Gebiete wieder miteinander, bindet das Gebiet an den Großraum Genf an und versammelt die gesamte Bevölkerung um neue, frei zugängliche Räume, umgeben von reicher Fauna und Flora.

Team

Der Europan-Wettbewerb bot die Gelegenheit, eine offene Gruppe aus Menschen zu bilden, die einander seit etlichen Jahren kennen und regelmäßig oder gelegentlich in Genf zusammenarbeiten. Unser Team teilt eine Vision zur Stadt, während wir unsere sich gegenseitig ergänzenden, multidisziplinären Fähigkeiten als Aktivposten einbrachten. Gemeinsame Gespräche und gegenseitiges Zuhören unter den Expert·innen unserer Gruppe aus Architektur, Landschafts- und Stadtplanung und Geografie führte zu einem inspirierenden Projekt, zur Schaffung einer lebendigen Stadt anzuregen. Die Motivation jedes Teammitglieds waren äußerst hilfreich, um unser Projekt für ein Gebiet vorzuschlagen, das wir gut kennen.
- Felix Brüssow (DE), Landschaftsarchitekt
- Stefania Malangone (CH), Architektin
- Oriane Martin (CH), Geographin, Stadtplanerin
- Kim Pittier (CH), Architektin
- Marc de Tassigny (CH) und Leonhard Kanapin (CH), Architekturbüro MDT architectes
- Nicolas Waechter (FR), Landschaftsarchitekt

Project

On the banks of the River Arve, between the boatmen and bathers, people scoured the riverbed looking for gold. To succeed in finding gold, they had to find the 'gold line', a path followed by the gold being pushed by the current. Rethinking Fontenette means thinking first and foremost about its gold line: the Arve, and its structuring nature as a major element guiding transformations in this district.

The 'Au fil de l'or' (Gold Line) gives more space to the waters of the Arve and its riparian zone. The project re-qualifies and enhances the location based on the surrounding nature, while reconnecting the different districts within it.

The banks of the Arve will become a new space for living, leisure time, relaxing, encounters, and strolling near the water, spending time on pontoons or pebble beaches, in observatories in the riparian forest, and in the new parks between the riparian zone and the first buildings. The combination of an enlarged riparian forest, new trees, spaces preserved from human use, and a new branch of the river for managing increasingly frequent flooding will create a new environment favourable to fauna and flora.

The new Artisanes district will be developed to the east of Fontenette. As a district with a long history of craftsmanship and artisanry, the Artisanes district will offer new activities related to these activities and to nature. The square will host numerous events such as a craftsperson and artisan market. Water features will enable children and adults to cool down during heat waves. The Parc des Orpailleurs and Place des Artisanes (Artisans Square) will unite the two sides of Veyrier Road, with its reduced traffic, thus creating a single neighbourhood.

The project promotes the inclusion of the entire population and reconnecting districts that are currently separated, thus linking the area to greater Geneva, and bringing the entire population together around new freely accessible spaces, in close proximity to a wealth of fauna and flora.

Team

The Europan competition was an opportunity to form an open group consisting for the most part of individuals who have known each other for several years and who collaborate regularly or occasionally in Geneva. Our team of seven young professionals shares a common vision for imagining the city based on the asset of our complementary and multidisciplinary skills. As architects, landscape architects, urban planners, and geographers, the dialogue and exchange between the specialists in our group have enabled us to propose an inspiring project with the aim of creating a living city. Our weekly meetings and the motivation of each member of the team have been a great strength in proposing our project for a location with which we are all very familiar.
- Felix Brüssow (DE), landscape architect
- Stefania Malangone (CH), architect
- Oriane Martin (CH), geographer, urban planner
- Kim Pittier (CH), architect
- Marc de Tassigny (CH) and Leonhard Kanapin (CH), architectural studio MDT architectes
- Nicolas Waechter (FR), landscape architect

AU FIL DE L'OR / GOLD LINE

Les bains de l'Arve et la ripisylve (végétation spécifiques en bord des cours d'eau) / Arve beach and the riparian vegetation

Plan du secteur / Plan of the sector   1: 2000

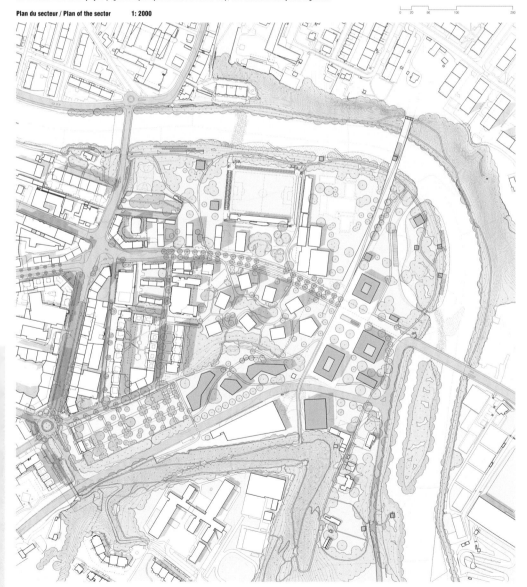

Préambule / Preamble

Le projet « Au fil de l'or » offre l'opportunité de vivre et d'expérimenter le quartier de la Fontenette et les bords de l'Arve d'une nouvelle manière. Donnant une plus large place aux eaux de l'Arve et à sa ripisylve, ce projet permet de requalifier et de valoriser ce secteur grâce à la nature environnante tout en reconnectant les différents quartiers entre eux. Le secteur accueillera de nouvelles activités, des espaces de loisirs, de détente, de rencontre et de déambulation ainsi qu'un nouveau pôle culturel et artisanal. À travers ces transformations, La Fontenette deviendra un espace liant les humains à la nature comme un nouvel écosystème générant de nouveaux usages et de nouvelles rencontres permettant de faire vivre ce secteur de Carouge à travers sa vitalité métabolique et inclusive.

"Gold Line" offers the opportunity to live and experience the Fontenette district and banks of the Arve in a new way. Giving greater space to the waters of th e Arve and its riparian zone, this project requalifies and enhances the sector thanks to the surrounding nature, while reconnecting the different districts with an. The sector will host new activities, leisure, relaxation, meeting and walking areas, as well as a new hub for artisanry and craftsmanship. Through these transformations, Fontenette will become a space linking humans to nature, a new ecosystem generating novel uses and encounters, and allowing this sector of Carouge to live through its metabolic and inclusive vitality.

Arve, Plage à la fontenette, 1955

Le parc des sports / Sports Park

Le parc des sports permettra à la population de venir profiter d'un espace de verdure pour se détendre à l'ombre des arbres, au soleil sur la pelouse ou sur des gradins au bord de l'Arve. La population pourra y pratiquer de nombreuses activités sportives en libre-service tout en profitant d'un nouvel accès à l'eau.

In the Sports Park, the population will come and enjoy a green space to relax in the shade of the trees, in the sun, on the lawns, or on the terraces of the banks of the Arve. The population will be able to practise numerous freely accessible sports activities while enjoying new access to the water.

Fontenette-plage / Fontenette Beach

Grâce à un élargissement de la ripisylve sur certaines zones actuellement dédiées au football et à la piscine de Carouge, Fontenette-Plage propose une grande promenade dans la ripisylve ponctuée de plages de galet maintenu à l'aide d'épis, de lieux de rencontre et de détente. De nouvelles activités seront également proposées dans un petit pavillon multi-usage.

Thanks to an enlargement of the riparian zone in certain areas currently dedicated to football and to the Carouge swimming pool, Fontenette Beach offers a long walk through the riparian forest punctuated by meeting places, relaxation areas and pebble beaches held in place by groynes. New activities will also be proposed in a small multi-purpose pavilion.

Parc des Orpailleurs / Parc of Orpailleurs

Ce grand parc est caractérisé par une pelouse, un bras d'eau de l'Arve et une île couverte de ripisylve. Le nouveau bras de l'Arve accueillera ses eaux lors des crues de plus en plus fréquentes en été. La population pourra profiter d'un nouveau lieu de fraîcheur pour se reposer sur un ponton, observer la nature, jouer dans l'eau, tremper ses pieds ou même se baigner en toute sécurité. Ce nouvel espace rappellera les bains d'Arve qui étaient très populaires à une époque où ses eaux vivifiantes étaient préférées à celles du lac permettant ainsi de renouer avec les activités historiques de la rivière.

The large Gold Panners' Park is characterised by a lawn, a branch of the Arve, and an island covered with riparian vegetation. The new branch of the Arve will accommodate its waters during the increasingly frequent summer floods. The population will be able to take advantage of a new place of freshness to rest on a pontoon, observe nature, play in the water, dip their feet, and even swim in complete safety. This new space will be reminiscent of the Arve baths, which were very popular at a time when its invigorating waters were preferred to those of the lake, thus reconnecting with the river's historical activities.

La Place des Artisanes / Artisane Square

La Place des Artisanes est entourée des deux bâtiments conservés et surélevés du bureau des autos ainsi que d'un nouveau bâtiment localisé de l'autre côté de la route de Veyrier afin d'en faire un seul et unique quartier. Elle proposera un nouveau lieu de vie et de rencontre. Accompagnée d'un écran végétal sur son pourtour et de plan d'eau, la place accueillera de nombreux évènements comme le marché des artisans. Une passerelle la reliera au nouveau bâtiment de l'autre côté de la route du Val-d'Arve avec des équipements publics et un parking.

Artisans' Square is surrounded by the two preserved and elevated buildings of the driver and vehicle licensing authority, and a new building located on the other side of the Veyrier Road, bringing these spaces together as a single neighbourhood. It will offer a new place to live and meet. Accompanied by water features and a vegetation screen around its perimeter, the square will host numerous events such as the craftsmen and artisan market. A footbridge will link it to the new building on the other side of Val-d'Arve Road with public facilities and a car park.

Le quartier des Auréas et le vieux cimetière

Le quartier des Auréas sera revalorisé en animant les rez-de-chaussée des bâtiments grâce à des programmes collectifs. De l'autre côté de la forêt urbaine, sur la moitié est de l'actuel cimetière, une proposition de quartier de logement pourra être réalisée ouvrant ainsi le quartier sur la butte de Pinchat.

The Auréa district and old cemetery area will be upgraded by animating the ground floors of buildings with collective initiatives. On the other side of the urban forest, on the eastern half of the current cemetery, a proposed housing area could be constructed, opening the area to the Pinchat hillock.

Le parc des Animaux

Le Parc des animaux permettra de maintenir et de mettre en valeur cet espace existant de découverte autour des animaux et des oiseaux de concours. Lieu familial par excellence, cet espace boisé sera revalorisé grâce à de nouveaux espaces de rencontre et une meilleure connexion avec le reste du quartier Fontenette afin d'en faire un lieu remarquable et inspirant permettant de faire co-habiter l'humain et l'animal.

The Animal Park will make it possible to maintain and enhance this existing space of discovery around animals and show birds. An ideal family-friendly setting, this wooded area will be upgraded with new meeting spaces and a better connection to the rest of Fontenette sector, transforming it into a remarkable and inspiring place where humans and animals can cohabitate.

AU FIL DE L'OR / GOLD LINE

Ripisylve
Riparian area

● Continuité paysagère
Landscape continuity

▨ Densification et reconnection du cordon de verdure du bord de l'Arve
Densification and reconnection of the vegetation on the banks of the Arve

■ Nouveaux bâtiments et bâti transformé ou surélevé
New buildings and transformed or raised buildings

Reconnexion
Reconnection

Connexion entre la Fontenette et Champel par un ascenseur.
Connection between la Fontenette and Champel with a lift.

Connexion et séquençage des places publiques ; de la Place du Marché à la Place des Artisanes, en passant par la place de la Fontenette.
Connection and sequencing of public places; from Place du Marché to Place des Artisanes, via Place de la Fontenette.

Connection à mobilité douce depuis le pont du CEVA jusqu'à Pinchat.
Connection with a cycling path from CEVA bridge to Pinchat.

Programmes
Programs

┄ Cordon de programmes publics se développant sur les berges de l'Arve.
Layer of public programs evolving along the Arve.

● Logement
Dwelling

● Commerce / Artisanat
Merchant / Craftmanship

● Loisir / Culture
Leisure / Culture

● Education
Education

Circulation
Circulation

Un tronçon de la Route de Veyrier est dédié uniquement à la mobilité douce et en amont est réduite à 30km/h et ne dessert que les parkings. Cela réduit fortement la circulation nuisible dans le secteur.
A section of the Route de Veyrier is dedicated only to soft mobility and reduced to 30 km/h and only deserve the car parking. This reduces traffic pressure in the area.

● Circulation routière
Traffic

◍ Riverain / Zone 30
Residents / 30km/h speed limit

┈ BHNS uniquement
Only BHNS

○ Mobilité douce
Non motorized mobility

① La ferme du Val d'Arve

② Parc des Orpailleurs

③ Fontenette-plage

④ Le parc des Sports

Rapports à l'Arve / Arve riverside

La ripisylve et les différents rapports à l'Arve / Riparian area and Arve riverside

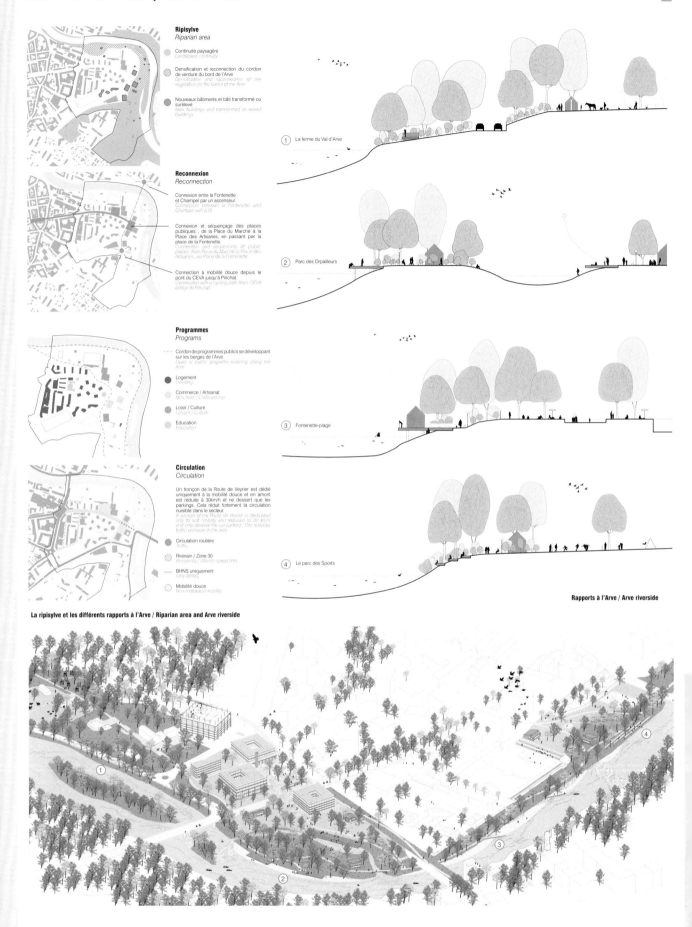

AU FIL DE L'OR / GOLD LINE

Place des artisanes / Artisans Square

Promenade au bord de l'Arve / Path along the Arve

"J'aime beaucoup venir ici les mercredis après-midi pour mon cours sur la biodiversité. On parle des plantes et des arbres et parfois on peut même voir des grenouilles et des oiseaux".

"I like coming here on Wednesday afternoons for my biodiversity class. We talk about plants and trees and sometimes you can even see frogs and birds."

"C'est vraiment un plaisir de venir travailler dans ce quartier. On est proche de la nature et c'est facile de venir à vélo".

"It's a pleasure to come and work in this area. We are close to nature and it is easy to come by bike."

"Grâce au marché sur la place des Artisanes je peux faire découvrir mes œuvres à tout le monde. C'est vraiment agréable de se sentir au cœur de ce quartier.

"Thanks to the market on Artisans Square I can show my work to everyone. It's nice to feel like you're at the heart of this neighbourhood."

**(B) Quartier des artisanes
Artisans district**

place		skateboard	
atelier mobile		restaurants	
nœud de circulation		discothèque	
arbres solitaire		épicerie	
fontaine		buvette	
évènements		marché artisanal	

**(C) Parc des orpailleurs
Gold panners park**

solarium		pelouse	
café/bars		arbres solitaire	
pavillons		cinéArve	
formations		jeux	
recherche		activités	
nage		barbecue	

**(D) L'île des orpailleurs
Gold panners island**

observatoire		pêche	
sensibilisation		ripisylve	
baignade		forêt	
kayak		jeux en forêt	
pontons		refuge faune	
sauna		milieu flore	

La place des artisanes et le parc des orpailleurs / Artisans square and gold panners park

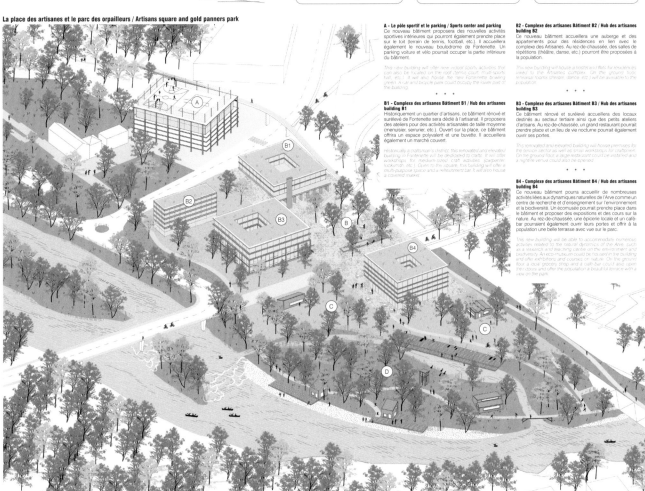

A - Le pôle sportif et le parking / Sports center and parking
Ce nouveau bâtiment proposera des nouvelles activités sportives intérieures qui pourront également prendre place sur le toit (terrain de tennis, football, etc.). Il accueillera également le nouveau boulodrome de Fontenette. Un parking voiture et vélo pourrait occuper la partie inférieure du bâtiment.

This new building will offer new indoor sports activities that can also be located on the roof (tennis court, multi-sports hall, etc.). It will also house the new Fontenette bowling green. A car and bicycle park could occupy the lower part of the building.

* * *

B1 - Complexe des artisanes Bâtiment B1 / Hub des artisanes building B1
Historiquement un quartier d'artisans, ce bâtiment rénové et surélevé de Fontenette sera dédié à l'artisanat. Il proposera des ateliers pour des activités artisanales de taille moyenne (menuisier, serrurier, etc.). Ouvert sur la place, ce bâtiment offrira un espace polyvalent et une buvette. Il accueillera également un marché couvert.

Historically a craftsman's district, this renovated and elevated building in Fontenette will be dedicated to crafts. It will offer workshops for medium-sized craft activities (carpenter, locksmith, etc.). Open to the square, this building will offer a multi-purpose space and a refreshment bar. It will also house a covered market.

B2 - Complexe des artisanes Bâtiment B2 / Hub des artisanes building B2
Ce nouveau bâtiment accueillera une auberge et des appartements pour des résidences en lien avec le complexe des Artisanes. Au rez-de-chaussée, des salles de répétitions (théâtre, danse, etc.) pourront être proposées à la population.

This new building will house a hostel and flats for residences linked to the Artisanes complex. On the ground floor, rehearsal rooms (theatre, dance, etc.) will be available to the population.

* * *

B3 - Complexe des artisanes Bâtiment B3 / Hub des artisanes building B3
Ce bâtiment rénové et surélevé accueillera des locaux destinés au secteur tertiaire ainsi que des petits ateliers d'artisans. Au rez-de-chaussée, un grand restaurant pourrait prendre place et un lieu de vie nocturne pourrait également ouvrir ses portes.

This renovated and elevated building will house premises for the service sector as well as small workshops for craftsmen. On the ground floor, a large restaurant could be installed and a nightlife venue could also be opened.

B4 - Complexe des artisanes Bâtiment B4 / Hub des artisanes building B4
Ce nouveau bâtiment pourra accueillir de nombreuses activités liées aux dynamiques naturelles de l'Arve comme un centre de recherche et d'enseignement sur l'environnement et la biodiversité. Un écomusée pourrait prendre place dans le bâtiment et proposer des expositions et des cours sur la nature. Au rez-de-chaussée, une épicerie locale et un café-bar pourraient également ouvrir leurs portes et offrir à la population une belle terrasse avec vue sur le parc.

This new building will be able to accommodate numerous activities related to the natural dynamics of the Arve, such as a research and teaching centre on the environment and biodiversity. An eco-museum could be housed in the building and offer exhibitions and courses on nature. On the ground floor, a local grocery shop and a café-bar could also open their doors and offer the population a beautiful terrace with a view on the park.

Fagerstrand (NO)

Standort

Fagerstrand ist ein zergliederter Küstenvorort, gekennzeichnet durch einen ungenutzten Industriestandort, einen Mangel an Plätzen, um Kontakte zu pflegen, und eine gefährliche Straßenkreuzung; jedoch mit dem Potenzial, ein neuer Knotenpunkt am Oslofjord zu werden.

Aufgrund von Veränderungen in der Wirtschaft hat die Natur die verlassenen Überreste des Erdölzeitalters zurückerobert und sie in Baumkathedralen und Nistplätze für Vögel verwandelt. Diese grünen Nischen bilden heute ein Niemandsland zwischen verschiedenen Bereichen, die für eine zukünftige Entwicklung vorgesehen sind. Hier ist die Gemeinde auf der Suche nach einem innovativen Plan, der die Bereiche verbinden kann und Fagerstrand, zu den Bedingungen der Natur, zu einem einzigen Ort machten kann.

Fagerstrand ist als an den Ballungsraum Oslo angeschlossener Bereich für eine städtische Verdichtung vorgesehen. Zwei große Entwicklungsstandorte, einer am Meer, der andere im Wald, sind durch einen grünen Korridor getrennt, der sich durch das Gebiet erstreckt, in dem sich das Zentrum befinden soll. Fagerstrands Identität ist mit einer intimen Beziehung zu Meer und Wald eng verbunden. Wie kann diese Identität erhalten werden, wenn der Ort umgewandelt und mit städtischen Eigenschaften intensiviert wird?

Der Standort lädt Bewerberinnen und Bewerber ein, Konventionen zu Vorstellungen von zentral und urban zu hinterfragen beziehungsweise zu überlegen, wie ökologische Prozesse und die bebaute Umgebung dazu beitragen können, soziale Ungleichheiten zu reduzieren und einen dynamischen Ort zum Leben für Menschen und andere Lebewesen gleichermaßen zu erschaffen.

Location

Fagerstrand is a fragmented coastal suburb characterized by a disused industrial site, a lack of places for socializing, and a dangerous road junction, but nonetheless has the potential to become a new hub along the Oslo fjord.

Due to changes in the economy, nature has reclaimed the abandoned relics of the oil age and turned them into woodland cathedrals and nesting sites for birds. These pockets of green now form a no man's land between various areas earmarked for future development. Here, the municipality is looking for an innovative plan that can interconnect the areas to make Fagerstrand feel like one place, in harmony with nature.

Fagerstrand is designated for urban densification as an area that is linked with the Oslo metropolitan area. A green corridor that stretches through the area where the centre will be located divides two large development sites, one on the seafront and the other in the forest. Fagerstrand's identity is closely tied to its intimate relationship to both the sea and the forest. How can this identity be retained as it is transformed and augmented with urban qualities?

This site invites Europan participants to challenge conventions regarding what being central and urban entail. The municipality asks participants to interrogate how ecological processes and the built environment can help reduce social inequalities and create a vibrant place to live for both humans and non-humans alike.

Bevölkerung   Inhabitants
ca. 3000

Betrachtungsraum   Study Site
246 ha

Projektgebiet   Project Site
57 ha

Equalines

Projekt

Fagerstrand bietet sich für eine Verdichtung an, mit der allerdings eine Reihe von Fragen verbunden sind: Wo soll sich das neue Stadtzentrum befinden? Wie kann der Schutz des unbebauten Landes mit dem Schutz privaten Eigentums in Einklang gebracht werden? Wie lassen sich die Eigenschaften ländlicher Streuung mit denen urbaner Dichte zusammenbringen?

Equalines beantwortet diese Fragen mit dem einfachen Prinzip der linearen Konzentration. Eine zentrale urbane Achse bietet durch die Etablierung einer starken lokalen Wirtschaft Möglichkeiten für alteingesessene wie auch für neue Bewohnerinnen und Bewohner. Eine renaturierte Küste stellt lokale Ökosysteme wieder her und zelebriert diese. Zudem bietet sie den Menschen von Fagerstrand die Möglichkeit, eine sich entwickelnde postindustrielle Landschaft entlang einer durchlässigen Uferregion zu erleben. Ein beständiges grünes Netzwerk erhält und erweitert gewachsene Lebensräume.

Die Grenzen zwischen bebautem und unbebautem Gebiet werden durch eine Vielzahl an Funktionen aktiviert, die die Durchlässigkeit zwischen kulturellen, wirtschaftlichen und ökologischen Abläufen verstärken. Potenzial für metabolische Lebensenergie wird durch kombinierte Flüsse von Lebensmitteln und Energie, aber auch von Tourismus, Freizeit und Unternehmergeist nutzbar gemacht. Diese Flüsse sind entlang zentraler Linien konzentriert, die mit ihren natürlichen Bewegungen übereinstimmen und Synergien zwischen ihnen anregen.

Der Fokus auf Linearität bietet für einen großen Teil der Bevölkerung Potenziale und erzeugt weniger Exklusion durch Randgebiete, die sich aus einem konzentrischen Modell ergeben würden. Das trifft vor allem im Fall von Fagerstrand zu, wo die bestehende räumliche Konfiguration bereits stärker linear als konzentrisch ist. Nicht zuletzt schafft die Kombination verschiedener Funktionen entlang einer Linie eine höchst durchlässige Umgebung.

Team

Wir lernten einander während des Masterstudiengangs für Stadtplanung an der TU Delft, Niederlande, kennen. Im Laufe unseres Masters entwickelten wir ein breites Spektrum an Spezialisierungen, denen wir heute in verschiedenen akademischen und professionellen Positionen nachgehen. Die Mischung aus Interessen und Disziplinen bot eine ideale Basis für die Zusammenarbeit bei diesem Wettbewerb. Es ist das erste Mal, dass wir an Europan teilgenommen haben. Wir betrachten den Preis als Motivation, unsere Designarbeit in unterschiedlichem Maß und an verschiedenen Standorten weiterzuführen. Wir sind überzeugt, dass Prozesse wie Europan unseren kontinuierlichen Austausch zwischen akademischer Welt und Praxis weiter verstärken können.

– Stefano Agliati (IT), Architekt Urbanist
– Henry Endemann (DE), Stadtplaner
– Lukas Höller (DE), Ladschaftsarchitekt
– Rebecca Smink (NL), Stadtplaner

Project

The planned densification of Fagerstrand gives rise to a set of urban planning-related questions: Where should the new centre of the town be located? How can the protection of unbuilt land be balanced with the protection of residents' properties? How can the qualities of rural dispersion be aligned with the qualities of urban density?

Equalines explores these questions based on a simple principle: linear concentration. A central urban axis offers equal opportunities for old and new residents by establishing a strong local economy. A re-naturalized seaside restores and celebrates local ecosystems, thus giving the people of Fagerstrand the chance to experience a thriving post-industrial landscape along a permeable waterfront. A robust green network preserves and expands continuous habitats.

The edges between built and unbuilt areas are activated by means of a variety of functions that enhance porosity between cultural, economic, and environmental flows. Potentials for metabolic vitality are harnessed by combining flows of food and energy, but also of tourism, leisure, and entrepreneurial spirit. These flows are bundled along central lines, which matches their natural movements and stimulates synergies between them.

The focus on linearity can offer access to opportunities to a large share of the population and results in less exclusion on the peripheries than a concentric model. This is particularly true in the case of Fagerstrand, where the existing spatial configuration is already more linear than concentric. Lastly, the combination of multiple functions along one line creates a highly porous environment.

Team

We met while studying in the master program in urbanism at the TU Delft, The Netherlands. During our masters studies, we developed a diverse range of specializations that we are now pursuing in academic and professional positions. The mix of interests and disciplines formed an ideal basis for collaborating on this competition. This is the first time that we are participating in Europan. We see the award as a motivation to continue our design work on various scales and in various locations. Moreover, we are convinced that competitions like Europan can further enhance our ongoing exchange between academia and practice.

– Stefano Agliati (IT), urban designer
– Henry Endemann (DE), urban planner
– Lukas Höller (DE), landscape architect
– Rebecca Smink (NL), urban designer

EQUALINES

HOW FAGERSTRAND CAN OFFER EQUAL OPPORTUNITIES THROUGH LINEAR CONCENTRATION

As Fagerstrand is posed for densification, a conventional set of "urban questions" arises: where should the new center of the town be? What is a suitable functional mix? How can the protection of unbuilt land be balanced with the protection of residents' properties? Furthermore, more place-specific questions come up: how can the strict separation between the industrial sites and the residential areas be loosened? How can the qualities of rural dispersion be aligned with the qualities of urban density? EQUALINES explores these questions through a simple principle: linear concentration.

Linearity is explored in this proposal through three dimensions: people, planet, and prosperity. This is derived from classic sustainability theory of the triple-bottom-line: social, environmental, and economic sustainability. It is also largely in line with the UN's conceptualization of holistic sustainable development. Therefore, these three layers are used here to explore the multiplicity of functions that can be associated with the framework of linear concentration.

The main spatial interventions and the lines that they create can be summarized as follows:
1. A new urban axis along the Fagerstrandbakken bundles the majority of densification, including business and community functions. Newly built compositions of point-houses are combined with infill developments.
2. The industrial site along the waterfront is opened up and re-naturalized into a wetland habitat. Singular structures from the old industry (including the silos) remain and form the centroids for new flows of leisure, energy, and food production.
3. The existing structure of pipes from the old industry is used for the distribution of produced and captured goods, such as biomass, algae, electricity, and water. The pipes are also used for the creation of a new trail along the water and through the forest – the Rørvei ("Pipe-Path").
4. The landscape around the Lillerud dam remains largely untouched. The expansion of the Pipe-Path allows for an experience of post-industrial remnants without harming the environment. Towards the east of the project site, careful interventions and permeable urban edges help to consolidate the most important green axes.

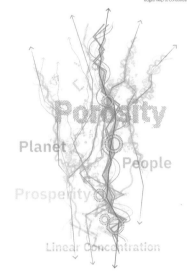

Conceptual representation of the seven main layers

Strategic Plan, 1:5 000

Bird's eye view, looking east from the wetland towards the town

A1

A2

A3

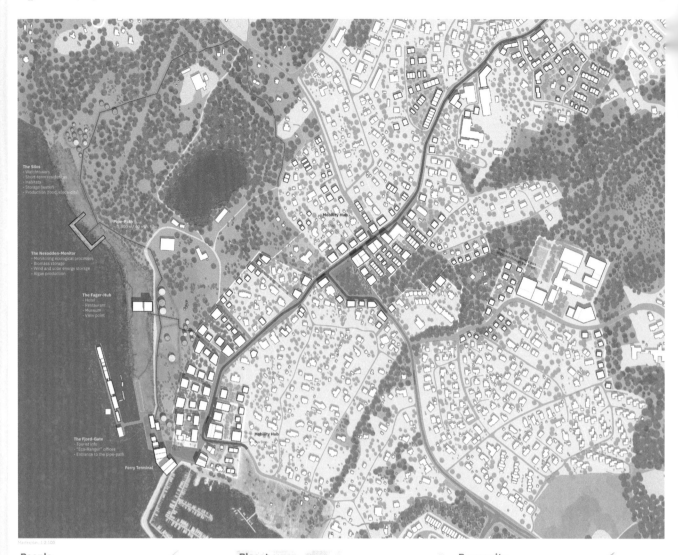

The Silos
- Watchtowers
- Short-term residences
- Habitats
- Storage (water)
- Production (food, electricity)

Pipe-Path
1,900 m / 40 min. hike

The Nesodden-Monitor
- Monitoring ecological processes
- Biomass storage
- Wind and solar energy storage
- Algae production

The Fager-Hub
- Hotel
- Restaurant
- Museum
- View point

The Fjord-Gate
- Tourist info
- "Eco-Ranger" offices
- Entrance to the pipe-path

Ferry Terminal

Mobility Hub

Mobility Hub

People

Planet

Prosperity

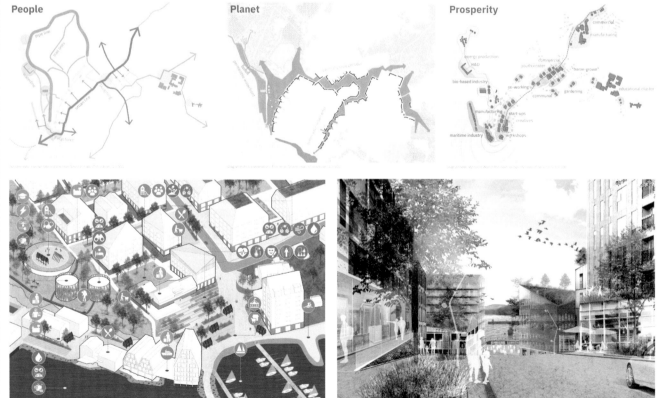

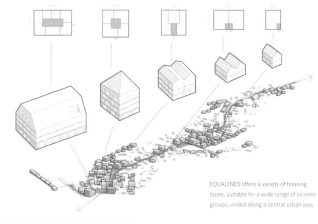

EQUALINES offers a variety of housing types, suitable for a wide range of income groups, united along a central urban axis.

Rain water is stored in the silos and used for irrigation of vertical farming. Electricity is generated from sun, wind, biomass, algae, and tides. Vertical farming in the silos provides food for locals and visitors. Residents and visitors can use the trail system for daily walks with different lengths. Tourists can spend a special night in one of the silo residences.

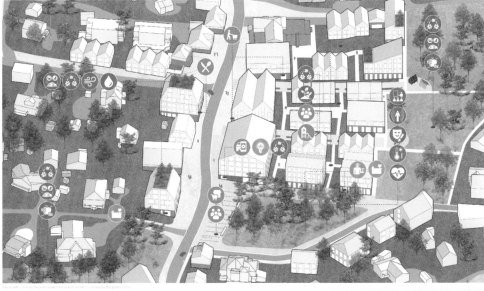

2025 - Nuclei
Urban development, the landscape, and the public space are first established in the most crucial points. 400-600 housing units can be realized in this phase, excluding the Sagstubben and Kveldsroveien development areas (outside the project area).

People
Planet
Prosperity

2030 - Spread-Out
Starting from the nuclei, development spreads out, increasingly forming the envisioned lines. An additional 100 - 250 units can be realized in this phase, still almost exclusively located around the urban axis.

People
Planet
Prosperity

2035 Fill-In
Infill developments expand the linearity, closing gaps in the urban axis, the wetland along the waterfront, and other landscape corridors. 50 - 100 units can be realized in various locations, depending on demand and availability of plots over time.

People
Planet
Prosperity

2050 - Consolidate?
The fabric can be further consolidated over time: freed-up plots can be used for further densification along the urban axis. Development is never "finished". There is always room for improvement - following the aspired symbiosis of people, planet, and prosperity.

People
Planet
Prosperity

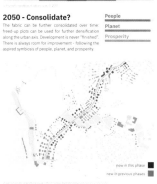

new in this phase
new in previous phases

Hjertelia (NO)

Standort

Als Reaktion auf die in Hjertelia vorherrschende Typologie der Einfamilienhäuser, welche die norwegischen Landschaft dominieren, soll für das Wettbewerbsgebiet eine nachhaltige Alternative entwickelt werden. Im Zentrum stehen dabei Mobilitätslösungen für Fußgängerinnen und Fußgänger und sowie Radfahrende. Durch die Beteiligung an Europan 16 will die Gemeinde Ringerike ermitteln, wie Hjertelia zu einem experimentellen Pilotviertel werden kann, das auf urbaner Landwirtschaft und sozialen Lebensformen basiert, die die Zugehörigkeit zu einer Stadt unterstreichen, die vor umfangreichen Veränderungen steht. Das ehrgeizige Ziel liegt darin, den Weg für weitere Entwicklungen innerhalb des Betrachtungsgebietes aufzuzeigen und so zudem mit neuen Beispielen zu einem allgemein verfügbaren Repertoire an Wohntypologien für die Zukunft beizutragen.

Insbesondere angesichts der Tatsache, dass der Bezirk eher für seine Landwirtschaft und die malerischen Felsschluchten bekannt ist als für seine trendigen Cafés, fragen sich viele, ob überhaupt jemand nach Ringerike übersiedeln würde, um dort eine Wohnung zu beziehen.

Wir wissen allerdings, dass sich eine urbane Identität in Hønefoss von urbanen Identitäten in großen Städten unterscheiden wird. Wenn Ringerike Bevölkerungswachstum, Klimawandel und technologischen Fortschritt in der Landwirtschaft ins Auge fasst, wird es um eine dichtere Bebauung nicht umhinkommen. Wie lässt sich eine neue Art urbaner Identität in einem peripheren landwirtschaftlichen Bezirk wie Ringerike ausdrücken?

Die Entwicklung von Hjertelia war umstritten, da das Gebiet aus Ackerland und Wald besteht. Die Entwicklung solcher vorstädtischer Waldgebiete und landwirtschaftlicher Anbauflächen ist für zahlreiche norwegische Kleinstädte charakteristisch und stellt auch auf globaler Ebene eine große Herausforderung dar. Der Flächennutzungsplan für Hjertelia und die angrenzenden Gebiete wurde von der Politik jedoch abgesegnet, und Teile dieses Areals werden bereits bebaut. Die lokalen Behörden wollen ihren Besitz in Hjertelia einsetzen, um ein ambitioniertes Beispiel für einfühlsame und standortspezifische Architektur und Außenräume zu entwickeln, die dazu beitragen, die Ökologie und die produktiven Eigenschaften der Landschaft zu verstärken.

Location

The aim in Hjertelia is to develop the site as a reaction and sustainable alternative to the typology of detached homes that dominates the Norwegian landscape. The development must be planned around mobility solutions for pedestrians and cyclists. Through Europan 16, the municipality of Ringerike wants to examine how Hjertelia can become an experimental pilot district based on urban farming and social forms of living that underpin belonging in a town undergoing large-scale changes. The ambitious goal is to show the way forward for further development within the study area, and, moreover, to contribute, with new examples, to a shared library of housing typologies for the future.

Many people are asking whether anyone would want to move to Ringerike in order to live in an apartment at all, since the district is better known for its agriculture and beautiful ravines than for its trendy cafés.

What we do know is that an urban identity in Hønefoss will be different from urban identities in large cities. To address population growth, climate change, and technological advances in agriculture, Ringerike will have to build denser. How can a new sort of urban identity be expressed in a peripheral agricultural district such as Ringerike?

The development of Hjertelia has been controversial because the area consists of farmland and forest. Developing such suburban woodlands and agricultural plots is common on the fringes of many small Norwegian towns and a major challenge globally. Politicians have nevertheless approved the zoning plans for Hjertelia and the adjacent areas, and parts of them are already under construction. The local authority wishes to use its property in Hjertelia to develop an ambitious example of sensitive and site-specific architecture and outdoor space that helps augment the ecology and productive properties of the landscape.

Bevölkerung   Inhabitants
ca. 9600

Betrachtungsraum   Study Site
60 ha

Projektgebiet   Project Site
3,7 ha

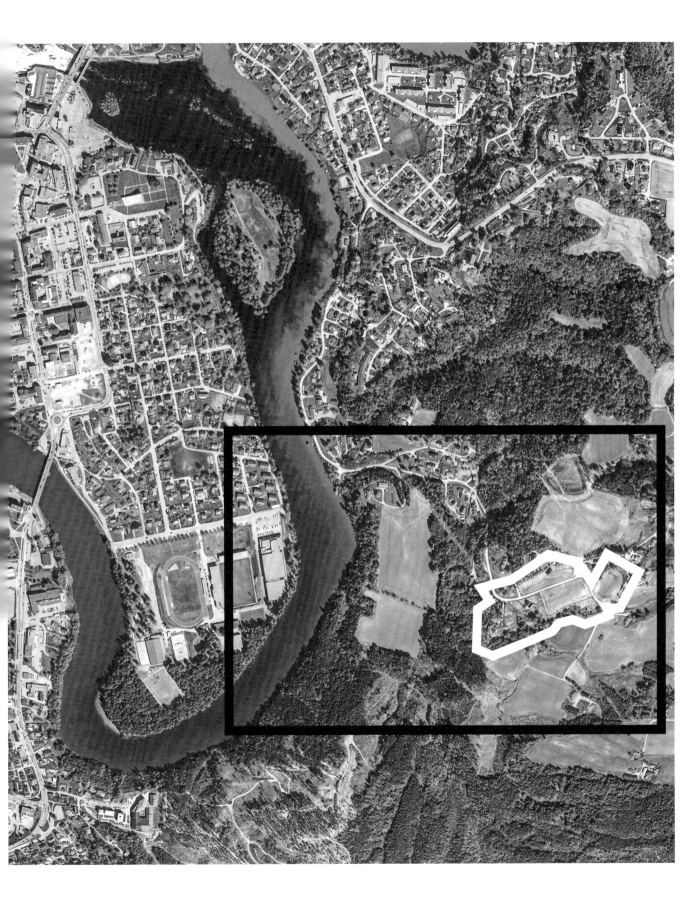

Født i skogen

Projekt

Ich bin im Wald geboren! Das ist eine Vision eines CO_2-neutralen Dorfes zwischen Bäumen und Feldern. Achtung: Dies ist eine unperfekte Utopie … oder Dystopie? … , die uns einiges abverlangt!

Bei der Ausweisung neuer Siedlungsflächen werden in der Regel Wälder abgeholzt, was zu Zersiedelung und Umweltzerstörung führt: Der Lebensraum von Tieren wird eingeschränkt, Biotope werden zerstört, und für das Klima wichtige Wälder gehen verloren. Bauen heißt typischerweise: Mensch gegen Tier! Das wollen wir ändern und schlagen vor, die Beziehung zwischen Mensch und Tier zu überdenken. Unser Projekt befasst sich mit der Solidarität mit Tieren in menschlichen Räumen und schlägt eine neue Art des Zusammenlebens vor: Tiere und Pflanzen erhalten die Erdgeschossfläche, und Menschen rücken eine Ebene höher.

Einfamilienhäuser verbrauchen viel Fläche, Baumaterial und Energie, sie verursachen Zersiedelung und damit noch mehr Verkehr und teure Infrastruktur, und sie zerstören so noch mehr Biodiversität. Ein norwegischer Bürger produziert etwa acht bis neun Tonnen Kohlendioxid pro Jahr. Unser Ziel ist es, eine Siedlung zu gestalten, in der es sich kohlendioxidfrei leben lässt.

Das Konzept der über dem Boden schwebenden Waldhäuser verbindet den Traum vom Wohnen im eigenen Einfamilienhaus mit dem vom Wohnen in der Natur und ist gleichzeitig nachhaltig. Dies wird erreicht durch:

– ökologischen Holzbau, der Kohlenstoffdioxid bindet ($-1,5\,t\ CO_2$)
– ein Mobilitätskonzept, das auf Fahrrad, Ski und Zufußgehen basiert ($-2,5\,t\ CO_2$)
– ökologische Lebensmittelproduktion – keine Monokultur! ($-0,5\,t\ CO_2$)
– Wiederverwendung von Regenwasser ($-0,5\,t\ CO_2$)
– Reduzierung des Energieverbrauchs – nur ein beheizter Raum ($-1\,t\ CO_2$)
– Reduzierung von Privatbesitz (wenig Stauraum, dafür mehr Gemeinschaftsbesitz, wie z. B. eine Waldbibliothek, Waldspielzimmer usw.) ($-1\,t\ CO_2$)
– Wiederaufforsten zwischen den Häusern ($-0,5\,t\ CO_2$)
– Vermittlung eines neuen ökologischen Denkens in der Waldschule ($-1,5\,t\ CO_2$)

Komm, lass uns in den Wald gehen und Pilze sammeln!

Team

Opposite Office zeichnet, schreibt, erfindet und baut architektonische Geschichten und Gebäude. Das aktivistische Architekturbüro wurde 2017 von Benedikt Hartl in München gegründet. Opposite Office beschäftigt sich mit architektonischen Fragestellungen an der Schnittstelle von Architektur, Soziologie und Politik. Die Arbeiten sind stets zwischen Realität und Fiktion angesiedelt. Opposite Office ist ein sozial und politisch motiviertes Büro, das räumliche und soziale Aufgaben miteinander kombiniert und so versucht, einen Beitrag zu einer gesellschaftlichen Debatte zu leisten. Die Arbeiten von Opposite Office wurden in über 100 Ländern veröffentlicht, ausgestellt und prämiert.

Beim Europan-Wettbewerb waren Benedikt Hartl, Thomas Haseneder und Theresa Eberl beteiligt.

Project

My birthplace is the forest! This is a vision of a CO_2-neutral village in the woods and above crofts. Attention: This is a nice chunk of an imperfect utopia… or dystopia?… which severely will limit us!

As a rule, forests are cut down when new areas are designated for housing, thus leading to urban sprawl and environmental degradation: The habitat of animals is restricted, biotopes are destroyed, and forests, which are of great importance for the climate, are lost. Typically, building means: man against animal! We want to change this and propose a rethinking of the relationship between humans and flora and fauna. Our project concerns solidarity with animals in human spaces and proposes a new form of cohabitation: the ground floor space is reserved for animals and plants, and human beings move up one level.

Single family houses consume a lot of space, building materials and energy, they cause urban sprawl and thus even more traffic and expensive infrastructure, thereby destroying even more biodiversity. A Norwegian citizen produces about 8 to 9 tons of carbon dioxide per year. Our aim is to design a settlement where you live carbon dioxide free.

The concept of forest houses that hover above the ground, combine the dream of living in your own detached house, living in nature and being sustainable at the same time. This is attained by the following means:

– ecological timber construction binds carbon dioxide ($-1.5\,t\ CO_2$)
– shared mobility concept reduces carbon dioxide ($-2.5\,t\ CO_2$)
– ecoglogical food production – no monoculture! ($-0.5\,t\ CO_2$)
– rainwater is used as water supply ($-0.5\,t\ CO_2$)
– energy consumption is reduced by sustainable energy concepts – only one heated room ($-1\,t\ CO_2$)
– materialism is discouraged through sharing economies – e. g. forest library, forest playroom ($-1\,t\ CO_2$)
– reforestation by planting trees between the houses ($-0.5\,t\ CO_2$)
– a new mentality of ecology is taught in the forest school ($-1.5\,t\ CO_2$)

Come on, let's go into the forest and collect mushrooms!

Team

Opposite Office draws, writes, invents, and builds architectural stories and buildings. The activist architecture office was founded by Benedikt Hartl in Munich in 2017. Opposite Office deals with architectural issues at the interface between architecture, sociology, and politics. The projects are always situated between reality and fiction. Opposite Office is a socially and politically motivated office that combines spatial and social tasks and thus attempts to contribute to social debates. Opposite Office's work has been published, exhibited, and received awards internationally in over 100 countries.

Benedikt Hartl, Thomas Haseneder, and Theresa Eberl were involved in the Europan competition.

Hjertelia (NO)

🌲🌲🌲 født i skogen

I am born in a forest! A vision of a CO_2-neutral village in the woods...

As a rule, forests are cut down when new areas are designated for housing, which leads to urban sprawl and environmental degradation: The habitat of animals is restricted, biotopes are destroyed and forests, that are important for the climate, are lost. Typically, building means: man against animal! We want to change that and propose a rethink of the relationship between humans and animals. Our project concerns solidarity with animals in human spaces and proposes a new way of cohabitation: Animals and plants get the ground floor space and humans move up one level.

Single family houses consume a lot of space, building materials and energy, they cause urban sprawl and thus even more traffic and expensive infrastructure, thereby destroying even more biodiversity. A Norwegian citizen produces about 8-9 tons of carbon dioxide per year. Our aim is to design a settlement where you live carbon dioxide free, where:

- 🌲 ecological timber construction binds carbon dioxide -1.5t
- 🌲 shared mobility concept reduces carbon dioxide by 2.5t
- 🌲 ecological food production (no monoculture!) -0.5t
- 🌲 rainwater is used as water supply -0.5t
- 🌲 energy consumption is reduced by sustainable energy concepts (one heated room) -1t
- 🌲 materialism is discouraged through sharing economies (e.g. forest library, forest playroom) -1t
- 🌲 reforestation by planting trees between the houses -0.5t
- 🌲 a new mentally of ecology is taught in the skog skole -1.5t

Of course, living in the city in multi-story buildings can be a sustainable solution, but the dream of living in nature, the dream of your own four walls, the dream of independence and the dream of adventure is very present in Norwegian culture. The desire of living in a detached house is part of the Norwegian dream, and more than 60% of Norwegians live in one. The problem: These detached houses don't deliver their inhabitants' desires.

- 🏠 instead of living „in nature", you live next to other ugly detached houses with coiffured gardens that have nothing to do with real nature.
- 🏠 instead of neighborly exchange and community, you get annoyed about the lawnmower on Saturday mornings.
- 🏠 instead of a happy family life, you split up and suddenly sit alone in a house that is far too big and far too expensive.
- 🏠 instead of isolated living, the house forms a community with a high grade of identification

So we asked ourselves, how can we combine the dream of living in nature in your own house, on the one hand, and sustainability and community on the other. The question is, how does the single-family home really become what we are seeking? And here is the answer...

- 🏠🏠 instead of clearing forests and destroying nature, the new housing typology will produce a new natural environment. New trees are planted to help protect the climate.
  Of course, renaturation of forests is not the biggest issue in Norway, but the new settlement should be a prototype and inspire communities in other countries!
- 🏠🏠 instead of carefully styled front gardens, you now really live in nature.
- 🏠🏠 instead of a solution that is entirely geared towards car traffic, we propose an innovative mobility concept that is designed as a combination of bicycles, electric vehicles, public ransport and especially sharing concepts. The final route to your home is only accessible by bike and on foot.
- 🏠🏠 instead of living in isolation, there is a distinct community based on sharing and help.
- 🏠🏠 instead of social segregation, the design of the different types of houses seek social mixture, integration and inclusiveness

Come on and let's go into the forest and collect mushrooms!

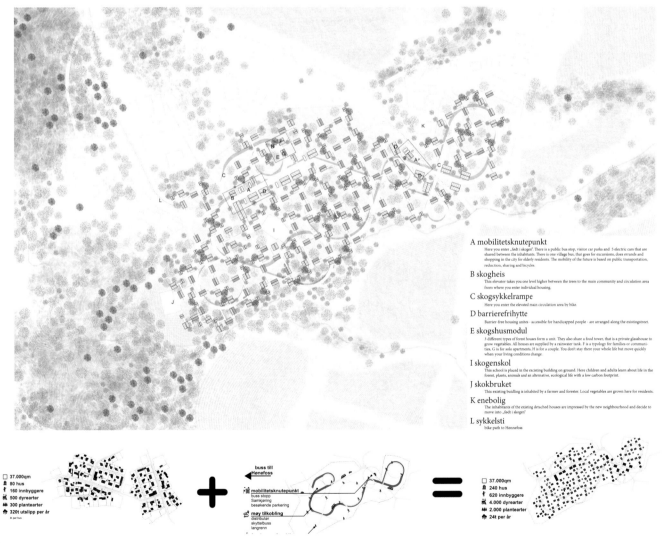

A mobilitetsknutepunkt
Here you enter „født i skogen". There is a public bus stop, visitor car parks and 5 electric cars that are shared between the inhabitants. There is one village bus, that goes for excursions, does errands and shopping in the city for elderly residents. The mobility of the future is based on public transportation, reduction, sharing and bicycles.

B skogheis
This elevator takes you one level higher between the trees to the main community and circulation area from where you enter individual housing.

C skogsykkelrampe
Here you enter the elevated main circulation area by bike.

D barrierefrihytte
Barrier-free housing unites - accessible for handicapped people - are arranged along the existingstreet.

E skogshusmodul
3 different types of forest houses form a unit. They also share a food tower, that is a private glasshouse to grow vegetables. All houses are supplied by a rainwater tank. F is a typology for families or communities, G is for solo apartments, H is for a couple. You don't stay there your whole life but move quickly when your living conditions change.

I skogenskol
This school is placed in the existing building on ground. Here children and adults learn about life in the forest, plants, animals and an alternative, ecological life with a low carbon footprint.

J skokbruket
This existing buidling is inhabited by a farmer and forester. Local vegetables are grown here for residents.

K enebolig
The inhabitants of the existing detached houses are impressed by the new neighbourhood and decide to move into „født i skogen"

L sykkelsti
bike path to Hønefoss

☐ 37.000qm
🏠 80 hus
👥 160 innbyggere
🐾 500 dyrearter
🌿 300 plantearter
🌲 320t utslipp per år
4t per hus

+

buss till Hønefoss

🚌 mobilitetsknutepunkt
buss stopp
Samkjøring
besøkende parkering

🚲 møy tilkobling
distributar
skyttelbuss
langrenn

=

☐ 37.000qm
🏠 240 hus
👥 620 innbyggere
🐾 4.000 dyrearter
🌿 2.000 plantearter
🌲 24t per år

Hjertelia (NO)

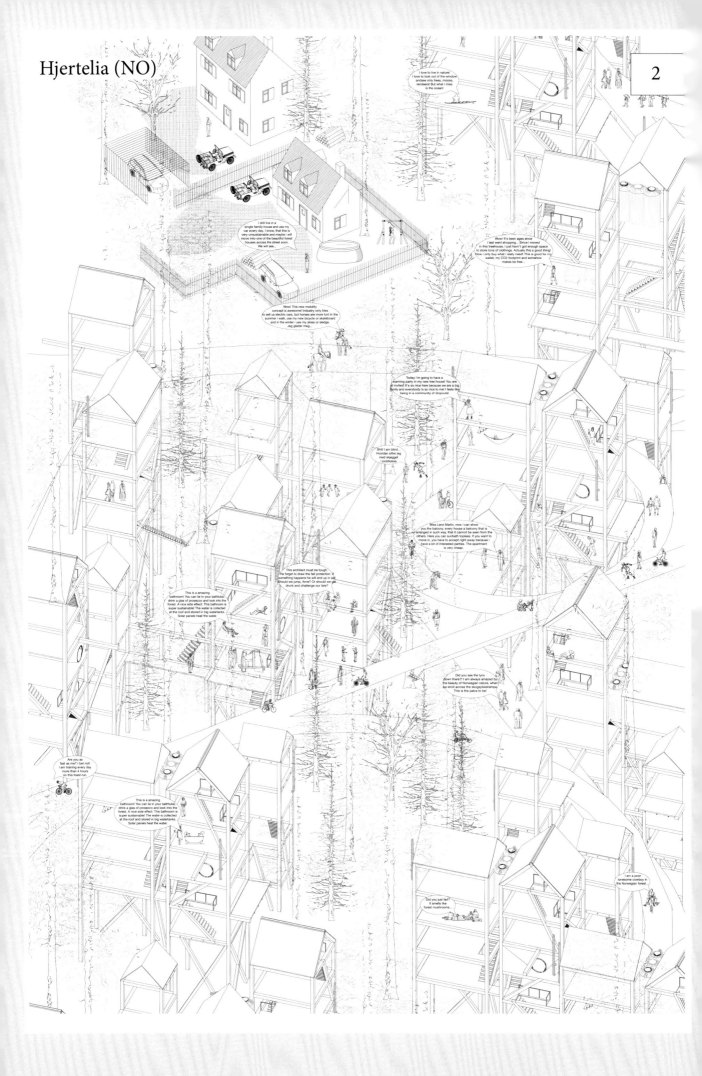

Hjertelia (NO)

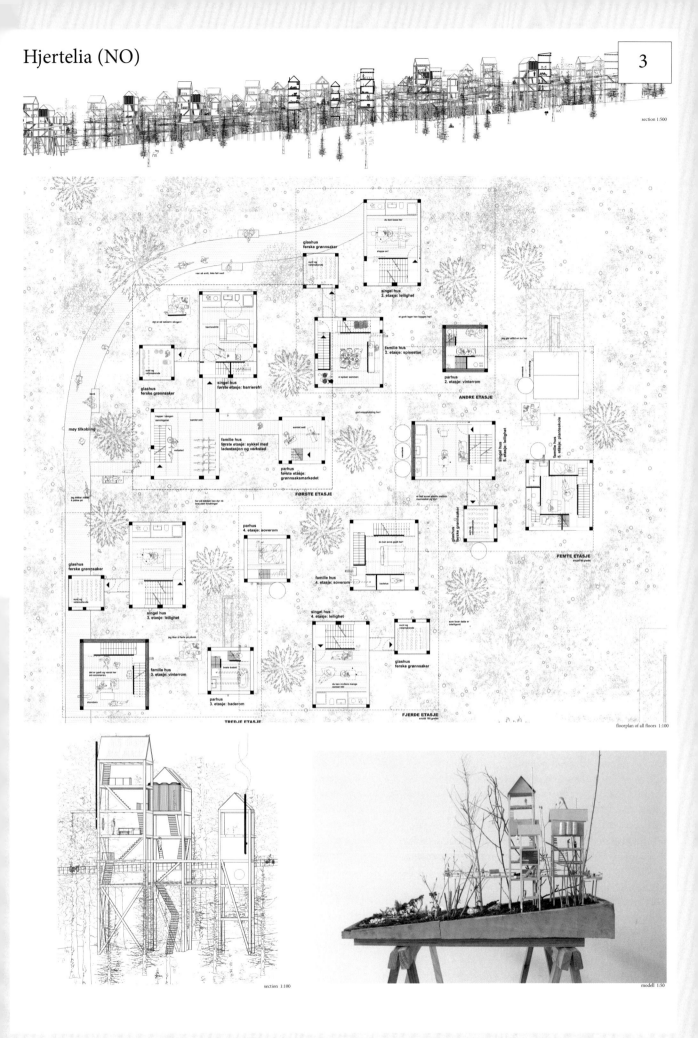

section 1:500

3

glashus
ferske grønnsaker

du kan kose her

slappe av!

singel hus
2. etasje: leilighet

det er så nakkert i skogen!

barnenhit!

et godt lager kan bygges her!

familie hus
2. etasje: spisestue

parhus
2. etasje: vinterrom

jeg går alltid en tur her

ANDRE ETASJE

singel hus
første etasje: barrierefri

glashus
ferske grønnsaker

møy tilkobling

trapper i skogen
renningstal

samlet sett

familie hus
første etasje: sykkel med
ladestasjon og verksted

parhus
første etasje:
grønnsaksmarkedet

FØRSTE ETASJE

god stoppikkling her!

singel hus
5. etasje: leilighet

familie hus
6. etasje: plantenskole

glashus
ferske grønnsaker

FEMTE ETASJE

parhus
4. etasje: soverom

du kan gjøre her!

familie hus
4. etasje: soverom

glashus
ferske grønnsaker

singel hus
2. etasje: leilighet

familie hus
3. etasje: vinterrom

parhus
3. etasje: baderom

TREDJE ETASJE

singel hus
4. etasje: leilighet

glashus
ferske grønnsaker

FJERDE ETASJE

floorplan of all floors 1:100

section 1:100

modell 1:50

Västerås (SE)

Standort

Västerås wächst, und man schätzt, dass die Bevölkerung in dreißig Jahren auf 230.000 Personen angewachsen sein wird. Mälarporten ist mit seiner Lage in der Nähe des Stadtzentrums, des Mälarensees und wichtiger öffentlicher Verkehrsknotenpunkte ein für die Entwicklung von Västerås bedeutsames Gebiet. Mälarporten bietet gute Möglichkeiten für die Schaffung eines völlig neuen Viertels, das sowohl innovativ als auch nachhaltig ist. 6000 bis 7000 Wohneinheiten und 10.000 Arbeitsplätze in gut gestalteter Wohnumgebung werden in dem Gebiet entstehen. Ein neuer Verkehrsknotenpunkt wird die Reisen nach und innerhalb von Västerås vereinfachen.

Die Aufgabe des Wettbewerbs besteht darin, flexible Lösungen zu entwickeln und Attraktivität und Aktivität zu schaffen – sowohl für diejenigen, die das Gebiet heute durchqueren und besuchen, als auch für diejenigen, die zukünftig dort leben werden. Dabei kommt es darauf an, dass die unterschiedlichen Lösungsvorschläge miteinander in Verbindung stehen und durch ein einheitliches Thema verknüpft sind, sodass sich das Gebiet von Anfang wie ein Stadtviertel anfühlt. Gut geplante temporäre Architekturen, Gebäude, Parks und Plätze tragen dazu bei, ein sicheres und attraktives Viertel zu schaffen, und fördern das Engagement und die Identifikation während der langen und komplexen Bauphase. Die Lösungen können sowohl standortspezifisch als auch flexibel sein.

Um die Ziele des Pariser Abkommens und der Agenda 2030 zu erreichen, brauchen wir eine starke Neuausrichtung unserer Städte. Dafür benötigen wir neue Denkweisen, um in kurzer Zeit weit voranzukommen. Die Stadt Västerås wünscht sich, dass Mälarporten eines der Projekte wird, die uns zeigen, wie das geht.

Die gleichen ehrgeizigen Ziele, die für das gesamte Projekt Mälarporten formuliert wurden, sollten auch während der Planungs- und Bauphase angestrebt werden. Die Stadt Västerås möchte zeigen, wie es möglich ist, ein Gebiet, das heute als verlassen und unpersönlich empfunden wird, auf dynamische Weise mit neuem Leben und Begegnungen zu füllen.

Das Gebiet soll viele verschiedene Zielgruppen anziehen und nicht nur diejenigen, die früh zuziehen. Das Gebiet muss Platz für alle bieten und für Menschen aus ganz Västerås und darüber hinaus interessant sein. Wichtige Aspekte zur Schaffung einer lebensfähigen Stadt, in der sich die Menschen gerne aufhalten und willkommen fühlen, sind Zugänglichkeit, Integration, Kreativität und Sicherheit.

Die Umgestaltung sollte aus den Bedürfnissen der Menschen erwachsen und sich daraus entwickeln. Die Bewohner sollten an der Entwicklung des Gebietes gestaltend mitwirken. Kinder und Jugendliche sind die Zielgruppen, die das Gebiet heute besuchen und entdecken, die hier aufwachsen und die sich entscheiden, hier herzuziehen, wenn sie erwachsen sind.

Es werden nicht nur die Menschen sein, die dem Gebiet Leben einhauchen. Heute gibt es kein Grün, und das Gebiet besteht aus undurchlässigem Boden. Damit die Stadt lebendig wird, müssen diese Flächen umgewandelt und mit neuer Vegetation und biologischer Vielfalt bepflanzt werden, um eine grüne und gegenüber dem Klimawandel widerstandsfähige Stadt zu schaffen.

Location

Västerås is growing and within thirty years from now the population will grow to an estimated 230,000 people. Mälarporten is an important area in this development, with its location close to the city centre, Lake Mälaren and important public transportation nodes. Mälarporten offers amazing possibilities to create an entirely new neighbourhood that is both innovative and sustainable. The area today consists of inaccessible land, offices and industries that in the future will host 6,000 to 7,000 housing units and 10,000 workplaces in well-designed living environments. A new transportation hub will simplify travels to and within Västerås, and also strengthen the link between the city centre and the water.

The competition task is to develop flexible solutions that create attractiveness and activity for those who pass through and visit the area today, as well as for those who move in early. It is important that the solutions are connected and linked to a unifying theme that makes the area feel like a city district from the beginning. The proposals need to show a clear concept that builds on and develops the identity of the area. Well-planned temporary architecture, buildings, parks and places aid in creating a safe and attractive neighbourhood and bring forth commitment and pride during the long and complex construction period. The solutions can be both site-specific and flexible. They could be rebuildable with add-ons so that they can be moved around in the area as it is being built, and at the same time create character, excitement and new dynamics.

In order to reach the goals in the Paris agreement and Agenda 2030 we need a powerful readjustment of our cities. This means that we need new ways of thinking and to take many steps forward within a short period of time. The city of Västerås wants Mälarporten to be one of the projects that shows us how.

The same high ambitions that are formulated for the entire project of Mälarporten should be aspired to also during the planning and construction period. The city of Västerås wants to show how it is possible to, in a dynamic way, fill an area that today is perceived as deserted and impersonal, with new life and meetings between people.

The area must provide places for everyone and attract different target groups from all over Västerås and beyond. Important aspects are accessibility, inclusion, creativity and safety in order to create a viable city where people want to be and feel welcome.

The transformation should grow and develop out of people's needs. The area should be developed together with the inhabitants, who will be co-creators. Children and young people are designated target groups to visit and discover the area today, for growing up here, and for choosing to move here when they grow up.

It will not only be the people that give life to the area. Today there is no greenery and the area consists of impermeable land. In order for the city to become alive and sustainable, these areas need to be converted and introduced with new vegetation and biodiversity in order to create a city that is green and resilient to climate change.

Bevölkerung   Inhabitants
ca. 154.000

Betrachtungsraum   Study Site
90 ha

Projektgebiet   Project Site
16 ha

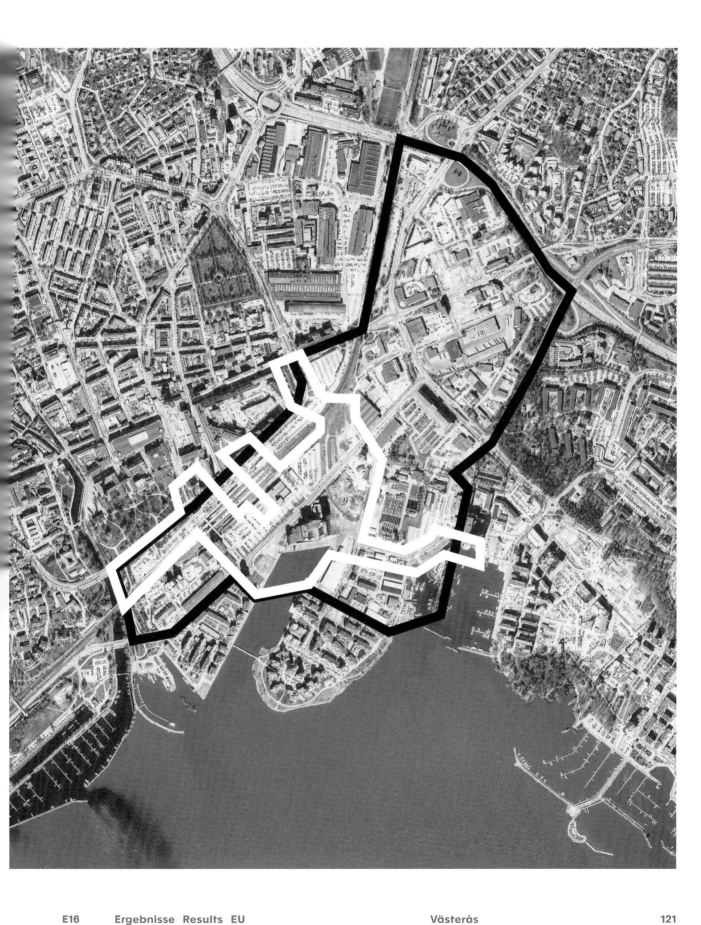

Vitality!

Projekt

Unser Team bietet dem Europan-Projekt Västerås einen metabolistischen Zugang zu nachhaltiger urbanistischer Entwicklung. Unsere Philosophie geht von einer vielschichtigen und rechtzeitigen Co-Evolution aus, bei der soziale und ökologische Bereiche ebenso in einer Synergie miteinander verbunden sind wie mit der Gemeinde Västerås. Wir gehen das Thema des Wettbewerbs von Europan 16 mit Vitalität an, von den Grundlagen der Architektur lebendiger Städte bis hin zu inklusiven Gemeinschaftsgebäuden.

Unser Plan für demokratische Beteiligung wird regenerative Rückkoppelungsschleifen anstoßen. Die Co-Evolution wird mithilfe von Themenpavillons stattfinden:

1 Sozial – für Zusammenkünfte, Veranstaltungen und Workshops
2 Grün – die Erde aus Kontaminierung, um sie zu düngen und Bäume zu pflanzen
3 Wasser – reinigende Wirkung von Algen auf verschmutztes Wasser, um einen Lebensraum für Wasserlebewesen neu zu beleben und Ökosysteme unter Wasser zu entwickeln.

Team

– Pino Heye (DE), Student der Stadtplanung
– Katharina Ipsen (DE), Architektin
– Cécile Kermaïdic (FR), Studentin der Architektur
– Wolfram Meiner (DE), Student der Architektur
– Tecla Spruit (NL), Anthropologin

Project

Our team offers Europan's Västerås site a metabolistic approach to sustainable urban development. Our philosophical concept is multi-layered coevolution in time, in which the social and the ecological are intertwined in synergy, as is the case for much of the municipality of Västerås. We address the themes of the Europan 16 competition with vitality, from the foundations of the architecture of living cities to inclusive community building.

Our plan for democratic participation will spark such regenerative feedback loops. This coevolution will take place based on themed pavilions:

1 Social: for gatherings, events, and workshops
2 Green: previously contaminated soil is fertilized and planted with trees
3 Water: algae helps purify polluted water in order to give rise to a new habitat for aquatic species and develop underwater ecosystems.

Team

– Pino Heye (DE), urban planning student
– Katharina Ipsen (DE), architect
– Cécile Kermaïdic (FR), architecture student
– Wolfram Meiner (DE), architecture student
– Tecla Spruit (NL), anthropologist

Västerås (SE) Vitality!

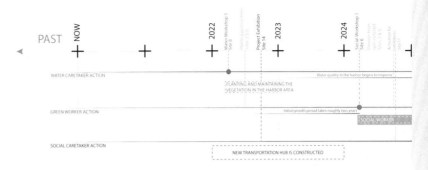

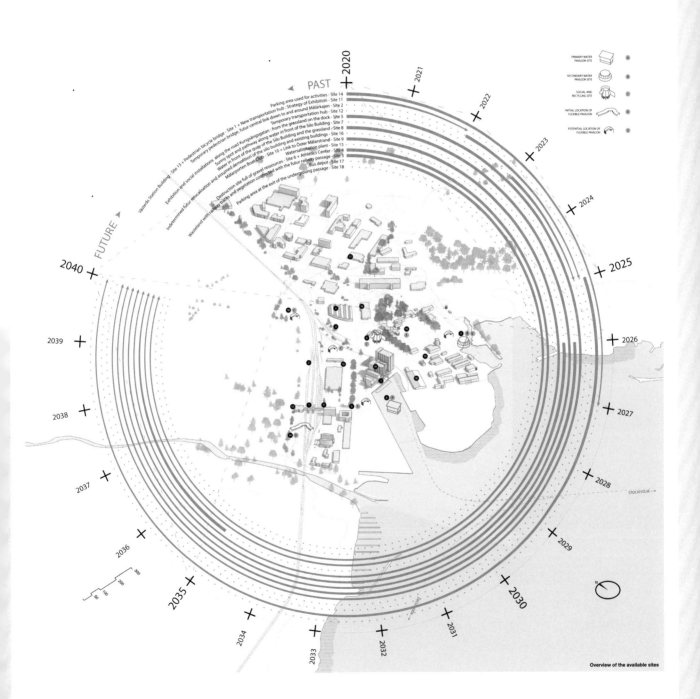

Overview of the available sites

Västerås (SE) Vitality!

PRECISE STRATEGY UNTIL THIS TIME   ACTION PLAN UNTIL 2034

2026 | 2027 | 2028 | 2029 | 2030 | 2031 | 2032 | 2033 | 2034

HARBOR IS DECOMMISSIONED

WATER CARETAKER ASSOCIATION IS ESTABLISHED DURING THE WORKSHOP

ASSOCIATION IS ESTABLISHED DURING THE WORKSHOP

THE NEW AREA BECOMES MORE POPULATED

Continuous resource management on site 6 starts

LARGE SCALE CONSTRUCTION STARTS

During off-season all pavilions become available to all members of the public as sites for events.

FACILITY CARETAKER ASSOCIATION IS ESTABLISHED DURING THE WORKSHOP

Map of Lake Mälaren

Weather Data of Västerås

WATER STRATEGY

Our immediate intervention starts in the harbor, at site 8, with the construction of the first floating pavilion. The location of the first pavilion allows ships to enter the bay until 2027.

The pavilions in the Malarporten bay will allow to host a variety of workshops about the topic of water, for example educational activities such as water cleansing. They will demonstrate the process of vegetalisation as a pedagogical tool for children and young adults. The events enable the inhabitants of Västerås to establish a personal relationship with the aquatic habitat. Finally, they will organize and fit into a global network of people, knowledge and skills.

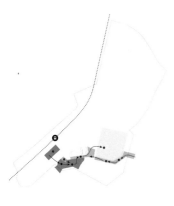

Relevant sites for the water strategy

Construction Detail 1:100

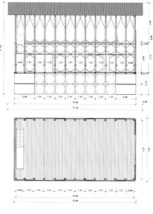

Construction Detail 1:100

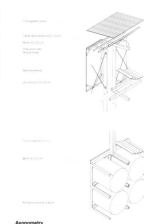

Axonometry

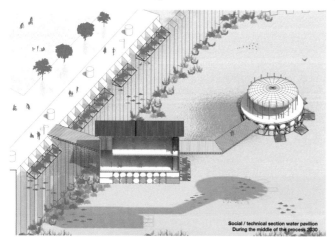

Social / technical section water pavilion
During the middle of the process 2030

Interconected metabolism
„Trophic Network"

WATER WORKSHOP1

BRIEF
The community of Västerås is invited to investigate the vast potential of the city's water sytem through the lens of metabolism, allowing participants to experiences the interplay of the different infrastructures that are often underappreciated in contemporary urban planning processes. The goal after one week of work is the development of a holistic strategy for Malarporten and the transformation by creating a system that integrates social, technological, and natural aspects.

FLOW IN VÄSTERÅS
Following a thorough analysis of city's water system and the formulation of a holistic strategy to increase the water quality using natural processes, participants will explore and conduct their own research which will form the basis for the design phase, tangible ideas for the transformation will be collected and further developed in groups. The collected research, design ideas and a map of the social resources will be presented during a public event on the last day of the workshop.

THE RESULT
Following the workshop, a strong network of supporters within the community of Västerås will form a new association and enable real change and transform the water system as caretakers of the water infrastructure. Their knowledge will grow through cohesion within the group and future workshops with similar, relvant topics.

Västerås (SE) Vitality!

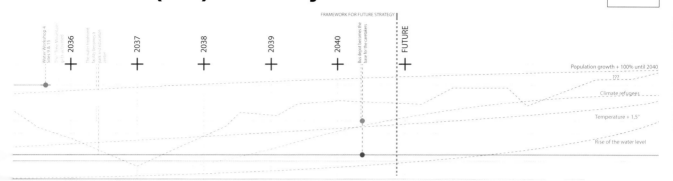

GREEN STRATEGY

First, this strategy will be experimented on the site 6 and 3.

Indeed, the will is to connect the exiting trees, that we will call the « Mountain » to link, spread and intensified the mountain forest. It will become a biodiversity reservoir, a new green habitat and a new parc for Vasteras. When the bus depot on the site 17, will be available in 2040, the process will move to that location. The first intention for the green strategy is to deal with polluted ground and fertilized the soil by growing a forest. Eutrophic elm-ash forests is in place on the shore of the Malaren lake.

The Fraxinus excelsior European Ash, the Ulmus glabra wych elm, and also Pedunculate English Oak, are in numbers. Those species will be planted to grow the forest. Especially, the European Ash and the peduculate Oak are tolerant to the climate change, resisting to heat of raising temperature's cities. The strategy of planting will be taking care by experts, biosphere specialists, landscape designers and gardeners, first plantation will be the pioneer trees.

They will have the responsibility to monitoring the place. This is the same strategy that is used for the water pavilions and growth of aquatic plants. Pioneer trees are the fast ones to settles on big destroyed landscapes. Those will be the first trees to grow. Those trees will prepare the soil for the next stage of growth. We need that intervention to grow the pioneers trees.

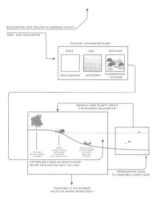

Schematic action plan
for the water improvement

Social pavilion during the first workshop in 2024

SOCIAL STRATEGY

The social pavilions purpose is to create social cohesion. The social events will starts in front of Vasteras Station, on the site 14 and site 11.

As the social pavilions links Vasteras Station to the destruction site, site 6, we will activate the Kungsängsgatan street, throughout exhibitions, events, interventions as sitting and meeting places and pavilions to create a link between the two location. Inclusion : Dynamics of inclusion and exclusion can become processes of home-making and of community-building by facing uncomfortable socio-cultural issues. It is easier to address these issues in a communal space which allows personal freedom of expression. We hope our pavilions will be such spaces.

To arrive at the point in which all individuals feel free as at home in a space certain thresholds need to be surpassed and worked (see diagram). At the start it will be the attractiveness and cosiness of the pavilions that will captivate citizens. They will have to be maintained, as to ensure their continual use. After using the space for a certain amount of time visitors will feel co-owners of the spaces and thus feeling free in them. This freedom allows for co-creation in space by discussing together on their use. This will lead to joint decisions which will constantly be re-evaluated in social interactions and the previously mentioned democratic processes. When individuals or groups feel excluded this process tends to go in reverse – see diagram. It is easy to expect the excluded to do all the work of home-making and fitting in through continual effort. However, home-making is a connective bridge between individuals in boundaries of respect and curiosity in understanding. Communication is key both to reach out and include, as well as to ask to be included in all ways an individual feels comfortable.

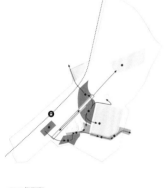

Relevant sites for the social strategy

Relevant sites for the recyling strategy

Water pavilion
Almost finished 2034
Original image
courtesy of Lars Hedberg

Thema 3
Lebendige Städte –
Wir brauchen Visionen

Topic 3
Living Cities –
We Need Visions

Thema 3
Lebendige Städte –
Wir brauchen Visionen

Topic 3
Living Cities –
We Need Visions

Schule als Gesellschafts- raum am Beispiel der Gemeinde Dettmannsdorf

Verständnis, gegenseitige Akzeptanz und ein selbst-kritisches soziales Miteinander beruhen auf Wissen, Begegnung und Austausch. In den städtischen und ländlichen Räumen heutiger Gesellschaften steht immer weniger nicht kommerzialisierter Raum zur Aneignung für jedermann zur Verfügung. Gesellschaftshäuser und Kulturbauten mit differenzierten Raumprogrammen sind praktisch aus unserem Alltag verschwunden, kleine Kommunen und Stadtbezirke können sich Bibliotheken meist nicht mehr leisten. Gleichzeitig erleben Zentralbibliotheken in großen Städten eine Renaissance als Arbeits-, Lern-, Denk- und Veranstaltungsräume und als Treffpunkte. Wir wissen längst um die Bedeutung der Bildung für gesellschaftlichen Wohlstand und die Gleichheit von individuellen Entwicklungsmöglichkeiten. Schulen sind heute neben Bibliotheken die letzten verbliebenen nicht kommerzialisierten Räume, in denen sich Menschen unterschiedlichen Alters und unterschiedlicher Herkunft begegnen.

Ein Beispiel aus Nordostmecklenburg zeigt, wie es einer kleinen Gemeinde aus eigener Kraft gelungen ist, sich mit dem Erhalt einer Schule als Lebensraum und als Sozialgemeinschaft zu revitalisieren.

Aufgrund einer Laune der Geschichte erzählen die maximal 120 Jahre alten Straßendörfer in der hügeligen Landschaft mit Alleen und weiten Räumen wenig von ihrer jahrtausendealten Siedlungsgeschichte, einzig die übrig gebliebenen Gutshäuser, in fast jedem Dorf, die Kirchen und Großsteingräber verweisen darauf, dass es hier auch schon zu früheren Zeiten Leben gegeben haben muss.

Die Gemeinde Dettmannsdorf liegt ca. 25 km östlich von Rostock und besteht aus sechs Straßendörfern, fünf davon ehemalige Gutsstellen, in einem Umkreis von drei Kilometern. Sind die Bauten von 1900 noch von einem gewissen gestalterischen Anspruch geprägt, ist alles Folgende auf den das Gebäude bestimmenden Zweck ausgerichtet. Aller begrenzter Charme entspringt dieser Vereinfachung.

Dies trifft auch auf die Bauten der Schule zu, die in den 1950er, 70er und 80er Jahren in der Mitte des Dorfes errichtet wurden, ohne dass jemand darüber nachgedacht zu haben scheint, wie sie zueinander oder zum Dorf stehen. Der Standort wurde 2003 als staatliche Schule geschlossen und 2005 von Bürgerinnen und Bürgern der Gemeinde und dem gemeinnützigen Schulförderverein Dettmannsdorf e. V. mit zwölf Schülern als Evangelische Schule im ehemals verlassenen Schulbestand wiedereröffnet. Die Akzeptanz einer freien Schule im sensiblen Mikrokosmos Dorf ist nicht selbstverständlich. Neben dem Pädagogischen war die Entwicklung in den folgenden Jahren stets davon geprägt, die Räume der Schule besser in die Dorfstruktur zu integrieren und alle Angebote auch für die Dettmannsdorfer und die Region zur Verfügung zu stellen.

In ersten Schritten der Aneignung wurden zwischen 2010 und 2012 zunächst die Fassaden der alten Schulgebäude aufgefrischt, die Außenräume neu gegliedert, ein ehemals unwirtliches Gefüge zum begehrtesten Ort erklärt und dem Schulareal mit einer Bühne eine neue

Mitte geschenkt, um die sich fortan alles Geschehen organisiert. Der Pavillon in offener Bauweise ist in zwei Räume gegliedert und wird von Flächen und Stützen aus Stahl und Holz gebildet.

Die Bühne kann verschieden genutzt werden – als überdachter Pausenraum an Regentagen, als Sommerklassenzimmer oder Tribüne bei Sportfesten, als allseitig offener Bühnenraum für verschiedene Veranstaltungen von Schule und Dorf usw. Im Zweifel ist die Bühne einfach nur ein Ort, von dem aus sich die Welt betrachten lässt und der je nach Wetter und einfallendem Licht anders in Erscheinung tritt.

Die Schule wächst bis 2017 auf 400 Schülerinnen und Schüler an und wird mit dem Neubau einer 1,5-zügigen Grundschule mit Gemeinschaftseinrichtungen für alle Klassenstufen und einem Jugendwanderquartier in Zwischennutzung erweitert. Der zweigeschossige Neubau begleitet die Außenräume der Schule: Er bildet den Auftakt zu deren Campus, schützt vor Witterung, fasst die Räume ein und ist Ort der Begegnung und des zwanglosen Austauschs. Er ist so gegliedert, dass an drei Seiten im Erdgeschoss entlang der Außenräume ein Gebäudeüberhang und im Obergeschoss zur Grundstücksgrenze ein Rettungsbalkon entstehen.

Man betritt das Gebäude vom Schulhof. Cafeteria, Mehrzweckraum und Bibliothek liegen als offener Raumverbund am Haupteingang und können über eine Schiebewand zu einer großen Veranstaltungsfläche verbunden werden. Weitere Gemeinschaftseinrichtungen wie Lehrküche, Bandraum und Werkstätten befinden sich ebenfalls im Erdgeschoss, mit direktem Zugang zu den Außenräumen. Die Gemeinschaftseinrichtungen stehen außerhalb der Schulzeiten der Dorfgemeinschaft zur Verfügung. Der Mehrzweckraum lässt sich in zwei unabhängige Schlafbereiche gliedern, sodass das Erdgeschoss in den Ferien als Jugendwanderquartier umgewidmet werden kann.

Im Obergeschoss gibt es den Kunst- und Musikraum für alle Schülerinnen und Schüler sowie die Räume der Grundschule mit Hort. Alle Klassenräume überblicken den Schulhof. Entlang einer inneren Enfilade liegt jeweils zwei Klassenräumen ein Gruppenraum gegenüber. Bei Bedarf lassen sich die Klassenräume einzeln oder gemeinsam über das Öffnen der Schiebewand mit dem Gruppenraum verbinden. So kann ein differenzierter Raum für individuelles Lernen geschaffen oder, bei Hortbetrieb am Nachmittag, im offenen Raumverbund gleichzeitig Spielen, Basteln und Lernen angeboten werden. Über die Enfilade, den eigentlichen Verhandlungsraum, besteht immer Austausch zwischen benachbarten Klassenraumgruppen sowie Zugang zu den dazwischen angeordneten Garderoben und Nebenräumen.

Die Schule ist inzwischen wegen ihrer Lernerfolge, der Digitalisierung und ihren Bildungsangeboten auch unter Pädagogen bundesweit bekannt. Im Dorf haben sich Geschäfte, Tankstelle, Friseur, Physiotherapie, Kosmetik, Restaurant, Kita und Seniorenwohnen, Zahnarzt und Allgemeinmediziner gehalten; die Einwohnerzahl, derzeit um die 1000, wächst, wie auch die Geburtenrate. Staatlich gewollt, gefördert oder unterstützt wurde das nicht, das Dorf hat es trotzdem getan.

Es gibt in der Gemeinde Dettmannsdorf mit ihren über 800 Vereinsmitgliedern in Sport, Kultur und Kirche, mit diversen Festivitäten, Veranstaltungen und der monatlich erscheinenden Dorfzeitung inzwischen so etwas wie

Bürgerstolz und ein vielfältiges Engagement in allen Altersgruppen. Über die Jahre ist das Bewusstsein gewachsen, dass die Gemeinschaft nur so gut ist wie das, was man selbst dazu beiträgt.

Die Evangelische Schule Dettmannsdorf belegt eindrucksvoll, wie wichtig es ist, die Räume der Schule in der Mitte der Gesellschaft zu halten und sie auch für diese zu öffnen. In Dänemark, Holland oder Japan weiß man längst davon und integriert in die Schulen Arztpraxen, Arbeitsämter, öffnet Bibliotheken und Mehrzweckräume für die Kommunen, verortet die Schulen so in der Mitte der Gesellschaft als nicht kommerziellen Begegnungsraum. Als Ort des Austauschs unterschiedlicher Altersgruppen und sozialer Schichten wird Schule so zur täglichen Übung von Gemeinschaft und gegenseitiger Verantwortung.

Unsere Gesellschaftsräume sind ein Spiegelbild dessen, was wir uns selbst zutrauen, was wir uns zugestehen und auch was wir von uns selbst einfordern. Räume können Handlungen begleiten und anregen oder unterbinden; einen wesentlichen Beitrag zu Würde, Selbstachtung und gegenseitiger Akzeptanz leisten – oder diffuse Empfindungen bestärken. Robuste und belastbare Gesellschaften brauchen Gemeinschaft stiftende Bildungsräume in ihrer Mitte.

Marika Schmidt
Dipl.-Ing. Architektin, Inhaberin mrschmidt Architekten GmbH, spezialisiert auf Schulbau, Auszeichnungen wie BDA-Architekturpreis Nike für soziales Engagement 2019, diverse Lehrtätigkeiten und Publikationen zur Architektur

School as a Communal Space Based on the Example of the Municipality of Dettmannsdorf

Understanding, mutual acceptance, and self-critical social coexistence are based on knowledge, encounters, and exchange. In the urban and rural spaces of societies today, ever less non-commercialized space is available for people to appropriate. Clubhouses and cultural buildings with differentiated spatial programs have practically vanished from our everyday life, and small municipalities and city districts are generally no longer able to afford libraries. Along with the disappearance of non-commercial, publicly accessible spaces from society, central libraries in big cities have been undergoing a renaissance as spaces to work, learn, think, attend events, and come into contact with people. We have long been aware of how important education is for social prosperity and an equality of possibilities is for personal development. Aside from libraries, schools are today the last remaining non-commercialized spaces in which people of different ages and backgrounds encounter one another.

One example from northeastern Mecklenburg shows how a small municipality has managed to revitalize itself on its own by preserving a school as a social community and living environment.

Due to a whim of history, the street villages, which are a maximum of 120 years old, in the undulating landscape of Mecklenburg, with its avenues and vast spaces, say little about their thousands-of-years-old history of settlement. The churches, megalithic tombs, and manor houses that have remained in nearly every village are the only things that make reference to the fact that there must already have been life here in earlier times.

The municipality of Dettmannsdorf is located roughly 25 km to the east of Rostock and consists of six street villages, five of them former estates, in a radius of three kilometres. With the passage of time, the structural level of the buildings has sunk. While the buildings from 1900 are still characterized by a certain design aspiration, everything that has followed is oriented towards the purpose that defines the building. All the limited charm arises from this simplification.

This also holds true for the school buildings that were erected in the centre of the village in the 1950s, 70s, and 80s, even though no one ever thought about what relationship the buildings should have to one another or to the village. The site was closed as a state school in 2003, and reopened as a Protestant school with twelve pupils in the previously abandoned school buildings in 2005 by citizens of the municipality and the non-profit Schulförderverein Dettmannsdorf e. V. The acceptance of an independent school in the sensitive microcosm of the village is not self-explanatory in any way. Besides pedagogical aspects, the development of the school in the years that followed was always shaped by the notion that the spaces of the school should be integrated more optimally in the structure of the village and that the range of offerings also be available for residents and the region.

In the initial stages of appropriation, the façades of the old school buildings were first refreshed between 2010 and 2012, the outdoor spaces restructured, a previously inhospitable framework clarifies, and the school grounds given a new centre with a stage, so as to organize everything that would take place from then on. The pavilion with an open architecture is structured into two spaces and shaped by surfaces and supports of steel and wood.

The stage can be used in various ways – as a roofed-over place for breaks on rainy days, a summer classroom, stands for sports festivals, and a stage space open to all sides for a range of events by the school and the village, and so on. In case of doubt, the stage is simply a place from which to observe the world, and takes on a different appearance depending on the weather and the incidence of light.

By 2017, the school had grown to have 400 pupils and been expanded with a new primary school building, with communal facilities for all the pupils and a youth hostel in interim use. The new school building accompanies the outdoor spaces of the school: it forms the start of the school campus, offers protection against the weather, frames the spaces, and is a place for informal exchange and encounters. The two-storey new building is structured in such a way that there is a building overhang along the outdoor spaces of the school on the ground floor and a rescue balcony on the upper storey towards the boundary of the site.

One enters the building from the school courtyards. The cafeteria, a multipurpose space, and library are situated as open interconnected spaces at the main entrance and can be put together to create a large area for events by means of a sliding partition. Other communal facilities, such as a teaching kitchen, band room, and workshops are also located on the ground floor, with direct access to the outdoor spaces. The village community has access to the communal facilities outside school hours. The multipurpose space can be structured into two independent sleeping areas, so that the ground floor can also be made into a youth hostel during holidays.

The upper storey has an art and music space for all the pupils as well as the rooms of the primary school. All the classrooms have a view of the school courtyard. Two classrooms each are situated opposite a group space along an internal enfilade. When necessary, one or both classrooms can be connected with the group space by means of a sliding partition, so that a differentiated space for individual learning is possible or pupils can play, do arts and crafts, and learn in the open interconnected space during the afterschool care operations. Via the enfilade, the real space for negotiation, there is always exchange between neighbouring groups of classrooms as well as access to the cloakrooms and ancillary spaces between them.

The school is meanwhile also well known by teachers throughout Germany as a result of its learning results, digitization, and educational offerings. Businesses, a petrol station, a hairdresser, a physiotherapy practice, a cosmetic salon, a restaurant, day nursery and housing for senior citizens, and a dentist and general practitioner have managed to hold on in the village, the number of residents has grown to roughly 1000 residents, and the birth rate has increased as well. This was not desired, funded, or supported by the state – but the village managed to do so anyway.

In the municipality of Dettmannsdorf, with its over 800 members of sports clubs, cultural associations, and churches, diverse festivities, events, and a village newspaper published on a monthly basis, there is now something like civic pride and multifaceted engagement in all age groups. Over the years, the awareness that the community is only as good as what one makes of it has grown.

The Evangelische Schule Dettmannsdorf impressively shows how important it is to keep school spaces in the centre of society and to open oneself up to them as well. This has long been common knowledge in Denmark, Holland, or Japan, and the doctors' practices, employment office, open libraries, and multipurpose spaces for the municipality that are integrated in schools situate them in the centre of society as a non-commercial space for encounters. As a place for exchange between different age groups and social classes, the school thus becomes an everyday exercise in community and mutual responsibility.

Our social spaces are a reflection of what we trust ourselves to create, what we allow ourselves, and also what we demand from ourselves. Spaces can accompany and inspire or inhibit activities, make a substantial contribution to dignity, self-esteem, and mutual acceptance – or reinforce diffuse perceptions. Robust and resilient societies need educational spaces that build community at their centre.

Marika Schmidt
Dipl.-Ing. architect, owner of mrschmidt Architekten GmbH, specialization in school buildings, awards including the BDA Architecture Prize Nike for Social Engagement 2019, diverse teaching activities and publications on architecture

1

2

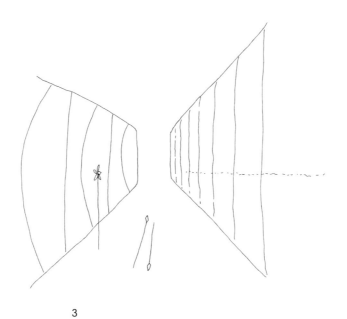

3

1	Schulgemeinschaft	1 School community
2	Schulgesellschaft	2 School society
3	Verortung	3 Localization

Zwischenräume – Prinzipien der Koexistenz für gemischte Typologien

Das Thema „Living Cities" zielt darauf ab, „lebendige, integrative und durchmischte Stadträume"[1] zu entwickeln. Ein Hintergrund für diese Zielsetzung ist die heutige Diversifizierung von Lebensmodellen. Zum Leben in der „Normalfamilie" sind neue Formen wie Patchwork-familien, Senioren-WGs oder das generationsübergreifende Co-Living hinzugekommen. Gleichzeitig haben sich die Arbeitsmodelle verändert. Durch die fortschreitende Digitalisierung und Globalisierung hat sich das ortsunabhängige Arbeiten mittlerweile etabliert. Wir müssen nicht mehr an dem Ort arbeiten, an dem wir auch wohnen. Wir müssen nicht mal mehr im Büro arbeiten. Wie wir sehen werden, hat die Vervielfältigung der Möglichkeiten zu leben und zu arbeiten auch die Gestaltung von architektonischen und urbanen Typologien beeinflusst.

Ein weiterer Hintergrund für das Thema von Europan 16 ist die Art und Weise, wie wir Stadtentwicklung betreiben. Angesichts des Klimawandels wollen wir die expansive, Flächen verschwendende und autoverkehrgetriebene Form des Städtebaus der Moderne hinter uns lassen, uns auf die Innenentwicklung und auf den Umbau der bestehenden Stadtsubstanz fokussieren, um so sparsam und effizient mit der kostbaren Ressource Boden umgehen zu können – ein wichtiges Projekt, das allerdings nicht ganz so einfach umsetzbar ist.[2] Die gesellschaftliche Vielfalt wird dadurch nicht mehr in der Fläche verteilt, sondern in einen bestehenden sozialen und räumlichen Kontext integriert. Es geht also darum, Koexistenz zu ermöglichen und zu organisieren: das Zusammenleben unterschiedlicher sozialer Gruppen im selben Raum.

Die gesellschaftlichen Entwicklungen stellen neue Anforderungen an Architektur und Städtebau. Hieraus sind in der letzten Dekade nicht nur neue Formen der koproduktiven Projektentwicklung entstanden. Es wurden auch neue Ansätze für dichte, gemischte und kontextuell integrierte Architektur- und Stadtraumtypologien konzipiert und erfolgreich umgesetzt, die versprechen, den vielfältigen Bedürfnissen der diversifizierten Gesellschaft gerecht zu werden. Ich möchte auf einige dieser neuen Typologien eingehen und ihre wesentlichen Entwurfsprinzipien erörtern. Die These, die ich dabei verfolgen werde, ist, dass in den Entwürfen solcher gemischter Typologien die Artikulation und bewusste Gestaltung von gemeinschaftlichen Zwischenräumen eine immer wichtigere Rolle spielt.

Beim Zusammenleben mehrerer Menschen müssen gemischte Typologien sowohl individuelle Freiheit, Eigenständigkeit und Rückzug für die Einzelnen ermöglichen als auch die Teilhabe am gemeinschaftlichen Leben zulassen. Ein Schlüsselprojekt, das den Diskurs zu neuen Wohnformen beflügelt hat, ist das Moriyama House des Architekten Ryue Nishizawa in Tokio. Es handelt sich hierbei um ein Mehrfamilienhaus, dessen Wohneinheiten nicht klassisch um einen Treppenhauskern angeordnet und geschossweise gestapelt sind, sondern auf einer Fläche verteilt werden. Die Wohneinheiten umfangen einen Garten, in dem Boxen mit gemeinschaftlichen Basisnutzungen wie Toilette, Bad oder Kochzeile verstreut sind.[3] Der gemeinschaftliche Zwischenraum wird durch die einzelnen Wohneinheiten begrenzt.

In ihnen kann man zu zweit oder allein wohnen. Sie verfügen auch über individuelle Außenräume auf den Dächern sowie eigene Toiletten und Kochzeilen. Diese scheinbar redundante Doppelung an Wohninfrastruktur gibt den Bewohnenden die Freiheit, am gemeinschaftlichen Leben im Garten teilzuhaben oder sich individuell zurückzuziehen.

Die Redundanz an (gemeinschaftlicher und individueller) Basiswohninfrastruktur finden wir auch im Clusterwohnen wieder – einer Wohntypologie, die im genossenschaftlichen Wohnungsbau in der Schweiz bereits vielfach umgesetzt wurde und mittlerweile auch in Deutschland beliebt geworden ist. Sie ermöglicht das Zusammenleben von unterschiedlichen sozialen Gruppen auf engem Raum. Es können dort zum Beispiel WGs aus Paaren von Seniorinnen und Senioren leben, denen das Einfamilienhaus nach dem Auszug der Kinder zu leer oder sein Erhalt zu aufwendig geworden ist. Gleichermaßen ist sie für WGs aus erwerbstätigen Alleinerziehenden, die sich die Betreuung ihrer Kinder teilen, für Singles oder für das Co-Living von all diesen Gruppen geeignet. Das Wohnprojekt von Duplex Architekten auf dem Hunziker-Areal in Zürich bietet beispielsweise eigenständige Ein- und Zweizimmerwohnungen mit Toiletten und Kochzeilen, zwischen denen ein gemeinschaftlicher Wohnraum mit derselben Infrastruktur liegt. Ähnlich funktioniert das Projekt Kraftwerk 2 von Adrian Streich Architekten, ebenfalls in Zürich. Hier sind die Wohncluster zwischen einem und vier Zimmern groß, was ein Zusammenleben von Singles, Familien und auch mehreren Generationen möglich macht. Beide Beispiele weisen tiefe Grundrisse auf, die im Geschosswohnungsbau sonst nicht üblich sind. In den inneren, dunkleren Bereichen werden die gemeinschaftlichen Zwischenräume angeordnet, die durch intelligente Lichtführung minimal natürlich belichtet sind. So können die erhöhten Kosten, die die redundante Infrastruktur erzeugt, durch zusätzliche verwertbare Geschossfläche abgefedert werden.

Ein weiteres Prinzip des Zwischenraums nutzen Gebäude, in denen Wohn- und Arbeitsräume gemischt werden. Neben flexiblen Wohnungsgrundrissen, die nicht mehr zwischen Arbeits-, Wohn- und Schlafzimmer unterscheiden, wird die Mischung durch semi-öffentliche Erdgeschosszonen erzeugt, die einen abgestuften Übergang zwischen öffentlichem Außenraum und privaten Wohnungen in den Obergeschossen schaffen. Das Projekt Spreefeld der Arbeitsgemeinschaft Silvia Carpaneto, fatkoehl und BARarchitekten in Berlin bietet in den Obergeschossen ebenfalls Clusterwohnungen an. Im Erdgeschoss befinden sich Gemeinschaftsküche, Gemeinschaftsräume für sportliche Aktivitäten wie Yogakurse oder für Veranstaltungen, Werkstatt, Büros und Arbeitsräume, die jeweils zur Wohnung hinzugemietet werden können. Solche Arbeitsmöglichkeiten im Wohnhaus sind durch die Etablierung von Homeoffice immer beliebter geworden. Man muss nicht in den engen Verhältnissen der eigenen Wohnung arbeiten und kann dennoch „zu Hause" bleiben.

Auch Bürogebäude sind mittlerweile gemischt und bedienen sich dafür gemeinschaftlicher Zwischenräume. Co-Working-Spaces sind flexible Großraumbüros, die klassische Bürozellen mit Bereichen für individuell anmietbare Tische mischen, um unterschiedliche Arbeitsformen zu ermöglichen. Je nach Bedarf können ein eigenes, abschließbares Büro, eine Arbeitsinsel mit mehreren Arbeitsplätzen oder nur ein Arbeitstisch gemietet werden. Zusätzlich werden gemeinschaftliche Nutzungen wie Küchen, Konferenzräume oder Lounges mit Tischtennisplatten angeboten. Alle für das Arbeiten notwendigen Services wie Internet, Drucker oder Kaffeeautomaten sind oftmals im Mietpreis enthalten. Das macht es für Menschen, die an einem Ort leben und an einem anderen kurzfristig und temporär arbeiten, sehr einfach. Sie müssen nur ihren Laptop anschließen und können sofort starten. Co-Working ersetzt mittlerweile auch bei großen Firmen wie Facebook, Zalando oder Axel Springer das klassische Zellenbüro. In den letzten Jahren haben diese Firmen ihre Headquarter als gigantische Arbeitslandschaften mit vielfältigen und flexiblen Arrangements von Arbeitsplätzen konzipiert, um jedem Projekt eine individuelle Team- und Arbeitsorganisation zu ermöglichen. Die Idee der experimentellen Bürolandschaften des Quickborner Teams aus den 1960er Jahren wird nun flächendeckend umgesetzt, mit dem Unterschied, dass die Räume des „New Work" zusätzlich gemeinschaftliche Zwischenräume zum Arbeiten, Essen oder Abhängen anbieten, um die Zeit im Büro und die soziale Bindung zum Unternehmen zu erhöhen.

Zwischenräume spielen auch auf städtebaulicher Ebene bei der Mischung von produzierendem Gewerbe, Wohnen und Arbeiten eine wichtige Rolle. Wurden diese konflikthaften Nutzungen bislang durch die Verteilung auf der Fläche getrennt, so machen es digitale und emissionsarme Produktionsmethoden mit 3D-Druckern oder Robotern nun möglich, sie vertikal zu stapeln, da das Wohnen durch die Produktion nicht mehr wesentlich gestört wird. Die Stapelung wird oft durch Sockeltypologien umgesetzt, die an amerikanische Hotelhochhäuser mit ausgedehnten Lobbys in den Sockeln erinnern. Im tiefen und schlecht belichteten Sockel können Nutzungen etabliert werden, die viel Platz und wenig Licht brauchen: produzierendes Gewerbe, Lager, aber auch Sporthallen, Werkstätten oder Ateliers. Darüber, vertikal getrennt, können gut belichtete Punkt- oder Zeilentypologien mit Wohnungen oder Büros Platz finden.

Auch beim Mischen von Wohnen und Produzieren braucht das Erdgeschoss als Schnittstelle zwischen den Nutzungen eine erhöhte Aufmerksamkeit. Es muss die störungsfreie gewerbliche Anlieferung sichern und gleichzeitig einen qualitätvollen und sicheren Außenraum für die Bewohnenden schaffen. Der siegreiche Wettbewerbsbeitrag der ehemaligen Europan-Gewinner JOTT architecture and urbanism für die IBA Heidelberg in Winnenden löst dies, indem der logistische Verkehr vom Fußgängerverkehr durch ineinander verschränkte, den unterschiedlichen Verkehren zugeordnete Stichstraßen getrennt wird. Als Kompensation für den verlorenen öffentlichen Raum im Erdgeschoss werden semiöffentliche Zwischenräume mit Gemeinschaftsgärten auf den Sockeln angeboten, die gleichzeitig als Puffer zwischen den vielfältigen Wohnformen im Obergeschoss und dem Gewerbe im Erdgeschoss dienen. Die Versammlung unterschiedlicher Gebäudetypologien innerhalb des Blocks bricht das etablierte städtebauliche Dogma der geschlossenen Blockrandbebauung ein Stück weit auf.

Wir sehen an diesem Beispiel – aber auch an zahlreichen anderen aktuellen Projekten –, wie sich im Städtebau der Fokus von der einheitlichen, äußeren Form (in die Nutzungen eingepasst werden) auf die Nutzungsperformance von Typologien verschiebt. Formale Heterogenität – mit ihrem Potenzial, jeder Nutzung optimale

Raumverhältnisse zu bieten – wird nun legitimes Mittel zur Erzeugung von Nutzungsvielfalt.

Bei gemischten architektonischen und urbanen Typologien dienen Zwischenräume als Puffer zwischen den unterschiedlichen Funktionen und sozialen Gruppen und gleichzeitig auch als soziale Schnittstelle für das Zusammenleben – der Zwischenraum ermöglicht je nach individuellem Bedürfnis Abstand und Nähe zugleich. Eine besondere Artikulation und Gestaltung von Zwischenräumen, Übergängen und Schnittstellen zwischen heterogenen Elementen, Nutzungen und sozialen Gruppen ist deshalb für die Organisation der Koexistenz unterschiedlicher sozialer und funktionaler Mischungen auf engem Raum entscheidend.

Ali Saad
Dipl.-Ing. Architekt, Senior Consultant im Cities Team von ARUP Deutschland, Doktorand und ehemaliger wissenschaftlicher Mitarbeiter am Labor für Integrative Architektur der Technischen Universität Berlin, Forschung zur Nutzungsvielfalt von architektonischen und städtebaulichen Typologien

1 Europan Deutschland „Wettbewerb E16 Thema". www.europan.de/archiv/e16/ (abgerufen am 12. Juli 2022); dieser Text basiert auf einem Keynote-Vortrag, den der Autor anlässlich der Einführungsveranstaltung des Europan-16-Wettbewerbs am 7. Mai 2021 gehalten hat
2 Angesichts des aktuell hohen und kurzfristigen Bedarfs an günstigem Wohnraum wird der Bau von neuen Stadtquartieren auf der „grünen Wiese" oftmals weiterhin betrieben, da diese Entwicklungsmethode im Gegensatz zum abstimmungs- und zeitintensiven sowie in der Regel teuren Bauen im Bestand konfliktfreier, schneller und auf wesentlich preiswerterem Boden vollzogen werden kann
3 Sie gehören dem Besitzer Herrn Moriyama, der ebenfalls in dem Haus wohnt und seinen Mitbewohnerinnen sowie Mitbewohnern erlaubt, sie mitzubenutzen. Vgl. Elser, Oliver/Rieper, Michael/Künstlerhaus Wien: Wohnmodelle: Experiment und Alltag. Berlin 2011, S. 133–155

Intermediate Spaces – Principles of Coexistence for Mixed Typologies

The topic 'Living Cities' aims at developing 'lively, integrative, and intermixed urban spaces'.[1] One background for this objective is the diversification of life models that is taking place today. Life in a 'normal family' has been supplemented with new forms like patchwork families, shared housing for senior citizens, or cross-generational co-living. Work models are changing at the same time. As a result of progressive digitization and globalization, location-independent work has meanwhile become established. We no longer have to work in the place where we also live. We even no longer have to work in an office. As we will see, this multiplying of options for living and working has also affected the design of architectural and urban typologies.

Another background for the topic of Europan 16 is the way in which we pursue urban development. Due to climate change, we want to leave the expansive, space-squandering, and car-friendly, modernist form of urban development behind us, and to focus on internal development and converting the existing urban substance in order to deal with the valuable resource of land economically and efficiently – an important project that is, however, not that easy to realize.[2] The social diversity described will thus no longer be spread out but instead integrated within an existing social and spatial context. It is hence about facilitating and organizing coexistence: having different social groups live together in the same space.

The aforementioned social developments have placed new demands on architecture and urban planning. In the past decade, this has not only given rise to new forms of co-productive project development. New approaches to creating dense, mixed architectural and urban typologies that are integrated into their context have also been successfully conceived and implemented and promise to be in a position to meet the multifaceted needs of a diversified society. I would now like to address some of these new typologies and discuss their main design principles. The hypothesis that I will pursue is that the articulation and intentional design of communal intermediate spaces is playing an important role in the design of such mixed typologies.

When many people live together, mixed typologies need to facilitate not just personal freedom, independence, and possibilities for individuals to withdraw, but also participation in communal life. One key project that has spurred the discourse on new forms of living is the Moriyama House by the architect Ryue Nishizawa in Tokyo. It is a multifamily dwelling whose living units are not arranged around a staircase core and stacked on top of one another in the classical manner, but are instead spread out across the plot of land. The living units are arranged around a garden in which boxes with basic communal uses, such as a toilet, bathroom, or kitchenette are distributed.[3] The communal intermediate space is bordered by the individual living units designed for one or two individuals. Each of them also has an individual outdoor space on the roof as well as a self-contained toilet and kitchenette. This seemingly redundant doubling of living infrastructure gives the residents the freedom to take part in communal life in the garden or to withdraw individually.

We also find a redundancy of basic (communal and individual) living infrastructure in cluster dwellings – a housing typology that has already been executed many times in cooperative residential construction in Switzerland and has meanwhile also become popular in Germany. It offers the possibility for various social groups to live together in a relatively small space. For instance, there might be shared apartments for older couples who found living in a single-family house too empty and expensive after their children moved out. It is also suitable as shared housing for working single parents who look after each other's children, for singles, or for the 'co-living' of all of these groups. The residential project by Duplex Architekten on the Hunziker Areal in Zurich, for example, offers self-contained one- and two-room apartments with individual bathrooms and kitchenettes and a communal living space between them with the same infrastructure. The Kraftwerk 2 project by Adrian Streich Architekten, which is also in Zurich, functions in a similar way. In it the residential clusters have between one and four rooms, thus enabling singles, families, and also multiple generations to live together. Both examples have relatively deep layouts, which are not common in multi-family building construction. Communal intermediate spaces are arranged in the darker, interior areas, and are naturally illuminated in a minimal way by means of an intelligently directed incidence of light. The additional usable floor area is thus able to cushion the increased costs that arise from the redundant infrastructure.

Another principle of intermediate space is utilized in buildings in which spaces for living and working are intermixed. In addition to flexible apartment layouts, which do not differentiate between workrooms, living rooms, and bedrooms, mixture is also generated by semi-open ground floor zones, which give rise to a graduated transition between the public outdoor space and the private dwellings on the upper storeys. The Spreefeld project by the Arbeitsgemeinschaft Silvia Carpaneto, fatkoehl, and BARarchitekten in Berlin also offers cluster dwellings on the upper storeys. A communal kitchen, communal spaces for sports activities like yoga courses or events, a workshop, offices, and workrooms, which can be rented in addition to an apartment, are situated on the ground floor. Such a range of work options in residential buildings has become more and more popular as a result of the establishment of working from home. It is not necessary to work in the cramped conditions in one's own apartment, but one can nevertheless stay 'at home'.

Office buildings have meanwhile also become mixed and also make use of communal intermediate spaces. Co-working spaces are flexible open-plan offices, which combine classic office cells with working zones consisting of tables that can be rented individually in order to facilitate various forms of work. Depending on the need, it is possible to rent one's own lockable office, a work island with several workplaces, or just one worktable. Furthermore, communal uses like kitchens, conference rooms, or lounges with table tennis tables are offered. All the services that are necessary for work, such as an Internet connection, printer, or coffee, are often included in the rental price. This makes things easy for people who live in one location and work in another temporarily and short-term. In principle, they only need to hook up their laptop and can start working immediately. Co-working is meanwhile also replacing the classic office cell at big companies like Facebook, Zalando, or Axel Springer. In recent years, these companies have conceived their headquarters as gigantic work landscapes with multifaceted and flexible arrangements of workplaces so as to facilitate an individual organization of the team and work for each project. The idea of experimental office landscapes conceived by the Quickborner Team in the 1960s is now being realized extensively, with the difference that the spaces for 'new work' also offer communal intermediate spaces for working, eating, or hanging out, in order to increase the time spent at the office and a social connection to the company.

Intermediate spaces also play an important role in the mix of manufacturing, housing, and work on an urban-planning level. While such conflict-ridden utilizations were previously separated by distribution across the area, digital and low-emission production methods with 3D printers or robotic arms are now making it possible to stack them vertically, since living is no longer substantially disturbed by production. The stacking is often executed on the basis of plinth typologies, which call to mind American hotel buildings with their large lobbies in the base. Utilizations that require a lot of space but little light, such as production and storage, but also sports halls, workshops, or studios, can be situated in the deep and poorly illuminated base. Above them, separated vertically, well-lit point tower or row typologies with apartments or offices can be placed.

The ground floor as an interface between utilizations also requires greater attention in the case of a mix of housing and production, since it must ensure disruption-free deliveries and also create high-quality and safe external space for the residents. The winning competition entry by JOTT architecture and urbanism, a previous winner of Europan, for the IBA Heidelberg in Winnenden resolves this by separating logistics traffic from foot traffic by means of interleaved cul-de-sacs allocated to the different types of traffic. As compensation for the public space that is lost on the ground floor, semi-public intermediate spaces with communal gardens are offered on the plinth and serve as a buffer between the multifaceted forms of housing on the upper storeys and the manufacturing on the ground floor. The bringing together of different building typologies within one block breaks to some extent with the established urban planning dogma of a closed perimeter block development.

Based on these examples – but also on numerous other current projects – we see how the focus in urban planning is shifting from a uniform, external form (into which utilizations are inserted) to the performance of typologies in terms of their multiple utilization. Formal heterogeneity – with its potential to be able to offer optimal space conditions for each utilization – now seems to be a legitimate tool for generating a diversity of uses.

In mixed architectural and urban typologies, intermediate spaces serve as a buffer between the different functions and social groups and simultaneously also as a social interface for living together – the intermediate space facilitates both distance and proximity depending on the individual need. A specific articulation and design of intermediate spaces, transitions, and interfaces between heterogeneous elements, utilizations, and social groups is thus crucial for the organization of the coexistence of different social and functional mixes in limited space.

Ali Saad
Dipl.-Ing. architect, senior consultant in the Cities Team of ARUP Deutschland, doctoral candidate and former research assistant at the Laboratory for Integrative Architecture of the Technische Universität Berlin, research on the range of uses for architectural and urban planning typologies.

1 Europan Deutschland 'Wettbewerb E16 Thema'. www.europan.de/archiv/e16/en/ (accessed: 12 July 2022). This text is based on a keynote lecture that the author presented on the occasion of the introductory event of the Europan 16 competition on 7 May 2021.
2 In light of the currently high and near-term need for affordable living space, the construction of new urban districts on a 'green meadow' frequently continues to take place, since such development methods often stand in contrast to generally expensive construction within the existing context, which also requires a lot of coordination and time, and such districts on a 'green meadow' can also be erected in a more conflict-free and faster way on land that is considerably less expensive.
3 They belong to the owner, Mr Moriyama, who also lives in the building and allows his fellow residents to use them. See Elser, Oliver/Rieper, Michael/Künstlerhaus Wien: Wohnmodelle: Experiment und Alltag. Berlin, 2011, pp. 133 – 55.

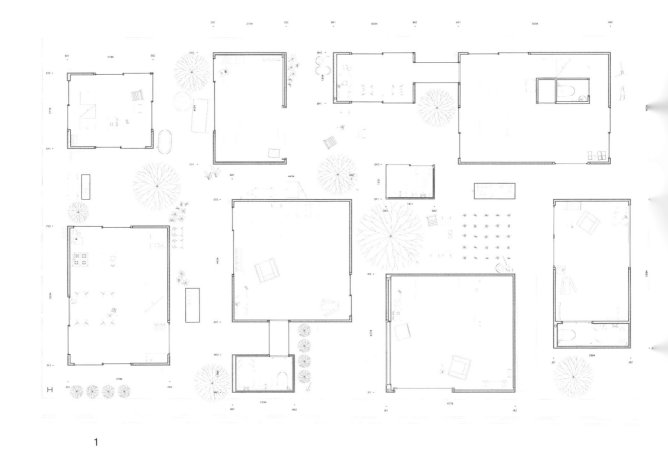

1

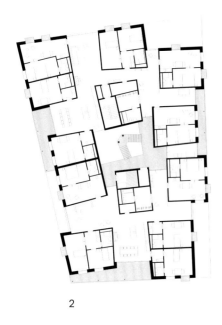

2

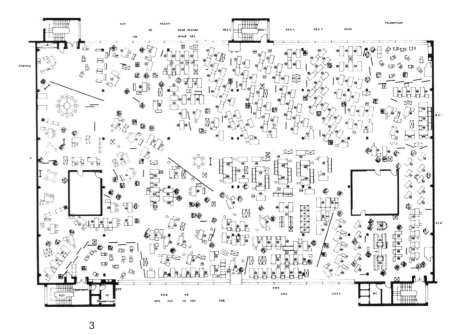

3

1 Moriyama House, Tokio,
Ryue Nishizawa, 2005

2 Haus A, Hunziker-Areal, Zürich,
Duplex Architekten, 2015

3 Grundriss C. Bertelsmann Verlag,
Gütersloh, Quickborner Team, 1961

4 Erster Preis Europan 14 –
The Productive City, Kriens,
Office Oblique, 2017

5 Erster Preis Europan 14 –
The Productive City, Kriens,
Office Oblique, 2017

6 Erster Preis Produktives Stadt-
quartier Winnenden, IBA'27
Stuttgart, Jott Architecture and
Urbanism, 2021

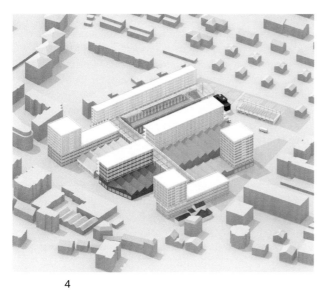

4

5

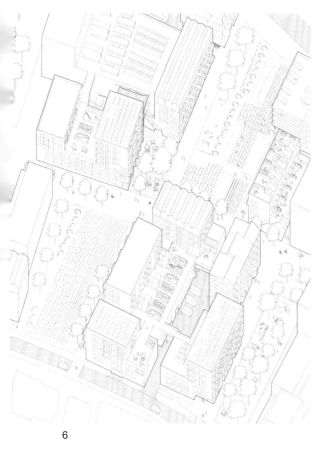

6

1   Moriyama House, Tokyo,
    Ryue Nishizawa, 2005
2   Haus A, Hunziker Site, Zurich,
    Duplex Architekten, 2015
3   Ground plan of the C. Bertelsmann
    Verlag building, Gütersloh,
    Quickborner Team, 1961

4   First prize Europan 14 –
    The Productive City, Kriens,
    Office Oblique, 2017
5   First prize Europan 14 –
    The Productive City, Kriens,
    Office Oblique, 2017

6   First prize Productive Urban
    District of Winnenden,
    IBA'27 Stuttgart, Jott Architecture
    and Urbanism, 2021

Europ(e)an Imaginaries

Wie es der Titel bereits andeutet, formuliert dieser Text die These, dass Europan-Projekte, in europäischen Städten und Landschaften angesiedelt, eine wichtige Rolle bei der Entwicklung nachhaltiger, zukunftsfähiger Vorstellungen davon spielen, was Städte sind, sein möchten und sein werden.

Imaginaries sind nicht einfach nur *images*, also Bilder, Collagen oder Renderings. Hier geht es nicht um Stadt-marketing oder Insta-Urbanismus. Imaginaries sind viel reicher, es sind ganze Vorstellungswelten. Sie werden aus Anregungen für, aus Aussagen über oder Kritik an der gebauten Umwelt und dem täglich dort stattfindenden Leben geformt. Sie sind von der Realität geprägt (oder von dem, was wir für real halten) und von der Vorstellungs-kraft (oder von dem, was unserer Ansicht nach real sein könnte, sollte oder vielleicht auch nicht sein sollte). Städte sind dabei nicht nur Schauplätze neuer Urban Imagi-naries, sondern verbinden das Globale, wie etwa die weltweite Urbanisierung oder den Klimawandel, mit dem Lokalen, mit Orten, an denen Menschen leben und wohnen. Es sind konkrete Räume, in denen Architektinnen und Planer bei der Umsetzung solcher Imaginaries physisch „in das System eingreifen", wie Donella Meadows das genannt hätte.

Die europäische Stadt (und damit auch die Europan-Stadt) ist natürlich nicht das einzige Modell städtischer Morphologie, aber sie tritt in Europa relativ häufig auf und hat eine lange Tradition. Seit der Zeit der Römer beher-bergte sie (nicht nur) menschliche Lebenswelten. Die Mauern, die mittelalterliche Städte umgaben, schützten freie Bürgerinnen und Bürger im Inneren vor der Ver-sklavung, die außerhalb der Befestigungsanlagen drohte. Bis heute können Mauern einhegen und ausschließen, sie können die, die sich darin befinden, schützen oder einsperren. Rem Koolhaas nannte 1972 sein später sehr bekannt gewordenes Diplomprojekt „The Voluntary Prisoners of Architecture", die freiwilligen Gefangenen der Architektur. Dieses Imaginary war von der Berliner Mauer inspiriert, die – für ihn damals überraschend – den „freien" Teil der Stadt umschloss, nicht den anderen.

In urbanen Vorstellungswelten ist die real existierende Stadt davon überlagert, wie Menschen sie wahrnehmen oder kollektiv von ihr träumen. Visionen können von Einzelnen angeregt und von vielen umgesetzt und er-fahren werden, wie etwa die Floating University von raumlaborberlin. Deren Geschichte begann mit Zeichnun-gen einer utopischen Struktur im noch existierenden Regenwasserrückhaltebecken des ehemaligen Flug-hafens Tempelhof, wo das Kollektiv einst zusammen mit dem Theater HAU (Hebbel am Ufer) eine temporäre Weltausstellung errichtet hatte. Diese vergessene Infrastruktur wurde zu einem Ort des Lernens, des Lehrens und der Cross Pollination, der gegenseitigen Befruch-tung – innerhalb und außerhalb der akademischen Welt. Dieser Ort, der ohne gesicherte finanzielle Unterstüt-zung noch immer unter prekären Verhältnissen arbeiten muss, ist ein gutes Beispiel für das, was ich als *probe-ability* bezeichne, die Fähigkeit, unwahrscheinliche Situationen zu erträumen, zu verwirklichen und auszutes-ten. Die Floating University könnte folglich als real gewordenes Imaginary betrachtet werden: Sie wird von zahlreichen Menschen betrieben, die dort unabhängig voneinander agieren, Geschichten und Narrative entwi-ckeln und sich so ins kollektive Gedächtnis der Stadt einschreiben. All dies verstehe ich als Teil einer Praxis, die als Worlding bezeichnet wird, die Kunst des Erfindens, Imaginierens und Ausprobierens von Methoden, „wie wir miteinander leben werden", wie Hashim Sarkis 2021 die Biennale in Venedig überschrieb – wo die Floating University ja bekanntlich hochverdient mit dem Goldenen Löwen ausgezeichnet wurde.

Mit der oben genannten Definition stehen Imaginaries dem sehr nahe, was früher vielleicht Utopie genannt worden wäre – oder Dystopie, je nach gewählter Perspek-tive. Ecumenopolis zum Beispiel, die von Konstantinos Doxiadis 1970 entwickelte Vision einer weltumspannenden Stadt, kann leidenschaftslos als folgerichtige Entwicklung betrachtet, bewundernd als technisch fortschrittliche Errungenschaft gepriesen oder besorgt als Schreckens-vorstellung wahrgenommen werden.

Interessanterweise gilt dies in ähnlicher Weise für eine ganze Reihe von Konzepten, Ideen und Vorschlägen, die in den 1960er und 1970er Jahren entstanden sind. Die Parallelen zur heutigen Situation sind unverkennbar: Auch damals waren sich die Menschen nicht sicher, was sie von der Zukunft zu erwarten hatten – mitten im Kalten Krieg, als ökologische Schäden immer deutlicher wurden und die fortschreitende Individualisierung Gesellschaften veränderte, die zugleich in rasantem Tempo immer wohlhabender wurden. Der technologische Fortschritt transformierte die Welt, überzog ihre Ober-fläche mit Infrastrukturen und Gebäuden und brachte etwaige Bedenken mit dem Versprechen einer besseren (einfacheren, weniger mühevollen) Zukunft zum Ver-stummen. Man nutzte dafür Bilder, *images*, wie eines aus dem Jahr 1970, das ein selbstfahrendes Auto zeigt, dessen Insassen entspannt miteinander spielen, während es zwischen robotergesteuerten landwirtschaftlichen Betrieben dahingleitet.

Dieses Beispiel macht einen weiteren interessanten Aspekt solcher Imaginaries deutlich: Sie müssen nicht kurzfristig realisiert werden, können aber mittel-oder längerfristig zur Entstehung mächtiger Sehnsüchte und Wunschvorstellungen beitragen. So wird heute die Eröffnung einer Autofabrik für angeblich klügere Fahrzeuge gefeiert, die ein US-amerikanischer Milliardär, der sehr gut darin ist, überholte Utopien als „Next Big Thing" zu verkaufen, mitten im Brandenburger Wald errichtet. Das ist symptomatisch für unsere Zeit – und die Macht vergangener Vorstellungswelten: Anstatt weniger und kollektiver zu reisen oder unseren Energiever-brauch zu reduzieren, färben wir lieber unsere nicht nach-haltigen Gewohnheiten grün und reden uns ein, dass es schon keine Probleme mit knappem Grundwasser, fehlendem Material oder Ressourcenkriegen geben wird. Dabei wissen wir es eigentlich besser.

Heutzutage hängen moderne Gesellschaften mehr denn je von Technologie ab. Doch die computerisierten, soziotechnischen Sphären scheinen weniger intelligent und noch weniger vorhersehbar, als unsere Väter und Großväter das vermutlich gehofft haben: Sogenannte Serious Games, Kriegsspiele, die am Beginn der digitalen Revolution standen, sind als ganz reale Bedrohungen zurückgekehrt, und europäische Städte werden im 21. Jahrhundert wieder zu echten, analogen Schlachtfel-dern. Auch wenn es uns nicht gefällt: Die Szenen, die ukrainische Städte unter Beschuss oder in Trümmern zei-gen, sind ein weiteres Urban Imaginary, eines, das besonders schrecklich ist und vor wenigen Wochen noch unvorstellbar schien. Menschen verlieren ihr Zuhause, ihr Leben oder ihre Familien, hier, mitten in Europa. Bewohnte Orte werden in Schlachten ausgelöscht, die so ziemlich alles infrage stellen, woran wir als gelernte Pazifistinnen und Pazifisten bisher geglaubt haben.

Dabei war ein solcher Krieg nicht unvorstellbar, weil es nie zuvor einen gegeben hätte: Der serbische Architekt Bogdan Bogdanović zum Beispiel hat sein ganzes Leben mit der Errichtung wunderbarer Gedenkstätten für die Opfer des Zweiten Weltkriegs im ehemaligen Jugoslawien verbracht, die an Orte und Menschen erinnern, die es nicht mehr gibt. In Skizzen für die Gedenkstätte Dudik bei Vukovar entwickelte Bogdanović die Vorstellung einer versunkenen Stadt, von der nach ihrer Überflutung nur noch die Spitzen der Türme sichtbar sind. Der realisierte Park bestand aus diesen symbolischen Turmspitzen, die zusammen mit Schiffen aus Stein einen mythologischen Ort bilden, umgeben von Rasen, Bäumen und einem herrlichen Garten. Bogdanovićs Arbeiten sind voller Symbolik und erinnern an schreckliche Ereignisse, sind aber nie als einschüchternde Monumente für die Toten konzipiert, sondern als Landschaften für die Lebenden, die es hoffentlich besser machen und besser haben als ihre Vorfahren.

Einige von Bogdanovićs schönsten Gedenkstätten wurden während des Jugoslawienkriegs in den 1990er Jahren selbst zerstört und verwüstet. Der Baumeister, der sich seinem Landsmann Slobodan Milošević mutig entgegenstellte und sogar kurz als Bürgermeister von Belgrad tätig war, ehe er ins Exil ging, fasste einige seiner Texte unter dem Titel „Die Stadt und der Tod" zusammen, in denen er die serbische Armee beschuldigte, nicht nur Menschen zu ermorden, sondern auch Städte zu vernichten – und damit die Zivilisation als solche. Wir hören heute wieder neue bzw. alte Begriffe wie Zivilisationsbruch und Zeitenwende, während unsere vermeintlich friedliche Welt in Trümmer fällt. Und das ist nicht die erste große Verunsicherung und Infragestellung unserer Lebensweise, sondern eine in einer Folge von dystopischen Entwicklungen wie der globalen Erderwärmung, einer Langzeitpandemie und dem Aufstieg autoritärer Regime.

Aber was, so könnten Sie fragen, hat das mit uns zu tun? Können Imaginaries die Welt wirklich verbessern oder sind sie letztlich doch nur Traumwelten, Wunschvorstellungen, Märchen?

Können wir, als Architektinnen und Urbanisten, als Planerinnen und Gestalter, überhaupt etwas zur Verbesserung der Verhältnisse beitragen? Liegt das in unserer Macht?

Ich bin davon überzeugt, dass wir das können,
– weil es unser Beruf ist, unser Metier, Geschichten über eine mögliche Zukunft zu erzählen;
– weil wir Städte bauen, wieder aufbauen oder umbauen;
– weil die europäische Stadt ein Modell für Zivilcourage und Kultur ist, und oftmals auch eine Bühne für zivilen Ungehorsam;
– weil es unsere Verpflichtung ist, Hoffnung zu geben, nicht nur jenen, die unter Kriegen leiden, sondern auch denen, die von Klimawandel und Energiekrise, Dürren oder schweren Regenfällen betroffen sind;
– weil wir in Systemen von Spekulationen und Gentrifizierung tatsächlich einen Unterschied bewirken können, indem wir Akteurinnen und Akteure des Gemeinwohls und der Gemeingüter, der commons, unterstützen, die wir alle teilen;
– weil wir dazu ausgebildet wurden, zu de-signen, also

zu ent-werfen, noch nicht vorhandene Situationen auf bestehende zu projizieren;
– weil wir dadurch Vorstellungen, Bilder, Modelle und Collagen alternativer Zukünfte liefern können, die in und von demokratischen Institutionen diskutiert und debattiert werden;
– weil wir Zerstörungen stoppen oder, wo das nicht mehr möglich ist, reparieren und so einen notwendigen Heilungsprozess beginnen können.

Wir können nicht nur, wir müssen all das tun – weil wir uns sorgen (because we care). Es gilt, Vor- und Fürsorge zu betreiben, für uns und alle, die mit uns leben und nach uns kommen.

Aber wie – so könnten sich jetzt junge Architektinnen fragen – können wir überhaupt einen Unterschied bewirken? Wem können unsere schönen Ideen und idealistischen Vorstellungen nutzen? Und wie – das fragen sich Stadtplaner, Bürgermeisterinnen oder Wohnungsbaugesellschaften – können wir eine gerechte Entwicklung unserer Städte unterstützen? Über welche Instrumente verfügen wir, um Teilhabe zu fördern? Wie können wir nachhaltigen Wohnraum für alle schaffen – und wie können wir andere davon überzeugen, dass dies eine absolute Notwendigkeit ist, und nicht nur nice to have?

Und jetzt stellen Sie sich bitte mal vor, welche Superkräfte Sie hätten, wenn Sie, junge Architektinnen und erfahrene Standortvertreter, zusammenarbeiten würden! Welchen Enthusiasmus, welche Erfahrung und welche Expertise könnten Sie beisteuern zu dieser leicht vermessenen Weltverbesserungsunternehmung!

Die Stadt ist, wie oben schon gesagt, der Ort, an dem sich das Globale und das Lokale begegnen. Sie ist der Ort, wo Konzepte und Pläne in Aktionen und Experimenten überprüft und evaluiert werden können. Wenn wir also aus dem Helikopter steigen (oder aus dem Raumschiff) und zurück auf den Boden kommen, dann könnte es sich lohnen, sich einige gute Beispiele aus 30 Jahren Europan-Praxis anzusehen, die zugleich ein europäisches Reservoir von vielfältigen Vorstellungswelten ist – und von denen gar nicht wenige tatsächlich gebaut wurden.

Beginnen wir mit einem Projekt von Froetscher Lichtenwagner für Europan 4 in Innsbruck: ein hybrider Standort, der aus einem Supermarkt, einem Wohnblock, einer Parkgarage und, ja, einem öffentlichen Platz besteht, den hier vorzuschlagen wohl kein professioneller Entwickler gewagt hätte. Das Projekt, das 1996 den Wettbewerb gewann, wurde zwischen 2000 und 2003 konkret geplant und bis 2006 umgesetzt.

Ein weiteres schönes österreichisches Beispiel ist die „Oase 22" von studio uek in Wien. 2007 für Europan 9 mit dem Anspruch eines nutzerzentrierten Designs konzipiert, verdichtet diese Wohnanlage eine ehemalige Schrebergartensiedlung. Nach dem Wettbewerb folgte ein weiterer, aus dem drei Architekturbüros ausgewählt wurden. Sie errichteten eine mäandernde Struktur aus drei Wohnblöcken, die durch einen Gemeinschaftsgarten auf dem Dach miteinander verbunden sind. Die Blöcke wurden gemäß dem Wiener Modell des geförderten Wohnbaus entwickelt und sind heute das Zuhause einer neu entstandenen Gemeinschaft.

Ebenfalls ein Beitrag für Europan 9 war unser eigenes, subsolar*s, Projekt für Spremberg. Trotz eines eher abstrakten Entwurfs für Verknüpfungen und Verbindungen, den wir in Hommage an Georg Simmel „Brücke und Tür" nannten, erhielten wir den Auftrag, die Freilichtbühne als Möglichkeitsraum für die Bürgerinnen und Bürger umzugestalten. Das war vermutlich die schnellste Europan-Umsetzung aller Zeiten, bei der nur zwei Jahre zwischen Gewinn des Preises und der Eröffnungszeremonie im Park lagen.

In Zagreb regte das Team openact im Rahmen von Europan 13 die Inbesitznahme der Flussufer durch temporäre Strukturen und kollektive Veranstaltungen an, während gleichzeitig an einem umfassenden Städtebauentwurf gearbeitet wurde. Dies ist ein gutes Beispiel dafür, dass unser Beruf selbst sich dieser Tage grundlegend verändert und wir manchmal eher Zeitpläne gestalten als Kronleuchter – und damit nicht nur den Prozess, sondern auch das temporäre Experiment und die *probeability* stärken.

Ein anderer, noch größerer Maßstab wird in einem Projekt des aktuellen Wettbewerbsverfahrens für die französische Stadt Niort deutlich. Das junge Büro Atelierkosmos nutzt wunderschöne Pläne und Zeichnungen, um Landschaftstypologien zu kartieren und ein ganzes Flussdelta zu regenerieren. Dieses Projekt lenkt die Aufmerksamkeit auf das, was wir leider immer noch häufig als Umwelt bezeichnen, als ob es etwas außerhalb unserer Körper Liegendes wäre – obwohl es sich um unsere Lebensgrundlage handelt.

Das Projekt „More-than-Farming Madrid" von furiistudio, ebenfalls ein Gewinner von Europan 16, bringt die (produktive) Landschaft zurück in die Stadt. Dabei geht es vor allem um das Züchten, Anbauen und Ernten von Nahrungsmitteln genau dort, wo sie auch konsumiert werden. Dies ist zwar keine neue Erfindung, aber eine profunde Strategie, um Treibhausgasemissionen durch den Bau von Treibhäusern genau dort zu reduzieren, wo Menschen leben, sich ernähren müssen, aber zugleich auch kümmern können.

Das letzte Beispiel in diesem Kaleidoskop gehört zu meinen Lieblingsprojekten: Die Excity, entworfen von Lluis Juan Liñán, Andrea Gimeno Sánchez und Josep Vicent Lluch Diaz für Warschau im Rahmen von Europan 14, wird aus dem Abfall errichtet, der im städtischen Stoffwechsel entsteht. Diese radikale Zuspitzung des Urban Mining ist ziemlich mutig, und ich hoffe sehr, dass wir in Zukunft mehr solcher „unbaubaren", mutigen und begeisternden Projekte sehen werden, die die Grenzen des Gewohnten produktiv verschieben.

Um diese Beispiele zusammenzutragen, habe ich das Europan-Archiv durchforstet, manchmal schmunzelnd, manchmal bestürzt ob der schnellen und umfassenden Transformationen dessen, was wir Planerinnen und Planer tun und wie wir es tun. Der erste Wettbewerb fand 1989 statt, dem Jahr des Falls der Berliner Mauer – also in der Prä-Internet-Zeit, was es beinahe unmöglich macht, Bilder aus dieser ersten Runde zu finden, obwohl einige Büros, wie zum Beispiel Mussotter Poeverlein oder Heide & von Beckerath, damals damit sehr bekannt wurden.

In Runde eins von Europan lautete das Thema Wohnbau (bzw. „Entwicklung der Lebensweisen und Architektur des Wohnens"), und es gab keine Standorte. Die Architektinnen mussten diese selber finden, und die Stadt belohnte die Gewinner dann mit einem Auftrag für etwas anderes. Manchmal träume ich davon, dass es wieder so sein könnte: dass Menschen, die ihre Stadt am besten kennen, sich mit dieser auseinandersetzen, Fragen an sie stellen oder Vorschläge für Orte machen, die noch unentdecktes Potenzial haben. Das alles natürlich parallel zu dem internationalen Flair, das alle zwei Jahre aufkommt, wenn – sagen wir – isländische Architekten, die in Portugal arbeiten, einen Vorschlag für Lwiw/Lemberg in der Ukraine einreichen.

33 Jahre sind eine lange Zeit, 16 Verfahren haben seitdem stattgefunden, an denen ungefähr 660 Städte und sicher Tausende Architektinnen teilgenommen haben, viele von ihnen mehr als einmal. Die eingesetzten Werkzeuge, aber auch die verfolgten Ziele haben sich im Laufe der Zeit verändert. Das ist nicht verwunderlich: Viele Dinge, darunter Europan und wohl auch die europäische Stadt, müssen sich ändern, um zu bleiben, was sie sind.

Seit mehr als dreißig Jahren bringt der Europan Wettbewerb unwahrscheinliche Verbündete zusammen: junge Architektinnen und Architekten mit idealen Vorstellungen auf der einen Seite und Vertreter von Standorten mit realen Problemen auf der anderen. Wir halten das noch immer für einen tollen Trick, um die Verwirklichung des Unwahrscheinlichen zu fördern, um transformative Fähigkeiten zu stärken und um neue mögliche Zukünfte zu öffnen, die, mit Ernst Bloch gesprochen, reale Zukünfte sein sollten, also eben nicht vollständig vorhersehbar und verfügbar.

Wir von Europan Deutschland sind daher schon sehr gespannt, wie sich die Ergebnisse dieser Runde in Ettlingen, Landshut, Schwäbisch Gmünd, Selb und Wernigerode entwickeln werden. Wir werden nach Kräften dazu beitragen, aus vorgestellten reale Welten entstehen zu lassen!

Saskia Hebert
Dr.-Ing. Architektin BDA, Stadt- und Transformationsforscherin, Mitinhaberin von subsolar* architektur & stadtforschung | Hebert und Lohmann PartG mbB, entwirft konkrete Räume und mögliche Zukünfte

Bei diesem Text handelt sich um ein leicht überarbeitetes Transkript des Vortrags im Rahmen der Preisverleihung E16 am 1. April 2022.

Europ(e)an Imaginaries

Europ(e)an Imaginaries: this title suggests that Europan projects, situated in European cities and landscapes, play a vital role in crafting sustainable, or rather 'futurable' narratives of what cities are, should be, and will become.

'Imaginaries', to be clear, are not just 'images'. This text is not about city marketing, or Insta-urbanism. Imaginaries are much richer, are worlds in themselves. They are crafted based on suggestions for and propositions or critiques of built environments and the everyday life that takes place there. They are informed by reality (or by what we think is real) and by the imagination (or what we think should or could, or even maybe should not, be real). This is important due to the worldwide growth of urban populations, because cities link the global with the local, and they are the places where architects and planners 'intervene in the system', as Donella Meadows might have put it.

The European (and thus also the Europan) city is of course not the only way that cities can be conceived, but it does have a quite long tradition. Since Roman times it has been sheltering human (and more than human) life worlds: the walls surrounding medieval cities protected the free citizens on the inside from being enslaved on the outside. In our times, walls still help keep people in or out, can imprison or protect. There is a well-known project by Rem Koolhaas, his diploma project 'the voluntary prisoners of architecture'. This imaginary was inspired by the Berlin Wall, which – surprisingly for him – surrounded the 'free' part of the city rather than the other one.

In imaginaries, the existing city is layered with the ways that people perceive or collectively dream about it. It can be suggested by some and crafted by many, as, for example, Raumlabor's Floating University. Starting with a series of drawings, their imagination hovered above the Tempelhof airfield, where they had previously erected a temporary World's Fair in cooperation with the HAU (Hebbel am Ufer) theatre, and then densified on the site of the rainwater basin on the other side of Columbiadamm. This forgotten infrastructure then became a place for learning, teaching, and cross-pollination – within as well as outside academia. Since it was created under precarious conditions, such as a lack of regular funding, the place is a good example of what I call 'probe ability', the capacity to dream and build and realize and test unlikely situations. The Floating University might thus be regarded as an imaginary that came into existence: it is supported by many individuals who tell stories and narratives and produce memories, for themselves and for others. All this is part of a practice called 'worlding', the arts of inventing, imagining, and trying out approaches to 'how we can live together', as Hashim Sarkis called the Venice Biennale of Architecture in 2021 – and where the Floating University was deservedly awarded the Golden Lion.

Based on the above definition, imaginaries are close to what has been called a utopian vision for quite a while – or, depending on your perspective, a dystopian threat. The Ecumenopolis concept, for example, in which Konstantinos Doxiadis proposed a city that would span the globe as an endless built structure, can be seen as an inevitable development, a technologically advanced achievement, or a horror scenario.

It is interesting that this can be said for a lot of concepts, or critiques, or visions that date back to the 1960s and 70s. Back then, people were also not sure what to expect from the future – as a result of the ongoing Cold War, the emerging manifestation of ecological deprivation, and the individualist differentiation that was changing societies as they grew wealthier. Technological 'progress' was rapidly transforming the surface of the world, covering it with infrastructure and buildings, and silencing any concerns with promises of better (easier, less burdensome) futures. There is a picture from 1970 depicting a driverless smart car travelling smoothly past farm factories while the people inside play games: here, we see another interesting aspect of imaginaries. While they do not have to be realized today, they can help construct powerful desires that materialize only after decades, as we can now see with the car factory being constructed in the former woods of Brandenburg by a US-American billionaire who is very good at selling out-dated utopias as the 'next big thing'. Instead of travelling less or reducing energy consumption, we prefer to 'green' our cars and our habitats, to do 'whatever it takes', and to tell ourselves that there will not be any problems with scarce water supplies, congestion, or material resources, even though we already know better. So beware of what you wish for, and what you tell others about it, because it might lead into a dead end in the long run, literally.

Today, modern societies are more dependent on technology than ever before. Unfortunately, the computerized sociotechnical sphere seems less intelligent and even less predictable than our fathers and grandfathers must have hoped: 'serious games', war games that stood at the beginning of the digital revolution, have returned as real threats, and European cities have once again become battlegrounds in the twenty-first century. Whether we like it or not: the scenes of Ukrainian cities under fire or in ruins show another 'urban imaginary', one that is particularly horrible and seemed unthinkable only a short time ago. People are losing their homes, their lives, or their children right here, in Europe. And cities are being practically eradicated in battles that seem irrational, violent, and archaic.

Of course this was not unthinkable because it had never happened before: We just forgot, probably because we wanted to. The Serbian architect Bogdan Bogdanović spent his whole life constructing beautiful memorial sites in former Yugoslavia, commemorating people and cities killed by fascists from Germany or their collaborators. In sketches for the memorial site at Dudik, near Vukovar, Bogdanović developed an entire imaginary of a sunken city, buried by a flood, with only the top of the towers remaining visible above the surface – and the park that was built consisted of just these peaks, along with ships made from stones depicting the remains a doomed city surrounded by a lawn and trees and a beautiful garden. Bogdanović's works, it must be said here, are full of meaning, but are by no means intimidating monuments, or 'Mahnmale' in German. The works are instead designed as landscapes for the living, who are able to enjoy spending time there and also to reflect on what happened in the past.

Ironically enough, some of Bogdanović's most beautiful memorial sites were destroyed or devastated during the Yugoslav Wars in the 1990s. Back then the city of Sarajevo underwent a 1,000-day siege, with snipers shooting civilian pedestrians on the main road from the surrounding hilltops, not unlike what is happening to the city of Mariupol today. Bogdan Bogdanović, who bravely stood up against his countryman Slobodan Milosevic and even briefly acted as mayor of Belgrade before being exiled, compiled some of his writings under the title Death and the City, in which he accuses the Serbian army of assassinating and murdering not only people, but also cities, and thus civilization. Today, we are again hearing those new / old words like 'Zivilisations-bruch' (breakdown of civilization) and 'Zeitenwende' (turning point), with our supposedly peaceful world falling into pieces that probably will be forgotten again very soon, not unlike the tombstones in the partisan cemetery in Mostar, Bosnia Herzegovina. Furthermore, other civilized certainties are already being shattered: with global warming, a long-lasting pandemic, and the rise of authoritarian regimes, our peaceful world seems to be destabilizing itself at a shockingly fast pace.

But why is this – or should this be – a matter of concern to us, here and now? Are imaginaries more than phantasy worlds, or fairy tales? Can they be of any relevance in such serious times – and, if yes, how?

I think they can,

– because it is our profession, our line of work, to tell stories of a possible future.
– because we build cities, or rebuild, or transform them.
– because the European city is a model of civil courage and culture, and often a stage for civil disobedience, even if people have to fear arrest or worse.
– because it is our obligation to give hope to all those who suffer not only due to wars, but also due to climate change and energy crises, drought and heavy rainfalls.
– because we can make a difference in systems of speculation and gentrification by supporting initiatives and stakeholders in the commons that we share.
– because we have been trained to de-sign, ent-werfen, to project different situations onto existing ones.
– because by doing so, we can provide images, pictures, models, and collages of alternative futures, to be discussed and debated in and by democratic institu-tions.
– because we have to stop the destruction and start the healing process.

In short: Because we care – Weil wir uns sorgen. This is our world, and everybody should do what he or she is best at to improve the situation, wherever they are. It is absolutely necessary to stabilize, to invent and test alternatives. It is mandatory that we prevent risks (German: Vorsorge) and care for others (German: Fürsorge).

But how can we do that? In what way, young archi-tects must ask themselves, can we make a difference? How can we foster regeneration and healing? Whom can we collaborate with in order to do so?

As city planners or as mayors or housing companies, it is necessary to ask oneself: How can we support an equitable development of our cities? Which tools do we have to encourage participation, or to integrate refugees? How can we build sustainable housing for everyone – and how can we convince others that this is an absolutely necessity and not simply something that would be 'nice to have'?

And now: if young architects and site representatives would work together, what superpowers they would have!

What great enthusiasm and expertise they could bring to the table, to this convivial round of improving the world!

And another very interesting question: What would they have to forget, to unlearn, to not do anymore?

These are transformative times, times that challenge our capacities to care and share, our talents, so that we can live on a damaged planet and reinvent our concept of being-in-the-world, because we have only one. One world for seven billion people, or perhaps one city, as Plan B proposes: a world-spanning city that is situated entirely in the comparatively thin layer of atmosphere wrapped around our planet like cling film.

The city, as stated above, is the place where the global meets the local. Furthermore, it is also the place where concepts and plans meet action and experiments, and where 'problems' (or challenges) meet 'visions' (or ideas). So if we alight from the helicopter (or get out of the spaceship) and put our feet back on the ground, it might be worth taking a look at some good examples from the thirty years Europan practice, which is also a European reservoir of concepts, critiques, questions, and suggestions.

Let us perhaps start with a project in Innsbruck by Froetscher Lichtenwagner for Europan 4: a hybrid place consisting of a supermarket, a housing block, a parking garage, and, yes, a public square that probably no professional developer would have dared to suggest there. After winning the competition in 1996, the project hibernated for four long years – to finally then be planned from 2000 to 2003 and realized until 2006.

Another beautiful Austrian project is Oase 22 by studio uek in Vienna. Conceived for Europan 9 in 2007 as a good example of user-centred design, this housing development densifies a former allotment garden area. After the competition, another one followed, from which a total of three architects were chosen to build a meander of three blocks interconnected by a rooftop community garden. The block has been developed according to the model of subsidized housing in Vienna and has now become a home for a new community.

Our own project for Spremberg was also a submission to Europan 9. With a rather conceptual design for links and connections called 'bridge and door', we were ultimately commissioned to redesign the open-air stage as a multifunctional 'space of possibilities' for the citizens who use it very creatively today. I believe that this was the fastest realization ever, with only two years between being awarded the prize and the opening ceremony in the park. Another project, the redesign of the intermodal access point at the Spremberg station square, took a little bit longer and was completed in 2014.

In Zagreb, as part of Europan 13, the openact team encouraged appropriation of the riverbanks by means of temporary structures and collective events, while working on a large-scale urban design scheme. This is a good example of how our profession itself is currently under-going a lot of change, designing calendars instead of chandeliers and promenades enhancing 'probe abilities'.

Yet another, still larger scale can be seen in a project for this year's competition for the French city of Niort. The young firm atelier kosmes uses these beautiful maps to discover landscape typologies and to regenerate an entire river delta. This project shifts viewers' attention to what is still called the 'environment', in German 'Umwelt', as if it were something external to our bodies – even though we know that it really is the foundation and the central condition of our livelihoods.

The project 'more than farming Madrid' by furiistudio, also a winner in Europan 16, which brings the (productive) landscape back into the town, is all about planting, cultivating, and harvesting food where it is consumed, in cities. This is not a new invention, but a profound strategy to reduce greenhouse gas emissions by building green-houses where people live and take care of them.

The final project in this kaleidoscope is one of my favourites: The 'ex-city', designed by a young Spanish team for Warsaw in the Europan 14 competition, is built from waste that is generated by its own metabolism. This radical concept of 'urban mining' is rather advanced, and I really hope that we will see more unbuildable but powerful, imaginative projects like these in the future, and that they might help encourage change for the good.

To gather these examples, I went back through the Europan archive, sometimes smiling, sometimes shocked by the changes and transformations visible. The first competition was held in 1989, in the year of the fall of the Berlin Wall – thus 'pre-internet', so that it is almost impossible to find images from that first round, although some firms from back then, like, for example, Mussotter Poeverlein or Heide & von Beckerath, have become quite famous in the meantime.

In round 1 of Europan, the subject was housing, and there were no sites: you had to find them, as architects, and the city would then reward the winners with a brief for something else. I dream of that concept being brought back at some time, since it encourages people who know their cities best to engage with them, parallel to the international flair that comes when, let's say, Icelandic architects working in Portugal send in a proposal for Lviv in the Ukraine.

Thirty-three years is a long time. Sixteen competitions have been launched since then, with the participation of around 660 cities and probably thousands of archi-tects, many of them more than once. The tools used, but also the aims presented have changed a lot over time. This is not surprising: a lot of things have to change in order to survive, including probably the European city, and certainly the Europan competition.

For over thirty years now, Europan has been pairing 'unlikely allies': young architects with great expectations and site representatives with real problems. We still think that this is a great trick to kick start a journey together on the road to the unknown, to encourage the unlikely to happen, to enhance 'transformative literacy' – and to open up new possible futures, that should, in the words of Ernst Bloch, be 'real' futures: with the scale of the problems piling up before us right now, we might indeed need fairy tales more urgently than techno-fixes that backfire, miracles instead of master plans, and collectively crafted Europ(e)an, or better worldwide imaginaries rather than out-dated utopias.

We are looking forward to seeing how the results of this session will develop in Ettlingen, Landshut, Schwäbisch Gmünd, Selb, and Wernigerode. We, the members of the Europan Germany non-profit organization, will help with this, whatever, no: wherever it takes… place!

Saskia Hebert
Dr.-Ing. architect BDA, urbanologist and transformation researcher, co-owner of subsolar* architektur & stadtforschung | Hebert und Lohmann PartG mbB, designs concrete spaces and possible futures

This text is a slightly refined transcript of the lecture given at the award ceremony E16 on 1 April 2022.

1

2

1 Floating University, 2018
2 Versunkene Stadt – Imaginary
  von Bogdan Bogdanović

3 Spomen-park, Dudik, 2014
4 Freilichtbühne Spremberg,
  Eröffnung 2010

3

4

1 Floating University, 2018
2 Sunken City – Imaginary by
   Bogdan Bogdanović

3 Spomen-park, Dudik, 2014
4 Open Air Stage in Spremberg,
   Opening 2010

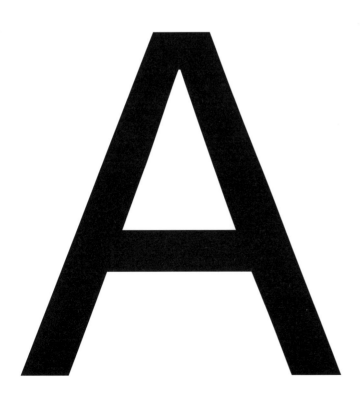

Anhang

Appendix

Jurys Juries

National

Bauherrenvertreter·innen Client Representatives
– Dr.-Ing. Timo Munzinger, Deutscher Städtetag
– Prof. Dr.-Ing. Iris Reuther, Senatsbaudirektorin der Freien Hansestadt Bremen, Leitung des Fachbereiches Bau und Stadtentwicklung

Architekt·innen / Planer·innen Architects / Planners
– Prof. Dr.-Ing. Thorsten Erl, metris architekten stadtplaner bda, Lehrgebiet Städtebau Universität Siegen, Siegen/Heidelberg, Vorstand Europan Deutschland
– Dr.-Ing. Saskia Hebert, subsolar* architektur & stadtforschung, stellvertretende Vorstandsvorsitzende Europan Deutschland
– Kyung-Ae Kim-Nalleweg, Kim Nalleweg Architekten, Berlin
– Anna Popelka, PPAG Architects, Wien und Berlin
– Ali Saad, Senior Consultant im Cities Team von ARUP Deutschland, Komitee Europan Deutschland
– Marika Schmidt, mrschmidt Architekten, Berlin

Person des öffentlichen Lebens Public Figure
– Kaye Geipel, stellvertretender Chefredakteur *Bauwelt*, stellvertretender Vorstandsvorsitzender Europan Deutschland

Stellvertreterin Substitutes
– Dr.-Ing. Irene Wiese-von Ofen, Vorstand Europan Deutschland

Ettlingen

Sachpreisrichter·innen Subject Judges
– Johannes Arnold, Oberbürgermeister der Stadt Ettlingen
– Christa Becker-Binder, Gemeinderätin Bündnis 90/ Die Grünen
– Christian Höglmeier, Geschäftsführer Albtal-Verkehrs-Gesellschaft, Ettlingen
– Christa Stauch, Gemeinderätin CDU

Stellvertreterin Substitute
– Kirstin Wandelt, Gemeinderätin SPD

Fachpreisrichter·innen Specialist Judges
– Jury Vorsitz Prof. Dr.-Ing. Thorsten Erl, metris architekten stadtplaner bda, Lehrgebiet Städtebau Universität Siegen, Siegen/Heidelberg, Vorstand Europan Deutschland
– Wassili Meyer-Buck, Amtsleiter Planungsamt der Stadt Ettlingen
– Anna Popelka, PPAG Architects, Wien und Berlin
– Annette Sinz-Beerstecher, Freie Landschaftsarchitektin
– Prof. Dipl.-Ing. Ludwig Wappner, Architekt und Stadtplaner, Karlsruher Institut für Technologie KIT

Berater·innen Advisors
– Dr.-Ing. Martin Berchtold, berchtoldkrass space & options, Karlsruhe
– Gerhard Ecker, Gemeinderat für Ettlingen, Freie Wähler
– Anna Eiden, stellvertretende Amtsleiterin Planungsamt der Stadt Ettlingen
– Stefan Wammetsberger, Koehler & Leutwein, Karlsruhe

Landshut

Sachpreisrichter Subject Judges
– Johannes Doll, Leitender Baudirektor Stadt Landshut
– Rolf-Peter Klar, Leitender Baudirektor Regierung von Niederbayern
– Alexander Putz, Oberbürgermeister Stadt Landshut

Stellvertreterin Substitute
– Verena Wocheslander, Bauamt Landshut

Fachpreisrichter·innen Specialist Judges
– Jury Vorsitz Josef Weber, Vorstand Europan Deutschland
– Prof. Dr.-Ing. Andrea Benze, offsea, Berlin, München, London, Professorin für Städtebau und Theorie der Stadt an der Hochschule München, Komitee Europan Deutschland
– Andreas Krüger, Belius, Komitee Europan Deutschland
– Dr.-Ing. Irene Wiese-von Ofen, Vorstand Europan Deutschland

Beraterin Advisor
– Katharina von Milczewski, Immobilien Freistaat Bayern, Regionalvertretung Niederbayern

Schwäbisch Gmünd

Sachpreisrichter·innen   Subject Judges
– Richard Arnold, Oberbürgermeister Schwäbisch Gmünd
– Julius Mihm, Bürgermeister Schwäbisch Gmünd
– Christiane Schoch, Vermögen und Bau Baden-Württemberg, Amt Schwäbisch Gmünd, Abteilungsleiterin Abteilung 6 Hochbau

Stellvertreter·innen   Substitutes
– Gerhard Hackner, Leitung des Amts für Stadtentwicklung Schwäbisch Gmünd
– Birgit Pedoth, Leitung der Abteilung Stadtplanung Schwäbisch Gmünd

Fachpreisrichter·innen   Specialist Judges
– Jury Vorsitz Prof. Dipl.-Ing. Florian Nagler, Florian Nagler Architekten, München
– Prof. Dr.-Ing. Thorsten Erl, metris architekten stadtplaner bda, Lehrgebiet Städtebau Universität Siegen, Siegen/Heidelberg, Vorstand Europan Deutschland
– Kyung-Ae Kim-Nalleweg, Kim Nalleweg Architekten, Berlin
– Julia Köpper, Octagon Architekturkollektiv, Leipzig

Stellvertreterin   Substitute
– Karin Sandeck, Architektin, München, Vorstand Europan Deutschland

Berater·innen   Advisors
– Brigitte Abele, Gemeinderätin, Fraktion Die Bürgerliste
– Dr. phil. Uwe Beck, Gemeinderat, SPD-Fraktion
– Prof. Dr. phil. Andreas Benk, Gemeinderat, Fraktion Die Linke
– Martin Bläse, Gemeinderat, CDU-Fraktion
– Thomas Kaiser, Gemeinderat, CDU-Fraktion
– Karl Miller, Gemeinderat, Bündnis 90/Die Grünen
– Karin Rauscher, Gemeinderätin, Fraktion Freie Wähler Frauen

Selb

Sachpreisrichter·innen   Subject Judges
– Helmut Resch, Bauamtsleitung Stadt Selb
– Margarita Vollmer, Gewinnerin E15
– Christian Wunderlich, Sachgebietsleitung Städtebauförderung Stadt Selb

Stellvertreter·innen   Substitutes
– Ann-Madeleine Gubitz, Stadt Selb
– Robin Thomä, Gewinner E15

Fachpreisrichter·innen   Specialist Judges
– Prof. Dipl.-Ing. Melanie Humann, Urban Catalyst, Berlin, Professorin für Urbanismus und Entwerfen an der TU Dresden
– Michael Rudolph, Station C23, Leipzig, Vorstandsvorsitzender Europan Deutschland
– Marika Schmidt, mrschmidt Architekten, Berlin
– Dr.-Ing. Irene Wiese-Von Ofen, Institut für Städtebau und europäische Urbanistik RWTH Aachen, Vorstand Europan Deutschland

Stellvertreterin   Substitute
– Karin Sandeck, Ministerialrätin des Bayerischen Staatsministeriums für Wohnen, Bau und Verkehr, München, Vorstand Europan Deutschland

Wernigerode

Sachpreisrichter·innen   Subject Judges
– Peter Gaffert, Oberbürgermeister Stadt Wernigerode
– Sandra Lewerenz, Geschäftsführerin, Gemeinnützige Gesellschaft für Sozialeinrichtungen Wernigerode
– Christian Zeigermann, Geschäftsführer, Gebäude- und Wohnungsbaugesellschaft Wernigerode (GWW)

Stellvertreter   Substitutes
– Uwe Albrecht, Stadtratsvorsitzender und stellvertretender Aufsichtsratsvorsitzender, GEE
– Michael Zagrodnik, Amtsleiter Stadt- und Verkehrsplanung Wernigerode

Berater·innen   Advisors
– Michael Bollmann, stellv. Teamleiter Wohnungswirtschaft, Gebäude- und Wohnungsbaugesellschaft Wernigerode
– Ralf Hesse, Architekt und Bauingenieur, Gebäude- und Wohnungsbaugesellschaft Wernigerode
– Luisa Storm, Assistentin der Geschäftsführung, Gebäude- und Wohnungsbaugesellschaft Wernigerode

Fachpreisrichter·innen   Specialist Judges
– Jury Vorsitz Prof. Dipl.-Ing. Anne-Julchen Bernhardt, BeL Sozietät für Architektur, Köln
– Dr.-Ing. Saskia Hebert, subsolar* architektur & stadtforschung, stellvertretende Vorstandsvorsitzende Europan Deutschland
– Christoph Heinemann, ifau Institut für angewandte Urbanistik, Berlin
– Josef Weber, Vorstand Europan Deutschland

Stellvertreter   Substitute
– Ali Saad, Senior Consultant im Cities Team von ARUP Deutschland, Komitee Europan Deutschland

Bildnachweise   Image Credits

Impressum Imprint

Herausgeber Editor
Europan – Deutsche Gesellschaft zur Förderung
von Architektur, Wohnungs- und Städtebau e. V.
Vesta Nele Zareh, Lola Meyer
Friedrichstraße 23A, 10969 Berlin
www.europan.de

Redaktionsteam Editorial Staff
Kaye Geipel, Saskia Hebert, Lola Meyer,
Michael Rudolph, Vesta Nele Zareh

Lektorat Editing
Kerstin Wieland

Englische Übersetzung English Translation
Amy Klement

Deutsche Übersetzung German Translation
Alexandra Titze-Grabec

Gestaltung Graphic Design
Simon Malz, Christina Schmid

Druck und Bindung Printing and Binding
Offizin Scheufele, Buchbinderei Spinner

jovis-Bücher sind weltweit im ausgewählten Buchhandel
erhältlich. Informationen zu unserem internationalen
Vertrieb erhalten Sie in Ihrer Buchhandlung oder unter
www.jovis.de.

jovis books are available worldwide in select bookstores.
Please contact your nearest bookseller or visit www.jovis.de
for information concerning your local distribution.

ISBN 978-3-86859-761-5 (Softcover)
ISBN 978-3-86859-801-8 (PDF)